HOW
CHURCHILL
SAVED
CIVILIZATION

HOW
CHURCHILL
SAVED
CIVILIZATION

THE EPIC STORY OF 13 YEARS THAT ALMOST DESTROYED THE CIVILIZED WORLD

BY JOHN HARTE

Skyhorse Publishing

Skyhorse Publishing books may be purchased in bulk at special discounts for sales promotion, corporate gifts, fund-raising, or educational purposes. Special editions can also be created to specifications. For details, contact the Special Sales Department, Skyhorse Publishing, 307 West 36th Street, 11th Floor, New York, NY 10018 or info@skyhorsepublishing.com.

Skyhorse® and Skyhorse Publishing® are registered trademarks of Skyhorse Publishing, Inc.®, a Delaware corporation.

Visit our website at www.skyhorsepublishing.com.

10 9 8 7 6 5 4 3 2 1

Library of Congress Cataloging-in-Publication Data is available on file.

Cover design by Rain Saukas
Cover photo: AP Images

Print ISBN: 978-1-5107-1237-9
Ebook ISBN: 978-1-5107-1241-6

Printed in the United States of America

*"The best-laid plans of mice and men
Often go awry."*

— *Robert Burns*

CONTENTS

AUTHOR'S PREFACE

THIS BOOK IS INTENDED TO RESOLVE the lingering mysteries about the circumstances that caused the Second World War and what transpired. It answers questions that have haunted many of the present generation in Britain, Germany, France, Russia, and the United States, and all English-speaking nations like Canada, New Zealand, and Australia. Some frequently asked questions are "How did it happen?" and "Why were the Allies unprepared?" or "Why did the British government disarm?" and "Why did they appease Hitler?" Then there is "Why did France collapse so fast?" or "Why didn't the British government accept Hitler's peace proposals?" and "What were the Nazis really up to?" Then there is the inevitable Jewish question: "Why us?" Many more unanswered questions remained hovering in the air, even after a number of important memoirs and histories of the Second World War were written. This book was designed to answer all of them.

The outbreak of the First World War in 1914 (which led almost inevitably to the Second World War) was recalled throughout 2014 as a milestone in the history of Western civilization. As Winston Churchill said at the time and wrote in his acclaimed history of the Second World War, it was a continuation of the previous one, in order to resolve the outcome.[1] That recent milestone celebrated the enormous courage of the Allied forces, and the leadership of brilliant generals in the second round, after a previous set had let everyone down—while the other side revealed the lowest depths of barbaric depravity to which Western civilization has ever sunk in its entire history. But how did it happen, and why? And furthermore, how could it have been avoided?

TV viewers and movie audiences in 2014 were treated to an almost end-to-end range of wartime documentary films and fictional Hollywood movies about both world wars. And numerous fiction and nonfiction books were published about both of them. None of them answered those questions, since their purpose was entirely different. But now that seventy years have passed since the end of the last world war—and despite its fascination for many middle-aged and older people—some younger ones who are now far distanced from it are likely to believe that its remembrance is all over and done with, already out-of-date and out of mind, and should perhaps be relegated to the distant past with Wellington's Battle of Waterloo and the American Civil War, to be disregarded by future generations as irrelevant to their own lives and times and society.

That would be a mistake. And it may even be because the populations and attitudes of some Western nations have been significantly altered by immigration from third-world countries since then. More than half of the populations of some Western nations will soon consist of people born elsewhere and dedicated to other cultures or religions and different values. As a result of immigration, Canadian society now embraces 140 different language groups, many from Asia and the Middle East. Some sources allege there are eight hundred in New York City. Why should they be interested in the past history of their newly adopted home, despite attempts to include them during the citizenship process? If they are not interested, it will be a tragedy of vast proportions that may turn back the clock—not for reasons of sentiment in the hearts of English-speaking peoples, but because the absence of that vital knowledge of how we managed to survive the onslaughts on our democratic Western civilization may make them vulnerable to the next new menace to their freedom and well-being, and their pursuit of happiness.

The reason they should be interested is because it could easily happen again. Whether the next global crisis arises from a vacuum created by the collapse of the U.S. economy, the implosion of the Chinese economy, weapons of mass destruction manufactured by Iran, or some other reason, like the ISIS terrorist attacks on Paris in 2015 remains to be seen. To recognize the signs, we need to know what happened last time and what brought it about. Understanding the past is the first step to understanding the future.

That is why this book reveals how close Britain came to appeasing the Nazi criminals and mass murderers who would have subjugated England

and put an end to civilized Western values. It also explains the mood of Britain's government when it voluntarily disarmed while turning a blind eye to German rearmament, in a naive hope that doing so would halt an arms race that might result in another world war. Instead, it hastened it. Britain was seen by its enemies to be weak and vulnerable and easy to invade and conquer. That crisis should act as a warning of how easily our liberty can be lost if it happens again in a different form.

Most historians candidly admit they still don't know what caused the outbreak of the First World War—only that key factors like complacency, ignorance, weakness, and paranoia played a significant role in triggering dangerous events that unrolled to make a world war suddenly inevitable. And yet, what history shows us, time and again, is that the world is always a dangerous place, displaying erratic ups and downs in one country or another. Generational changes and short memories produce complacent attitudes, while new young or immigrant populations lack the hard Intelligence data of devious politics and diplomacy, or the firsthand experience of all-out Total War. Nor might they possess a realistic cynicism about the flaws, delusions, and reckless impetuosity of human nature—so that warning signs go unrecognized or are ignored.

Perhaps the most significant thing about the First World War was that the most accomplished politician of the time, Winston Churchill, was convinced that Germany would not provoke a war with England. He had been invited to Prussian army maneuvers by Kaiser Wilhelm and, after inspecting the German troops, decided they were out-of-date and posed no threat to Britain. He even described the Kaiser as "a well-meaning man." His judgment turned out to be wrong. Only four years after his well-intentioned remark, the Germans contrived the Agadir crisis to test the political climate, and the Kaiser ordered new Dreadnought-class battleships. Churchill was now First Lord of the Admiralty, and it caused him to reconsider his previous impression, since Britain's naval dominance as a sea power was essential to connect and protect an empire spread around the world. On the other hand, Germany was a land power with military chiefs of staff always fearful of a possibility of being encircled on the continent of Europe. Was the Kaiser acting out of personal vanity for want of a costly luxury he meant to have, or was Germany planning for war with Britain? The answer came when the German War erupted a year later.

And perhaps the most extraordinary thing about the Second World War with Germany was that Winston Churchill was the only politician who saw it coming, while most influential cabinet members, like the prime minister and the foreign secretary, continued to appease Hitler whenever he threatened to send German troops to invade another neighboring country. Their actions encouraged the German dictator's ambition to dominate Europe. Then he would have enough power to threaten the rest of the world. This book describes how it was left to Winston Churchill to save civilization almost single-handedly and how the outcome could have gone either way.

Another factor likely to distract the attention of future generations from the first warning signs of a catastrophic war, or terrorist acts as sudden and unexpected as 9/11, is the continual distraction and addiction to mass market digital devices operated by artificial intelligence. Mobile smartphones, the Internet, and social media in particular, divert millions of viewers from the realities of the outside world into an alternative world of entertaining fantasies and illusions about themselves and what is happening in cyberspace, instead of guarding against *real* threats to our survival as they arise.

This book was written to commemorate all those who sacrificed their lives in two world wars, and to caution readers that it could very easily happen again if we are not constantly alert to the signals. Good fortune is unlikely to favor us forever without a clear-sighted perceptiveness of the world and the realities of the fragile human condition. The easiest way to do that is by making an effort to learn the lessons of history. When we do, we immediately see how we are always poised on moments of danger to our freedom that could very easily take a turn for the worse. A Third World War could happen in the blink of an eye if we are unprepared for it.

Despite "the unachievable pursuit of prescience," this book explains the past in order to cast insights on the future.[2]

But its main purpose is to provide an account of Winston Churchill's actions and their intended consequences—as well as some of the unintended ones—for readers who are unlikely to read a military or political history of six hundred to eight hundred pages, or the entire six volumes of Winston Churchill's account of *The Second World War* with its five thousand pages, and are now too far away from the time in which it took place to understand it without a reminder. I have pared down the details of this fascinating and appalling epic story of how our civilization was almost destroyed to a more accessible length, without omitting the major events that led to the war, or those that were instrumental in achieving military victory by the Allies.

The American War in the Pacific against Japanese armed forces is barely mentioned here because, except for the opening engagements in Singapore, it was a separate war in which neither Winston Churchill nor the other protagonists featured in this book were involved.

Whenever we explore the documentation of his time, Winston Churchill's name is likely to show up. He seems to have been always alert to possible dangers from every source. We sense the superiority of his energy, his sense of responsibility, and the anxiety that drove him to take charge. Churchill was Minister of War when the First World War ended in 1918, and military budgets are typically cut with a sense of relief by bureaucracies. But he was adamant that the budget for the Secret Service should be doubled instead. He explained that reducing secret service activity when Russia and Germany "were in turmoil would be foolhardy." He wrote, "No-one can foresee what the next few months may bring forth and it is vital to see that there is no diminution in the quality and quantity of information now being supplied."[3] That statement is as vital today as it was then.

—*John Harte, Ottawa 2016.*

ENGLAND AT THE CENTER OF THE WORLD

───────

THIS EPIC TRUE STORY BEGAN NOT so very long after the peaceful and light-hearted Edwardian era in England, during the reign of the cheerful King Edward VII. Known by his family as "Bertie," he was relaxed and flippant. He enjoyed a gentlemanly wager on a hand of cards and spoiled his mistresses with bottles of champagne. He lent his name to Edwardian England and became an engaging role model for many of his subjects. Even after he passed away and was followed by the stiff and responsibly serious King George—a naval officer who ordered his family around like the crew of a battleship and had no sense of humor—the lighthearted, good-natured Edwardian outlook continued until the outbreak of the First World War.

The typical Edwardian sense of playful fun with chums of the same sex was mirrored by silly but humorous writers like Jerome K. Jerome and P. G. Wodehouse. It involved laughing playfully at each other's eccentricities. Grown-ups often behaved like innocent children with their pranks, sometimes flying their kites in the park on a Sunday afternoon. It was a complacent era of frivolity and jollity, a cheeky and disrespectful age with irreverent comedians on the music hall stage. Edwardians loved dressing up in funny costumes and posing in living pictures or *tableaux vivant*, playing party games like charades or amateur theatricals, and being invited to fancy dress parties. They had to entertain each other before radios and movies were invented. And they loved ridiculing the pretensions of self-important authority figures, as a reaction against the pomposity of the previous Victorian era.

Humorous novelist and short story writer P. G. Wodehouse, who grew up in the Edwardian world, wrote continuously about men-boys who never grew up (except only for Psmith—"a grown-up among boys"). It was a world without the three unmentionables: religion, politics, and sex, which were too tiresome even to contemplate. Money was mentioned frequently, but only as a means of continuing the languid Edwardian life of privileged boyhood, without assuming heavy adult responsibilities. It was an age of perpetual Peter Pans—the boy who never grew up.

"Wodehouse's London was a place where aristocrats chased actresses, where American money pursued British class, where bookmakers and barmaids mixed on equal terms with cabinet ministers and newspaper editors, and where everyone read the *Sporting Times,* better known as the 'Pink 'Un', one of the most popular newspapers of the day."[1] It was a fun-loving society.

To find out what more serious Edwardians were like, we have to go to Edwardian novelists we can trust. They too testify to the innocent Edwardian charm. But, in *Mrs. Dalloway,* for example, Virginia Woolf viewed the world of men though puzzled eyes, since women had little or no choice but to marry. And men often seemed strange to them—particularly the odd young men suffering from shell shock after war in the trenches.[2] E. M. Forster's Schlegel sisters and Mrs. Wilcox in *Howards End* focus on the importance of the home in Edwardian life, and caution readers about connecting with strangers who may not be "our sort." Despite that, they "saw a little more clearly than hitherto what a human being is, and to what he may aspire." They also sought to reconcile the inner life and the material world around them.

Both of those classics bring back the gallant Edwardian past, when gentleness, grace, dependability, and courage were valued. According to *Mrs. Dalloway,* young men were often gauche, generally awkward with women, hopeless around the house, and didn't know what to do with their hands. Some needed attachments to keep them occupied, like a pipe that frequently required filling, a cigarette that needed tapping on a slender silver cigarette case, or they fiddled with a penknife that included an implement for removing stones from horses' hooves. It was a sentimental reminder of the vanishing horses in the wake of the railways and motor cars that simplified travel, and the recent war that had resulted in the slaughter of hundreds of thousands of horses on the battlefields. But right up until the Second World War, some workhorses still remained—lonely ones pulling milk carts through suburban streets and pairs of more powerful ones with broad chests for the far heavier carts of coalmen and dustmen and the breweries. Humane and charitable horse troughs filled with drinking water still stood on the corners of major streets in the 1940s.

Those restless and awkward but eager young men went to the trenches in the First World War. The women nursed them when they were wounded, or worked in munitions factories. Most young men were naturally reserved. The closest many came to intimacy was playful bantering with women or camaraderie with other men. It would be sentimental to imagine that was the norm, but the Edwardian era would be closer to paradise than any other in British history. Then came the First World War, after which there was nothing to joke about and it was no longer possible for anyone to smile.

World War II

Whereas the Victorian era had been a period of exploration and adventure, of aspirational heroes risking everything for the sake of discovery and recognition, Edwardians were more conscious of the arts and modernity, and the discovery of the unconscious mind. All conspired to form the post-Edwardians, for whom aspiration was not quite dead. It would die with the hopes of a young generation on the battlefields.

Edwardian silk top hats gave way to more utilitarian bowlers, and then the more casual and debonair trilby hat for the middle and upper classes between wars. Cloth caps were for the countryside and the working classes. Manners and clothing became less formal. But even until 1940, many men and women still wore smart kid gloves to avoid germs when they went out. Women abandoned decorative wide-brimmed Edwardian hats for more practical ones in a new era of open vehicles, which gave them confidence that they were in tune with the times.

The First World War had been over for nearly a decade by now. And although hardly a family in the British Isles had been left untouched by grief at the bleak deaths of loved ones on the Western Front—or in the air or at sea—new inventions like bicycles, automobiles, telephones, electric kitchen appliances, the radio, and portable gramophones prompted some people to feel that it was time to get back to a normal life again, that perhaps the dead wouldn't mind so much if they sought amusements and made an effort to smile again. After all, England was still the center of the world in the arts and commerce and industry and sports. And the British Empire was still spread out all over the maps, with islands and even entire continents identified as British by bright pink shading. Britain still ruled the waves. Everyone knew it was the biggest empire that had ever existed. And the world was safer than it had ever been before—except, of course, for the stormy Continent on the other side of the Channel, which had always been a problem.

Nevertheless, who could be anything other than hopeful about the future when there were tea dances and nightclubs, jazz, cocktail bars, and cricket still played on village greens? Edwardian Englishmen were enraptured by cricket and couldn't get enough of it. There was boating on the Thames in Maidenhead and punting on the River Cam, and the cheerful light entertainment of Hollywood movies that had only just begun to talk. The new music and dance steps resulted in an era of entertaining in the home, of jazz records, and cheerful singing on the silver screen. It encouraged a happy-go-lucky, complacent attitude that allowed the whole thing—another world war—to happen all over again.

The British government took little notice of the heavy political storm clouds gathering over Europe. Nor did isolationist America concern itself. The English were closer to it, but not easily panicked by other people's delusions. They were an undemonstrative lot, shy of connecting with strangers, but nevertheless good at comradeship. Perhaps that was why they were suited to battle.

Whatever was about to happen then, it was comforting to recall the innocence of the past Edwardian era, with its youthfulness and happy childhoods, its lighthearted games in the parks in mild spring weather, and its warm summers that came as a welcome surprise after all the cold and dampness of English winters—when a coal fire in the bedroom was as essential as one in the living room. Memories of rare glows of friendly summer sunlight were cherished while toasting crumpets over the flames on the end of a telescopic fork, while a thrill of a lost golden age surged into their hearts and offered hope for the future. How green was England then![3]

But by the 1930s, England was experiencing an economic recession and large-scale unemployment, with industrial strikes and hunger marches in London with hundreds asking for work; then, there were the lineups for free food at soup kitchens and ex-servicemen with their medal ribbons from the First World War—attempting hopelessly to sell matches or pencils, even apples, on street corners—embarrassed to be seen in such a shameful state and desperate for a few coins, sometimes with a sleeve pinned up to obscure where an arm had been. As with comradeship in the First World War, it brought Britain's social classes closer together in the knowledge that they were all one.

As the lines of the jobless grew in Britain, the United States, and Germany, eminent British economist John Maynard Keynes informed other modern economists in a Chicago audience that "we are today in the middle of the greatest catastrophe—the greatest catastrophe due almost to entirely economic causes—of the modern world."

At the end of 1930, the U.S. banking system faltered and was on the verge of collapse. Some major banks closed their doors for fear of withdrawals in excess of funds. Governor of the Bank of England, Montagu Norman, DSO, suffered from a nervous breakdown under the strain and claimed that the capitalist system would be wrecked within the year unless drastic measures were taken.[4] Faced with a world financial crisis that he viewed as heralding the collapse of Western civilization, he fled abroad for rest and care, while "armies of the unemployed now haunted the towns and cities of the industrial nations."[5]

Despite Montagu Norman's reputation for wisdom—because he had been so often right—one of his critics was Keynes. Another was Winston Churchill, who lost much of his savings in the 1929 Wall Street crash. He wrote to his former secretary, "Everyone I meet seems vaguely alarmed that something terrible is going to happen financially."

Gathering Storm Clouds

What the unsophisticated and decent young men and women of England had no way of knowing was that the present British government was one of the weakest in British history, particularly during a period that would be described as "the low dishonest decade."[6] Prime Minister Ramsay MacDonald headed a Conservative coalition government, although it was really Stanley Baldwin who held the reins of power. The stubborn Neville Chamberlain performed the main administrative functions as Chancellor of the Exchequer starting in 1931. It was their complacency that would cause Britain to be vulnerable to the threat of invasion by bigger and better-trained and better-armed German troops. Meanwhile, rule on the continent of Europe had been turned upside-down by the emergence of police states dominated by uncompromising and ruthless criminal dictators.[7]

As the threat of a second world war brewed on the Continent, Britain's politicians spent much of their time distracted by Indian policy involving the hatred between Muslims and Hindus, and Home Rule in Ireland with its hatred between Catholics and Protestants. How to keep them apart was a continual problem. Meanwhile, there was considerable unrest in Germany when its cabinet fell in May 1932. The German Chancellor hoped to be supported by President von Hindenburg, the national hero of the recent World War, and the political right wing in the Reichstag.

But the rabble-rouser and rising warlord Adolf Hitler was backed by thirteen million voters. And now he felt he was as powerful as the Italian dictator Mussolini, who had marched on Rome with his black-shirted army of Fascist thugs and intimidated and taken control of the government. Hindenburg had nothing but contempt for this hate-filled opportunist who evidently had the same idea for Germany. But five million were unemployed in Germany, and major street riots that heralded a possible civil war caused Hindenburg to change his mind and accept Hitler as a temporary measure, since he hoped to tame him with the burdens of office.

Instead, the Nazi Minister of the Interior, Hermann Göring, made four thousand arrests overnight, including the Central Committee of the Communist Party, and confiscated secret arms belonging to communists throughout Germany. Consequently, the Nazi Joseph Goebbels was able to organize an electoral campaign that effectively eliminated their main opposition. The Nazi vote secured 288 seats, giving them a majority of 37. Chancellor Hitler was given emergency powers for four years. January 30, 1933, marked a new order when Hitler became Chancellor of Germany and immediately set to work to eliminate all his political rivals. And the new Nazi order promptly suspended all civil liberties, allowing no rights for anyone.

"And now," Hitler said with a grim look of self-satisfaction at the parliamentary opposition, "I have no further need of you."

According to Churchill's view of the situation, Hitler represented the dark and primitive side of life that lay dormant in the hearts of a horde of the most furious, brutal, ambiguous, and ill-fated nation in Europe.[8]

President Roosevelt took office in 1933—the same year that Hitler became Chancellor of Germany. And, like Hitler, Roosevelt did not take charge of an industrial powerhouse but faced the daunting prospects of an economic collapse. Roosevelt's initial response was to put the American people to work. He was appalled by Hitler and by his audiences that responded to the dictator's hate-filled outbursts like wild animals. The President believed it would not be possible to contain Hitler, and that the best guarantee of peace was to arm America and support the democracies.[9]

The Third Reich

On April 12, 1934, Germany's Minister of Defense, General Werner von Blomberg, met the new German Chancellor, Adolf Hitler, on board the *Deutschland*, where he made a secret pact that the army would support the Führer on the condition the military would retain control over all military matters. But that was not what happened.[10]

The Third Reich was no longer a parliamentary democracy nor a parliamentary system of any kind. The new Nazi laws created a sole dictatorship, and Hitler's only answer to opposition was murder. He had already put into effect his premeditated plan for constructing Dachau's death camp in preparation for the mass murders of anyone who opposed him.

But the MacDonald-Baldwin government in Britain continued to close its eyes and ears to the gathering storm in Europe and carried on enforcing severe reductions and restrictions on Britain's modest armaments. Disarmament was praised and encouraged in the House of Commons by all spokesmen for the political parties, in an illogical belief that disarming would discourage an arms race on the continent of Europe. Consequently, the British air estimates displayed a total lack of understanding by the government and the opposition as to what was happening across the Channel. Britain was only the fifth air power, and the Air Ministry had not manufactured a single new aircraft that year.[11] It prompted Winston Churchill to rise in the House and warn the government of the risk of war.

One result of the government's languid attitude toward Germany with its seventy million Germans allowed to rearm and prepare for war was that the British public shared the same lack of interest in German rearmament. And as early as March 23, 1933, Churchill raised in Parliament Germany's ill treatment of minorities and the persecution of Jews.

He would write that the lack of wisdom of the British government and the French government's weakness had few parallels in history. He described what he saw as an irrational, unrealistic, and dangerous situation. He became more and more alarmed as events unrolled in Germany and the government failed to react. But, as he continued to criticize the slow pace of Britain's rearmament, he was erroneously regarded by some as a warmonger. Churchill's was not a lone voice, however, and it was easy for his critics to claim that the reason was Britain's poor economy. More to the point, as far as he was concerned, was Britain's state of unpreparedness to protect its population, which should have been the priority.

He could see all the great work of previous generations of thinkers, soldiers, economists, scientists, and industrialists being eroded by mediocrities.[12] That was the case in India, Germany, southern Ireland, and Palestine. Britain's low dishonest decade was a period of complacent indifference and mediocrity, in which more energetic and less scrupulous nations recognized an opportunity to exploit the British Empire's weakness. Churchill, with his mind steeped in history, would have known what had happened twelve centuries earlier, when the Roman Empire collapsed; the Muslim Arabs had erupted and defeated Persia, the Middle East, and Byzantium, resulting in the first Caliphate and the Ottoman Empire. Just as the loss of the previous *Pax Romana* had led to chaos all over the world for centuries, he could foresee the collapse of the British Empire creating a similar power vacuum in Europe.

Bureaucratic administrators of Britain and the United States were completely absorbed in the day-to-day affairs of their departments and too shortsighted in their tunnel vision to see the whole picture of what was happening outside of their particular daily sphere, and how it could threaten world peace. Britain was complacently unaware and the United States was aloof and isolationist. What Churchill hoped was that the United States would inspire French and British politicians to act. But America had its own economic problems after the Great Depression. And the course of events tumbled rapidly downhill while Churchill grew even more distressed at the policy of the government, when false sentiments by politicians were blithely accepted or passed in the House of Commons without being challenged by responsible members of the government or leaders of the opposition.[13]

In 1933, a motion was passed by students of the Oxford Union: "This House refuses to fight for King and country." And the Peace Pledge Union renounced war the following year. Then, on October 25, the Socialist candidate for East Fulham said, "British people demand . . . that the British government shall give a lead to the whole world by initiating immediately a policy of general disarmament." Such incidents resulted in a view that Britain had declined. And Hitler had no doubt that the British had become decadent.

To some of the smaller nations of Europe that looked to Britain for leadership, it seemed inconceivable that the British people had lost their flair and drive after generations of social and industrial progress and military victories on scores of foreign battlefields.

Meanwhile, the Japanese population had grown to seventy million. Inflation and the cost of living had risen and production was down, endangering their economy. They needed coal and iron, which came from China. Their main policy now turned to asserting control over the sources. Japanese troops landed in Shanghai in January 1932 and, in spite of Chinese resistance, penetrated deeper inland in 1933. As for the authority of the League of Nations, it was shown to be unable to offer any physical support when its collective strength was needed.

Churchill accused all political parties in Britain of enjoying composing treacly platitudes to conceal the unpleasant facts of reality in order to seek popularity and political success. And both leaders of the coalition government shared an ignorance of Europe that blinded them to its glaring problems. As for Stanley Baldwin, he shared the complacent pacifism that was typical of the Liberal and Labour-Socialist Parties. As Churchill put it afterward with hindsight, it conveyed an image of British foolishness, irresponsibility, and guilt, which encouraged its enemies to let loose on the world all the horrors and miseries that were likely to be even worse than any others in history.[14]

Churchill's answer to the problems erupting all over the world was to seek a "grand alliance" to stop the chaos and bloodshed he felt was inevitable. But neither America nor Soviet Russia was willing to go to war. Both had to be attacked first. It was inconceivable to Winston Churchill, who had grown up in an imperial age at the end of the Victorian era in which patriotism, courage, and service to one's country were the prime virtues. He would have enjoyed the patriotic fervor of a military marching tune popularized in Victorian music halls.

We're the soldiers of the Queen, my lads
Who've been, my lads, who've seen, my lads
In the fight for England's glory lads
When we've had to show them what we mean:
And when we say we've always won
And when they ask us how it's done
We'll proudly point to every one
Of England's soldiers of the Queen.

Military brass bands frequently played that stirring march at rural fairgrounds. It would have attracted millions of village boys into uniform and drawn them into wars in foreign countries. British colonies teemed with their tombstones in secluded plots of hallowed ground not so dissimilar from their own village churchyards. It was still played occasionally on the music hall circuits, right up to the beginning of the Second World War, and used as patriotic background music for a few early films extolling the British Empire and its fearless and victorious imperial forces. It could be heard on Sundays in public parks that featured a raised bandstand on which uniformed musicians proudly played their brass instruments, beat their huge drums, and clashed their cymbals, while girls and boys sat around it in deck chairs, holding hands and listening to the lively military music, all unaware of the trouble brewing on the other side of the English Channel.

2

THE MASTER OF GERMANY

GERMANY'S CHIEF OF STAFF WAS ERNST Röhm. He headed the SA—known as the Brownshirts. He was already in charge of three million storm troopers. But he was an ambitious man and had been pressing for control of the entire armed forces. Given the power, he would over-arch Adolf Hitler and pose a threat. Himmler, Heydrich, and Göring were fearful of his power and ambition. They convinced Hitler of the Brownshirt leader's disloyalty. Disloyalty was a characteristic that raised the traditional German rage called *Wut* in Hitler's chest.[1] He was more than merely receptive to their fear; he decided he had to act at once to stop anyone from becoming too independent, too powerful, or too popular, since they could become a threat to him personally. There was only one answer—they had to be liquidated as traitors.*

Hitler led the liquidation squad himself, after ordering all the leaders of the Brownshirts to be called to a meeting and disarmed between June 30 and July 2, 1934.

The Brownshirt leaders were transported to Stadelheim prison in Munich, where SS men shot them to death in a blood purge. Different sources claim that 150 to 401 were murdered so that Hitler could use the incident as a warning to any rivals who might disobey him. It became known as the "Night of

---

* Heinrich Himmler, a leading member of the Nazi Party, was appointed by Hitler to administer the Third Reich. He led the infamous SS and set up and managed the concentration camps. Reinhard Heydrich, known as "the hangman," was a high-ranking Nazi who organized the Holocaust. Hermann Göring, the leading member of the Nazi Party, was commander of the German air force.

the Long Knives." The pattern was set so that all armed forces knew Hitler had only one answer to opposition—instant death. Or, if he felt particularly vindictive, slow torture beforehand, so that death came as a release from all the pain. No compromise was possible.

The massacre, Churchill wrote, showed that Hitler would stop at nothing. Churchill did his best to convey that conditions in Germany were no longer those of any civilized state and added that so-called concentration camps were already in operation.[2]

A significant factor that ensured Hitler's dominance was a political system of proportional representation that fragmented opposition parties so that not one was strong enough to oppose him. It should have been clear to everyone that the German Third Reich was no longer a parliamentary democracy nor a parliamentary system with an opposition party. Hitler had destroyed all opposition. The steady advance of civilization in Europe had been halted and the clock turned back by what Churchill called the master of Germany. Despite the fact that murdering everyone who disagrees with you on a massive scale was a sure sign of a psychopath, it was not something that was recognized by the British cabinet, or France, who continued their normal diplomacy as if Germany were still a civilized nation.

But law and order had not only broken down inside Germany. Austrian Nazis mobilized on July 25, 1934, and an armed group entered the Chancellery in Vienna. Engelbert Dollfuss, who led the Austrian government, was struck by two revolver bullets and left to bleed slowly to death. The Nazis seized control of the broadcasting station to announce the resignation of the Dollfuss government and Dollfuss's replacement by a Nazi-backed puppet. But Chancellor Schuschnigg acted quickly to restore order in Austria. And in Italy, the new system of proportional representation also put the Fascist dictator Mussolini in power without effective opposition.

On August 19, the German electorate voted for Hitler to combine the responsibilities of both Chancellor and President, with 89.9 percent voting yes. While lulling the suspicions of the world through his diplomats and with his own smooth talk, Hitler secretly ordered Germany's armed forces to prepare themselves for war in Europe sooner rather than later and set about increasing the number of German military divisions.[3]

But the instinctive reaction of the British cabinet was to dismiss the saber rattling across the Channel as typical foreign shenanigans by upstarts. Britain's ruling class felt little sympathy for vainglorious imposters of any kind and were suspicious of foreigners, like the unreliable French and unstable Italians. As humorist P. G. Wodehouse wrote to his stepdaughter in 1925, "Mummie and I have come to the conclusion that we loathe foreign countries. We hate their ways, their architecture, their looks, their language, and their food." As for the rabble-rousers, they had seen them before and were unimpressed. Some were more impressed by Germany's science and technology and Prussia's obsessive compulsion for law and order at any cost. But Germany was no longer the Prussia of the former military Junkers: they were now Nazis sworn to obey their new warlord Adolf Hitler. And a languid and dismissive tendency existed among some of Britain's ruling classes, who were happy to let foreigners get on with what they had to, as long as it didn't interfere with Britain.[4]

But the young and idealistic foreign secretary, Anthony Eden, thought differently about the Nazis. They had betrayed civilized ideals. He wanted to live in a pure and ethical society. So he would have no truck with appeasing villains. The Nazis were beastly and it was cowardly to encourage bullies by giving in to them. No good would come of it!

The lean, politically experienced and steely Chancellor of the Exchequer, Neville Chamberlain, was more pragmatic and thought otherwise. His job was to balance the nation's books and he knew that Britain was in an economic crisis and could not afford to go to war with Germany. So did the tall and cadaverous Lord Halifax, who remarked that the world was full of evil and one had to be realistic and come to terms with it. He had no arguments with Hitler. Neither of them showed the smallest degree of imagination of what might happen.

Appeasement

The British ruling class was riddled with appeasers and pro-Nazis. Britain's ambassador to Germany, Sir Nevile Henderson, was one of the most rabid appeasers. There were estimated to be two thousand pro-Germans in Britain. The Anglo-German Fellowship Society was founded in 1935. Anti-Semitism was subtle but barely concealed and malicious. Jews were a useful scapegoat to blame for anything, since they had no country of their own or power to resist the slanders. What the aristocracy and landed gentry were more afraid of than Hitler was Communism. It was only a dozen years or so since Communist Russia had seized all private property there. So Britain's landed gentry were scared of losing their estates if Communism was not suppressed. They applauded Hitler's strong hand. As for senior staff of British intelligence services between the two world wars, they viewed Soviet Russia and Stalin as the greatest enemy, whereas the rising Adolf Hitler was regarded as "a disagreeable fellow but a potential ally."[5]

French Foreign Secretary Pierre Laval believed that France must avoid war at all costs. The military power he, too, distrusted was Soviet Russia. He sought arrangements with Mussolini in Italy and Hitler in Germany, whose policies he had no trouble with.

In December 1934, Italian troops clashed with Abyssinian soldiers at a well on the border of Italian Somaliland, as a pretext to claiming Ethiopia (as Abyssinia was also known).

More than a decade later, in his memoirs, Winston Churchill would explain that no one could judge the policy of the British government without bearing in mind the passionate wish for peace that dominated the emotions of the uninformed and misinformed British people. There were so many who felt that way after the horrors of the First World War that any party or politician who took any other attitude would be threatened with political destruction. But he added that it was no excuse for political leaders who failed to do their duty. For those who understand history as Churchill did, the past was closer than most people thought—and so was the future.

Not long afterward, he warned the House of Commons that he feared the day when the present rulers of Germany would be powerful enough to threaten the British Empire. He called on Prime Minister Baldwin, who had the power to take action. And Baldwin agreed to ensure that Britain's air power would no longer be inferior to the air forces of any country within striking distance. But the Opposition, including Socialist Clement Attlee, declared that they denied the need for increased air power.

Winston Churchill saw the danger to Britain of such unrealistic obstinacy, and he wrote after the event with absolute certainty that if Britain and France had each maintained parity of arms with Germany, they would have been twice as strong together, and Hitler's term of violence might have been stopped at the outset without losing a single life. But now it was too late. He warned that Britain's weakness did not only involve the British Isles but also the stability of Europe.

In March 1935, Germany publicly repudiated the Versailles Treaty, which prevented them from rearming. Six months later, Hitler turned all German Jews into vulnerable victims by removing their civil rights and making them unemployed, whether in government, universities, industry, or commerce. A year later, Hitler further violated the Treaty by sending German troops to the industrial region of the Rhineland, which was supposed to be a demilitarized zone. The troops had orders to return to base if they were opposed by French or British forces. Since they were not, they took possession of the industrial zone.

Now Churchill brought up the air estimates again in the House of Commons, in a belief that Prime Minister Baldwin's advisers were not telling him the truth. And he was sure they did not know the facts anyway. He believed the Germans were already as strong militarily as Britain, and would probably be twice as strong by the end of the year. The cabinet made the position public in April. But neither Parliament nor the public heeded the warning. And Hitler had time to apply pressure on his munitions factories and military training schools to increase their productivity.

Nevertheless, Churchill was considered alarmist when he quoted his own figures for the strength of the German air force and said that the real situation was probably even more serious. Soon afterward, Hitler revealed the actual constitution of Germany's air force, claiming that Germany possessed air parity with Britain. He also declared that national service in the German army was now compulsory—always a signal of imminent war.

Shortly afterward, Ethiopia appealed to the League of Nations about Italian threats to their territory. Meanwhile, the U.S. government wished everyone well and promptly dismissed the chaos in Europe from its mind.

A War Hypothesis

Although Britain still carefully adhered to the terms of the 1919 Treaty of Versailles, Germany did not. The British Admiralty discovered that the last two German pocket battleships being constructed—the *Scharnhorst* and the *Gneisenau*—were far larger than the Treaty allowed, and of an entirely different type. They were light battle cruisers, or commerce destroyers of the highest class, and obviously designed to destroy and sink unarmed merchant ships. Churchill pointed out that Hitler was placing Germany in a stronger position for war with Britain in 1939 or 1940 by building battleships of that class and continuing to build more U-boats.

The evidence was met by an irrational impulse by the British Admiralty, which responded by making an Anglo-German naval agreement without consulting France (Britain's ally) or the League of Nations. Winston Churchill wrote how dangerous it always is for members of the armed forces to play at politics, where they are lost in a sphere with quite different values.[6] He immediately condemned the agreement and warned the House of Commons that they would be amazed and shocked if they knew how much Germany had actually spent that year preparing for war. He described the whole of Germany as a mighty arsenal ready to be mobilized. But no one could obtain the actual figures, so his rhetoric was brushed aside by Sir Samuel Hoare.

It was Hoare's first speech as foreign secretary on July 11, 1935, when he replied, in effect, not to worry, since France's naval fleet was 43 percent bigger than Germany's, and the same size as the Royal Navy's. By doing so, Hoare permitted, even authorized Germany to build to its industrial capacity for another five or six years. It signaled the resurrection of Germany as a military power. And the establishment of conscription in Germany challenged the Treaty of Versailles.[7]

Churchill wrote that at that stage he was forced to assume a hypothesis that Great Britain, France, and Belgium were allies about to be attacked by Germany.[8] Consequently, the prime minister invited Churchill to join the newly formed Committee of Imperial Defense on Air Defense Research.

The question Churchill placed before his scientific adviser Professor Lindemann and his colleagues in the Technical Sub-Committee was how to protect Britain's civilian population from attack from the air. Scientists in Britain, the United States, France, and Germany had already considered the effects of using radio waves echoing back from bomber aircraft or from other metal objects. Radio direction-finding was later known as radar. But it was assumed it would take five years to detect enemy aircraft by radar. So a chain of stations was constructed for experiments on Britain's east coast, centered on Dover. Locating ships by radio was explored, too. The stations were already being constructed by March 1936, and the Air Ministry would create a coastal chain by 1939. Following enemy aircraft after they had flown inland required the Royal Observer Corps to link up with telephone exchanges. Ground-controlled interception stations set Britain ahead of everyone else in the technology although it was still in its infancy.

It would take four years for radio-detection methods to be used. Meanwhile the Luftwaffe flew special listening equipment up Britain's coast on the Graf Zeppelin to discover if British radar existed.

When Sir Samuel Hoare became First Lord of the Admiralty in 1936, he directed his officers to discuss naval matters with Churchill, since Churchill had experience as First Sea Lord in the First World War. The problem with making the navy more effective in its armaments was the length of time inevitably taken by works in progress. For example, gun turrets had to be ordered by 1936, since any further delay would reduce the five ships required to come up to strength to only two. Although it was agreed that the ideal complement would be nine sixteen-inch guns in three turrets—rather than ten fourteen-inch guns in four turrets—there would be an unacceptable delay in placing larger guns in the first five battleships. And each vessel would take five years to build.

On November 5, 1937, in a four-hour meeting, Hitler informed senior executives of the German armed forces about his plans. He warned them that expansion of territory could not be carried out without risks. They included short wars against Britain and France up until 1943–45, after which the world would be prepared with defenses. He would defeat Czechoslovakia and Austria at great speed, but he did not expect France to retaliate without Britain's support.[9] Now, when Hitler took over the role of War Minister, it placed him in complete control of all of Germany's armed forces.

By 1938, Churchill was shown the naval version of radar by the First Sea Lord. It was called *Asdic*. It sent sound waves through the water to discover the existence of submarines and echoed back from whatever steel structure they might meet. Churchill was pleasantly surprised by its clarity and force; it was even better than he had imagined.

But Britain not only lost air parity in the meantime; it was also threatened by Italy joining Germany in an axis of power and enabling Hitler to reach his goal of war. Meanwhile, Mussolini's threat to Abyssinia was almost as primitive and brutal as Hitler's propensity to mass murders. Both were devoid of twentieth-century ethics and continued to turn back the clock of progress. According to Churchill, the Italian dictator's aim was not only territorial gains, but also personal prestige. He sought Italian authority in Europe by building an Italian empire. And no discussion or argument or warning from Britain would make any difference to the dictator's brutal aggression against unarmed tribesmen, who were half-naked warriors armed only with spears. According to Churchill, Mussolini, as well as Hitler, regarded the British cabinet as frightened, flabby old women who could do nothing more than bluster, since they were no longer capable of fighting a war.[10]

As a result, Italian warships moved through the Suez Canal in considerable force, with nearly a quarter of a million troops and with considerable supplies, toward the Abyssinian frontier, without being stopped. Then, surprising everyone, even Churchill, on August 24, the British cabinet announced that it would uphold its treaty with Abyssinia under the Covenant of the League of Nations.

On the same day, Hitler signed a Nazi-Soviet pact—despite his intention to invade Russia at a chosen time in the future. In *Mein Kampf*, he had written that alliances are made only as part of the struggle—meaning that alliances borrow more time to prepare for war.[11]

Britain had already introduced conscription into the armed forces for men aged twenty to twenty-one at the end of April. But was Britain prepared? Churchill sent an urgent message to Sir Samuel Hoare, who was now foreign secretary, to ascertain whether he knew where the fleets were and whether they were in battle order. Were they adequate? Were they capable of rapid and complete concentration? Had the fleet been formally warned to take precautions? He seemed to imagine he was still First Lord of the Admiralty in the last war. Even so, his advice was gladly sought because of his experience.

Anthony Eden, who was now Minister for League of Nations Affairs and almost the equal of the foreign secretary, had rallied members of the League in the direction of sanctions against Italy if Mussolini invaded Abyssinia, since Italy depended on war materials from overseas, which members could sanction, if they chose to.

Nevertheless, Mussolini—no doubt hoping for a quick victory—launched his armies on Abyssinia, stating boldly that he "would not tolerate the imposition of any sanctions that hampered the invasion of Abyssinia: he would go to war with whoever stood in his path."

Britain's Would-Be Dictator

Having failed in most careers, Oswald Mosley intended to be England's dictator. He had been at the peak of his power in 1933, when he organized a big Fascist rally at Earl's Court Exhibition Hall. He was still a handsome, debonair, and virile young man with the glitter of a fanatic in his eyes. He had assumed a dashing mustache in imitation of the swashbuckling Hollywood movie idol Douglas Fairbanks, but darker and thicker, with a more military flair. He had posed triumphantly on the stage in a splendid tailor-made black uniform with a peaked cap that lent him a military air. Everything about him was copied from someone else. As well as his mustache, there was his self-confident strut at the head of his marching Blackshirts, in imitation of Mussolini. And his black uniform was copied from Hitler's Gestapo or Nazi storm troopers.

He was listed in *Who's Who* as Sir Oswald Mosley, the fourth Baronet of Ancoats. He had been taught to be a leader. But when he failed as a Conservative member of Parliament, he became convinced that his career would take off much quicker in the Labour Party with the ailing Ramsay MacDonald government. MacDonald was physically and mentally ill and incoherent in speech. No one knew what he was going to say or what he had just said. Evidently Mosley saw himself as a possible candidate to replace him as prime minister. But MacDonald passed his office on to his old crony, Stanley Baldwin.

Veteran statesman Lloyd George had coined a derisive name for the sterile identical-twin governments of Stanley Baldwin and Ramsay MacDonald, who took turns in office. They were almost indistinguishable with their syrupy platitudes offered to the public as substitutes for action. He called their limited imagination "MacStanleyism." Coddling the public by concealing the truth in order to take turns in office "was rotting the fabric and the vitals of the Empire. And had to be stopped."

Prime Ministers MacDonald and Baldwin and Chancellor Chamberlain were motivated largely by fear of wrecking Britain's economy, whereas Winston Churchill was motivated by fear of Britain's defeat at the hands of its enemy, and an invasion by mass murderers. Compared with the two prime ministers and the Chancellor of the Exchequer, who were unimaginative mediocrities still living in a previous and more accommodating era, Churchill was a modern visionary.

Mosley had resigned from the Labour Party to form his own political party, which he called the "New Party." But it failed, and he became a three-time loser. Then he saw how the histrionic Italian journalist, Benito Mussolini, took power in Italy by force of arms. Mussolini had hired a private army of black-shirted thugs to march on the king's palace at their head. King Victor Emmanuel was intimidated by Mussolini's armed bodyguards and asked him to form a new government.

Mosley visited Mussolini in Italy and invited Hitler to his wedding to the beautiful but empty-headed Lady Diana—one of the celebrated Mitford girls. But in England, he was considered to be unreliable and untrustworthy, particularly with other men's wives.

But Mosley was a smooth talker. Seeing how Hitler's power was built up on anti-Semitic propaganda and rhetoric, he spread the same lies to Britain's riffraff. But England scorned him as an ambitious opportunist—a ruthless manipulator and exploiter of gullible and rebellious youths.

That was before his Fascist rally at Earl's Court, when anyone who asked questions or objected was grabbed by his Blackshirts and hustled outside, where they were beaten with truncheons or brass knuckles in a back alley. According to some newspaper stories, the gutters outside ran with the blood of his victims. True or exaggerated, the British public was suspicious of him. Nevertheless, he decided to play his trump card by goading East End Jewish residents to riot—then he would be seen to take charge of the situation. It would bolster his leadership.

The Art of Deception

Meanwhile, in a speech given on May 21, 1936, Hitler declared that "Germany neither intends nor wishes to interfere in the internal affairs of Austria, to annex Austria, or to conclude an Anschluss." It was his usual double-talk to pacify opposition by concealing his real intentions beneath a manifest lie. It always worked. In this case, it would turn out that the annexation of Austria was one of his major priorities.

Hitler knew from the beginning of his political career that dictatorships can move much faster than republics or democracies—it is the difference between the rule of one and the rule of several. And, as British Prime Minister Baldwin was to remark to the House, "A democracy is always two years behind the dictator." Baldwin had said it several times before and now remarked on it again, since his purpose was to claim that he had long understood Britain's situation vis-à-vis German aggression, but it would not have been wise or politic to ask the country for a mandate to rearm at that time. He gave the game away when he added, "I cannot think of anything that would have made the loss of the election from my point of view more certain."

What he meant by that was, "If I'd told voters the truth about what was going on, they wouldn't have reelected me." The House was shocked. And Baldwin was treated with disdain.

Churchill called it a revelation of the prime minister's indecent motives. But everyone in the British cabinet was still polite and gentlemanly, and the government continued to conceal the truth from the public behind the usual treacly platitudes.

Meanwhile, the numbers forecast by Churchill's small team of helpers and researchers for a possible wartime economy reached pessimistic conclusions. There was no doubt by now that Britain was four years behind Germany in the production of war weapons and equipment. A breakdown of numbers of all arms, armaments, aircraft, tanks, battleships and submarines, battle equipment, and spare parts, appeared in a thesis by future President John F. Kennedy when he was a student. He turned it into a book, published in 1938 as *Why England Slept.*[12] He most likely obtained the statistics from his father Joseph Kennedy, who was the ambassador for the United Sates in England. Four years were projected to have all the weaponry ready for use. And Joe Kennedy didn't think Britain had a hope in hell of surviving for even a quarter of that time. As he warned the American President, Britain was finished.

3

A FORCE OF NATURE

CHURCHILL'S ATTENTION TO DETAILS WAS EXTRAORDINARY when one considers how busy and successful he was as one of the highest paid journalists in England, and as an author earning double the income of the prime minister. *Collier's* magazine paid him for articles on defense and the economy. And he was contracted to the *Daily Mail* for his weekly articles. He had already written a biography of his father, Lord Randolph Churchill, and the first two volumes of a biography of his ancestor the Duke of Marlborough, and there was an expected contract to write the *History of the English-Speaking Peoples,* with a hefty advance. He was also under contract to Alexander Korda to write a screenplay for a proposed film on King George V. All of it acted as a springboard for his celebrity as a politician—in much the same way as one of Churchill's role models, Benjamin Disraeli, had written a popular romantic novel about a hero in Queen Victoria's time, and was also considered to be the best Progressive-Conservative prime minister that Britain ever produced.

Politicians elected to power perform many different functions in order to protect the population, regardless of which sector voted them into office. And the array of worldviews in the British government in 1937 was varied in the extreme, from the wiry and self-opinionated Prime Minister Neville Chamberlain—who became prime minister in May—to the pragmatic Lord Halifax, and the idealistic Foreign Secretary Anthony Eden. The energetic and warlike Winston Churchill was still only an MP and held no influential cabinet position that might have provided him with power. Although an outsider, he was a powerful force of nature who could not be ignored. And his range of skills and experience, and his energy, were extraordinary in one individual.

Churchill was a brilliant communicator, whether as a political orator in the House of Commons, or as a popular journalist, or a historian. With his military and ducal background as a descendent of the famous Duke of Marlborough, who never lost a single battle, he could engage with and be respected by the most influential leaders in the world. And he was mightily persuasive in conversation. He had previously served in the First World War as Home Secretary and Lord of the Admiralty, so that—like General Montgomery who had served on the battlefield in World War I—he was more experienced in war than most people at the time. It enabled him to view the broad picture and interpret it as a visionary, and also be cynical and critically nit-picking, and dismissive of incompetence or lazy-mindedness in others. He also possessed another attribute that many leaders did not—it was a sense of broad humor that sometimes even restrained him from his impulsiveness to get right into the thick of the action, which he loved. Fortunately for everyone, except Britain's enemies, he was an obsessive-compulsive, histrionic workaholic who was always driven to demonstrate his importance through the performance of his talents on the world stage.

Winston Churchill was unique, in background and abilities. "I knew that he had been amazingly brave as a young man, and that he had seen bloodshed at first hand, and been fired at on four continents, and that he was one of the first men to go up in an airplane. I knew that he had been a bit of a runt at Harrow, and that he was only about five foot seven and with a thirty-three-inch chest, and that he had overcome his stammer and his depression and his appalling father to become the greatest living Englishman. . . . It is also true that, without Churchill, Hitler would almost certainly have won."[1]

Winston's father had been Lord Randolph Churchill, a former First Lord of the Admiralty in Asquith's Liberal government, and Chancellor of the Exchequer. His mother, Lady Randolph Churchill, had been the wealthy and beautiful New York heiress and socialite Jennie Jerome, whom Churchill had adored.

Churchill was thrilled by war. As a small child he'd played for hours on the floor with 1,500 toy soldiers.[2] While training for a commission in the army at Sandhurst, he had dreamed of being nineteen in 1793 and having over twenty years to fight against Napoleon's Grand Armée. In 1895, he had been a subaltern in the Fourth Hussars at the age of twenty-one. He had been stationed in Cuba, been attached to the Malakand Field Force—followed by the Tirah Expedition. As an officer in the Twenty-Fourth Lancers, he had charged on horseback at Omdurman with a saber. His actions as a war correspondent in the South African Boer War ended in his being taken prisoner by the Boers and escaping with a reward for his capture on his head. He was the only man with access to the British cabinet who had experienced personal combat in a war at first hand. War was his natural element, and he loved it.

Those Cabinet Ministers and Winston Churchill would influence what would happen in Britain and in the world affairs of Europe, particularly in Nazi Germany and Fascist Italy. Each member of the cabinet had his own particular viewpoint and personal mission that differed from the others. For Chamberlain, it was "to come to friendly terms with the dictators of Italy and Germany. And he conceived himself capable of achieving this relationship." Churchill worked with him for several years and knew his idiosyncrasies and his special abilities. Chamberlain came from a long line of famous political leaders. He had been Lord Mayor of Birmingham in 1915 and chairman of the Conservative Party, as well as serving as Chancellor of the Exchequer in Ramsay Macdonald's national government, and was largely a bureaucratic administrator. The three insular old cronies in the cabinet (Ramsay MacDonald, Baldwin, and Chamberlain) had worked together almost in isolation from the real world outside, while they had played out an old-fashioned game of provincial politics. But the world had become more sophisticated and brutal than they were able to comprehend. Times had changed without them noticing. Their time was now marked by Britain's war buildup against the might of Hitler's Nazi Germany.

A Question of Principles

Chamberlain believed in compromise and was prepared to recognize Mussolini's claims on Italy's conquest of Abyssinia. And he was ready to offer colonial concessions to Hitler. Where the word *appeasement* originated in British politics is difficult to determine, but it would gradually become a dirty word that tarnished everyone involved in it, from Chamberlain and Halifax to other rulers, like the British aristocracy and the landed gentry, and other pro-Nazis or admirers of German history. It became synonymous with cowardice. When Anthony Eden became foreign secretary, he would have none of it. Nor would Churchill.

Eden saw any arrangement with Italy as part of a general Mediterranean settlement to include Spain, all of which should be reached with close sympathy for France. Differences in the British cabinet became sharper by autumn 1937, when Chamberlain believed that Eden was obstructing him from opening discussions with Germany and Italy. Eden felt that Chamberlain was being too hasty to compromise with the dictators when Britain was too weak militarily to be in a strong bargaining position. Churchill sided with Eden and admired his courage and resoluteness, often remarking that his heart was in the right place.

The actions of the British cabinet were very naturally influenced by the spectrum of attitudes of its members. While Foreign Secretary Eden wanted to live in an ideal world, Chamberlain recognized Britain's economic, political, and military limitations, and preferred to use diplomatic expediency, whereas Lord Halifax was prepared to throw in his lot with the Nazis. Churchill adamantly insisted that the only way to win against Hitler's territorial acquisitiveness was by bargaining from a position of strength or obtaining victory in war.

Although the advantages of a diversified team are supposed to be the collective results of varied new ideas, the reality is that its more powerful members suppress contributions by the least powerful in order to have their own way. In this case, the most powerful was the prime minister, whose previous experience had only involved compromising with other opinions from reasonably cooperative and well-intentioned individuals when mayor of a provincial city in a parliamentary democracy. Chamberlain possessed very limited experience and outlook of European affairs. So it could be said that Eden didn't stand a chance against Chamberlain's naive belief that he could deal with two cynical and ruthless dictators who would not hesitate to use the utmost violence to get their own way. And Halifax was ready to give in to them. Without Churchill, there can be no doubt the war of words would have been lost, and those words would bind Britain to becoming a slave state in a Greater German Empire.

The disagreement of principles began to come to a head in January 1938 when Eden was on vacation in the South of France, and the American undersecretary of state, Sumner Welles, visited the British ambassador in Washington with a confidential message from President Roosevelt to Chamberlain. The President was deeply anxious at the deterioration of the international situation and wished to consult the British government on a plan to invite certain government representatives to Washington to discuss the underlying causes. Chamberlain replied that "His Majesty's Government would be prepared, for their part, if possible with the authority of the League of Nations, to recognize de jure the Italian occupation of Abyssinia, if they found that the Italian government on their side were ready to give evidence of their desire to contribute to the restoration of confidence and friendly relations."

Back in England, Eden, who had devoted himself to improving Anglo-American relations, was perturbed at what he considered to be Chamberlain's chilly rebuff of American overtures and support. Meanwhile, the U.S. President responded to it by saying he was gravely concerned that Britain might recognize the Italian position in Abyssinia. He believed it would only encourage undesirable Japanese policies in the Far East and also harm American public opinion toward Europe. President Roosevelt was running a personal risk by making overtures to Britain against his own domestic policy, which was not to involve the United States in the gloomy European drama that was unfolding. Powerful American political forces preferred a policy of isolationism from being caught up in the momentum of centuries of European hatreds and fears.

But Eden knew it could be a matter of life or death for Britain.[3] So his confidence in the future was at its lowest ebb when he went back to Paris to meet with the French in January, and they discussed the necessity of including Spain in any approach to Italy. The following month the Italians expressed their willingness to open discussions. But with Italy's refusal to discuss their position toward Austria, the conversation faltered and collapsed. Chamberlain agreed to new talks in Rome, but Eden was opposed to continuing to appease the dictators. With such serious differences of opinion between them, it seemed inevitable that one of them must resign.

After much soul-searching and deliberation with himself, Eden rejected the inaction of the British government and its tendency to appease Hitler. In a debate in the House of Commons on February 21, he rose to remark that "I do not believe that we can make progress in European appeasement if we allow the impression to gain currency abroad that we yield to constant pressure." He resigned and was instantly replaced as foreign secretary by Halifax. Now there was no one in the cabinet to oppose their policy of appeasing Hitler and Mussolini.

Chamberlain grew despondent when Franco's Fascist armies drove deeper into the Communist-occupied part of Spain. Gazing at a wall map, he decided that Czechoslovakia would be Hitler's next target for invasion and annexation because of its German-speaking populations. But when he studied the map, he had to admit that Britain could do nothing to prevent the Germans from conquering it, too. As would happen in Austria, the German-speaking people in Czechoslovakia would welcome the Nazis. It was another example of the drawback of democracy compared with dictatorship; the Nazis seemed to be everywhere at once—the Rhineland, the Sudetenland, Austria, Spain, Czechoslovakia. It was a result of the collapse and breakup of the multicultural Austro-Hungarian Empire in 1918.

Hitler described his tactics to acquire more territory as "the salami method"; as long as you take a thin slice at a time, no one objects. And it is too late after the whole salami has been eaten up. This piecemeal strategy is a divide-and-conquer tactic of using menacing threats to overcome opposition and achieve alliances. It had begun with his 1933 decree to suspend civil liberties in Germany and eliminate potential rivals by murdering them.

The Home Front

There was always plenty of mystery and entertainment available in London. It was the biggest capital city in Europe. The West End was a popular shopping center. Mayfair contained some of the most expensive and elegant town houses for the rich, and luxury hotels at which to serve them. It was bounded by Park Lane and Hyde Park, Piccadilly and Green Park, and Regent and Oxford Streets. Few ventured into the mercantile and financial district of the City unless they worked there. And there were few or no residents living in that area. Beyond it was the East End, where poorer folk lived. Docklands, Wapping, and Limehouse were inhabited largely by those who worked on the River Thames or in the docks. An aura of mystery still lingered over the river traffic and warehouses along the banks of the Thames, from Edgar Wallace's sixpenny thrillers and Sherlock Holmes detective mysteries.

The West End of London was surrounded by vast suburbs of middle-class homes. But few people hopped on to a red double-decker bus or into the Underground railway system to travel further afield than their own neighborhood. The subway system stretched for miles to the outer reaches of the suburbs, some built as recently in the northwest as the 1930s. But it was of no interest unless you lived there—other than for Hampstead Heath, which provided breathing space for a day's outing. Nor were the closer respectable suburbs of Clapham or Peckham Rye, Balham, or Brixton and Croydon of much interest to anyone else. They would be helplessly lost in streets of narrow row houses that looked exactly alike mile after mile.

Each neighborhood had its own local pubs and churches, parks and community halls, and movie theaters, so that local communities generally remained in their own localities, like separate villages, rather than exploring more central areas like the West End. Idle youths with time to kill leaned against lampposts at street corners, cigarettes drooping limply from the mouth, as they aimlessly teased any girls who passed by—occasionally receiving a cheeky retort—while they waited for the pubs to open.[4]

Suburban block after suburban block consisted of identical row houses and look-alike two-family homes, built by long-forgotten Victorian or Edwardian tract home builders to last forever. Although every one of the residents inside might like to imagine they were different from anyone else—even unique— they had long since been categorized and classified by statisticians or municipal councils as working class or lower middle class. (The middling sort lived elsewhere in more distinguished neighborhoods closer to downtown.) Many were Cockneys, a tribe of city dweller who had survived the streets of the metropolis from before Queen Victoria's time, and had been recorded for posterity by the persistent researcher of the streets, Henry Mayhew, who lived at the time of Charles Dickens. He profiled them in three volumes that he called *London Labour and the London Poor*, after pacing the streets himself. That was also the time that former Prime Minister Benjamin Disraeli recognized that London consisted of "Two Nations"—the haves and the have-nots.[5]

Mayhew categorized them then as "those that will work, those that cannot work, and those that will not work." Among them were Irish crossing sweepers who cleared away the dung from horse-drawn vehicles, and illiterate young female Irish lasses who had no education or skills and relied on seduction on the streets or in public houses for survival. There were Jewish old-clothes men, children called mudlarks who dredged the muddy banks of the Thames at low tide for anything they could find, London chimney sweeps, dustmen, sewer hunters, coal-heavers, street musicians, street artists, dock laborers, watermen, steamboat men, cab drivers and bus drivers, and London's vagrants. Most had moved up the social and economic ladder by now, or fallen by the wayside. Those that survived now worked on the railways, on London's buses or taxis, or the extensive Underground train system. Or they ran machinery in factories, labored in warehouses or workshops, or undertook clerical work in offices. Some bought, some sold, while the more literate wrote out invoices.

Unemployed male youths could still be distinguished by two of Mayhew's distinct categories: "Those that will work" and "Those that will not work." The latter were rebels against family and society who were envious of anyone else and ready to pull them down. They were the ones who joined the black-shirted youths of the British Union of Fascists, often with criminal records.

The Battle of Cable Street

On Sunday, October 4, 1936, a number of people in the know drove to the East End, or gave each other rides, by way of Cable Street, which ran due east from Tower Hill. The neighborhood was grim and gray with no redeeming features—an area of run-down local storefronts, warehouses, and tenement buildings, the apartments often lacking toilets or bathrooms.

Mosley's proposed march to take possession of the East End had been well publicized. If anyone asked their way in the neighborhood, they would likely be told that the Fascist rally was planned to be somewhere around Dock Street and Christian. It was marked by the presence of the Metropolitan Police, who were out in larger numbers than usual. Crowds of pedestrians milled around with some unfathomable purpose or simply hung around street corners to wait and see what might happen. Mosley had chosen the area for his march because of its Jewish population, who had been advised to keep well away from the route and not allow themselves to be baited.

The noise and activity increased closer to the proposed venue, where some people were building barricades. Drivers of cars and trucks who saw what was going on backed out of the streets or did a fast detour to leave the neighborhood altogether.

Most opposition to the Fascist marchers was considered likely to come from Communists who were better organized than local residents, mostly Jewish working class, Cockneys, or Irish laborers. The Communist Party had pasted posters on some walls to rally workers and anti-Fascists to protest or fight against Mosley's provocation. Some roads had been blocked off by abandoned trucks and other vehicles, as well as improvised barricades that reminded some people of the French Revolution in Paris—a specter that had haunted the West ever since.

It seemed like there were more police than protesters—thousands of uniformed constables and a number of mounted police. Even before Mosley and his Blackshirts appeared, foot police were wading in to push back some of the crowds, supported by police on horseback. Crowds booed them and jeered them. Although many of the police came from the same neighborhood, some of the women in the tenements began to empty the contents of chamber pots onto their heads whenever they were pushed close enough by the crowds.

A great deal of energy and adrenaline seemed to have been pumped up among the forward protesters around the barricades and the women in the tenements. A double-decker London bus had been overturned as part of the barricades. Anger mounted as some people high up in the tenement windows saw the approaching cavalcade of cars and the leading Blackshirts in the procession. Police pushed the crowds further back and watched out in case vehicles were set afire.

As soon as a leading car in the procession appeared, boos and jeers and shouting from thousands of protesters almost obliterated the enthusiastic singing from the marching Blackshirts who followed it. Police did their best to protect the uniformed Mosley, who stood up in his car, grinning confidently and making a stiff-armed Fascist salute. Some police charged the barricades, while others arrested individual men or women in the wriggling crowd. It took half a dozen constables to carry one man away, reinforced by three or four mounted police, followed by cries and shouts from bystanders and the women leaning out of tenement windows. Despite police numbers and the intimidating horses, the police force seemed to be almost defenseless against attackers who wielded clubs, iron bars, and what looked like broken chair legs. A few people scattered handfuls of tiny, three-cornered steel caltrops onto the road, with their painful upright spike designed to topple cavalry horses. The horses slipped and fell, whinnying in protest and creating pandemonium in some areas.

Evidently Mosley had been warned by the Home Secretary or the police to tone down his usual provocative performance from a platform or his open car. Even so, he waved his arms in flamboyant imitation of Hitler and shouted as loud as he could. But he was barely heard above all the angry noise from the crowds. The most active people were the police pushing back the crowds. Instead of protecting the community, they fought against them. There seemed to be about five thousand police to protect about half that number of Fascist marchers. The anti-Fascist crowds who had come looking for a fight numbered up to about a hundred thousand. Some attacked the police, while Mosley's open car was hurriedly waved on ahead by traffic cops to prevent it stopping. Instead, Mosley and his private army were directed back toward the City.

Fights continued long after the Fascist brigade had gone. Some men held rocks in their hands and looked for victims. A few sported brass knuckles. There were running battles with the police. People complained that instead of protecting the residents from the Fascists, the police had orders to protect Mosley and public property, that authority was in the hands of the wrong people. It pushed them into the welcoming arms of the Communist Party, since none of the other political parties showed any interest in helping them.

What had the Fascist marchers achieved? A show of force on one hand and an equal show of resistance on the other. It was a stalemate, except that the British Union of Fascists would obtain plenty of media publicity and new recruits from the unemployed masses. The march on the East End certainly produced plenty of publicity, but a shrewd move by the Home Secretary addressed the matter of recruiting by implementing a Public Order Act of 1936 only a few months later, which banned uniforms for political parties. The result was that the rank and file of British Fascists shrank dramatically instead.[6]

4

THE ART OF DECEPTION

The Conservative Party Conference was held on the day Mussolini's forces attacked Abyssinia. And, at the general election, Prime Minister Baldwin spoke strongly of the need to rearm. But in order to appeal to the large number of the electorate who wanted peace, not war—a research survey had been carried out that showed conclusively that most people in England wanted never to see a war again—he made another speech, this time to the Peace Society, stating, "I give you my word there will be no great rearmaments." He was therefore able to obtain the votes of those who were prepared to go to war and those who were not. The result was that Baldwin's Conservative government won the General Election.

It also helped that, due to Eden's diplomacy, Britain led the League of Nations against Italy's invasion of Ethiopia. Emperor Hailie Selassie was now in exile. He appealed to the League and was feted wherever he went in attempts to find allies to remove the Italian invaders. The British public was particularly sympathetic toward this lean and tiny "Lion of Judah," compared with the unusually tall and long-boned Abyssinian warriors in their regal togas, usually seen on Movietone News at the movie theater vainly waving their spears at Italian air force planes dropping bombs on their villages.

Since the electorate had now granted it another five years to govern, the new Conservative government was obliged to come to terms with reality. Sir Robert Vansittart, now at the Foreign Office, kept a steady eye on Hitler, but Baldwin was convinced that it was most prudent to keep the peace at any price, particularly as Germany was now allied with Fascist Italy. And the French government had already entered into a Franco-Italian agreement in January.

As Churchill saw it, if the British Admiralty used its naval power to defeat the Italian navy and closed the Suez Canal, Britain could influence the situation in Europe from a position of strength. But the British government had declared it would not go to war for Abyssinia, whatever happened. Baldwin was good at righteous indignation to protect himself and his party in the House, but not at war.

Mussolini, with his histrionic posturing, was also good at mimicking righteous indignation. But now that he was pressured by sanctions, it was said he was ready to compromise. He was already in bad odor internationally for using poison gas against the Abyssinian civilian population. But he was not prepared to make large concessions since his forces were defeating the Abyssinians. Vansittart was drawn into the Abyssinian conflict, although he was far more concerned with the German threat. Perhaps a peace offer could be made in which Abyssinia retained 80 percent of its territory. Instead, to everyone's shock, Sir Samuel Hoare and Laval had come to their own terms over Abyssinia. And Baldwin, once respected, was suddenly despised by all for what looked like his double-dealing. The Hoare-Laval Pact of December 1935 gave permission for Italy to possess two-thirds of the territory it conquered in Ethiopia and approval to expand its colonies in Africa. In exchange, Ethiopia would be allowed a small strip of land with access to the sea.

As far as Churchill and Eden were concerned, Hoare had acted dishonorably. Not surprisingly, he was known as "Slippery Sam" by his intimates. He was forced to resign when the underhanded agreement became public, and he wept openly like a whipped prep-school boy in Parliament. The Hoare-Laval Pact was trashed, and the House graciously accepted the prime minister's apology. British politics were still polite and considerate and civilized. In fact, Hoare had simply been following the appeasement policy of the cabinet, in which he supported Chamberlain and Halifax and was part of their inner circle advising them on foreign policy. Another pro-German appeaser was the British ambassador to Germany, Nevile Henderson.

Had Britain stood firm against Hitler and Mussolini instead of appeasing them, war could have been averted. All six of them carried a heavy burden of guilt. MacDonald, Baldwin, Hoare, Henderson, Halifax, and Chamberlain— different though they were, they shared numerous characteristics—they were all eager for power. All were smug and complacent, pompous and self-opinionated; all were competitive, and all were shaped by the past and appeared to be aged before their time with the burdens of hypocrisies. Seen through modern eyes, they all possessed the appearance of undertakers preparing Britain for burial. Their close similarities were probably why they were chosen for office; they had grown up and been educated among the same social class with the same values, prejudices, attitudes, and opinions. Each of them was "one of us."

However faithful they might have imagined they were toward England, each had been involved in deceits as politicians: it goes with the territory. Hoare had been employed by MI5. And they accepted the necessity of deception while waging wars of words with foreigners, of whom each had a very low opinion. They very likely considered themselves fortunate to belong to an island race, separated from barbarians by the English Channel and the Atlantic Ocean—in an ideal location if a nation is powerful enough to be independent of others. But that was the crux of the problem, since they had allowed Britain to be eroded of its power and therefore its independence by their own incompetence.

Anthony Eden became Foreign Secretary at the end of December. Meanwhile, Mussolini's forces swiftly annexed the whole of Abyssinian territory with brutal efficiency. And Britain lost face. An article in the *Münchner Zeitung* provided fair comment on the situation on May 16, 1936: "The English like a comfortable life compared with our German standards. This does not indeed mean that they are incapable of sustained efforts, but they avoid them so far as they can, without impairing their personal and national security."[1]

One result of all the turmoil was that the League of Nations was embarrassed by the breakdown in collective security that it had been founded to guarantee. And a new mood emerged in England, in which those formerly committed to peace at any price—like Liberals and Socialists—now began to contemplate war against Fascist and Nazi tyranny with equanimity. As Churchill pointed out, with tongue in cheek, the British nation, more than any other country, is occasionally ready to fight for a cause when it is convinced that it will not benefit materially from it. His observation was unarguable, since that attitude of philosophical detachment had been encouraged among Britain's classical scholars who looked romantically toward ancient Greece.

What surprised Churchill was that the government didn't seize the opportunity provided by this change of heart. He felt that the government could have more eagerly and enthusiastically led the nation forward by showing a more positive attitude toward the emergency. But the British government retained its policy of moderation to keep things quiet. And yet, Churchill maintained that if Germany were allowed to rearm without the Allies and the former associated powers interfering actively, a Second World War was most likely. The longer the government postponed a trial of strength, the worse would be Britain's chances of stopping Hitler without going to war. And then there was a likelihood that the British would suffer a dreadful ordeal even if victorious. The crux of the matter was that Britain had condoned Hitler and Germany's growing power by not acting when it should. The battle for peace was now virtually lost. Hitler was now free to strike. But where?

Columns of about thirty-five thousand German troops streamed across the border of the Rhineland at noon on March 7, 1936, simultaneously with an announcement that Hitler intended to reoccupy the region that had belonged to Germany before its defeat in the Great War. They entered all the main German-speaking towns and were greeted with joy by the populations. Meanwhile, German diplomats made conciliatory proposals intended to cover up their invasion with ambiguous language. It was a breach of the Pact of Locarno. The French were shocked, since it, and another peace treaty, had been intended to protect their sovereignty. The Rhineland was vital to France.

All Eyes on England

Churchill claimed the Rhineland invasion could have been avoided if the Allies had been more alert and less complacent. After all, the French army possessed nearly a hundred divisions and an air force—and was still falsely believed to be the strongest in Europe. And he had no doubt that if the government had mobilized, Hitler would have been compelled by his own general staff to withdraw. He was convinced France's was the only army in Europe big enough and strong enough to drive the German invaders out of the Rhineland. And there was no doubt in his mind that the Allies of the previous war still possessed superior strength.

French Foreign Minister Flandin met with the British, saying, "The whole world and especially the small nations today turn their eyes toward England. If England will act now, she can lead Europe. You will have a policy, all the world will follow you, and thus you will prevent war. It is your last chance. . . . If you do not stop Germany by force today, war is inevitable."

At which Lord Lothian objected languidly by murmuring, "After all, they are only going into their own back garden."

After Hitler's successful coup, the dictator announced, "All Germany's territorial ambitions have now been satisfied."

Germany's violation was debated on March 26. Eden stood up for the restoration of the Pact of Locarno. But the cabinet was disinclined to oppose Hitler's breach of the Pact, despite Churchill's claim that Hitler's violation of the Rhineland was serious because it threatened Holland, Belgium, and France.

Meanwhile, German Foreign Minister Neurath talked to the American ambassador in Moscow on May 18, 1936, revealing that, "the youth of Austria was turning more and more toward the Nazis, and the dominance of the Nazi Party in Austria was inevitable and only a question of time."

People began to draw together in England at the realization of the threat of Germany's military power and its deceit and lack of ethics. Whether the public realized that Germany was led by a madman or not, Churchill did. And he knew that psychopaths are incurable liars who can't be trusted—that they are isolated from reality by their delusions.

At the same time, there was a problem of responsibility, service, and leadership with the new young King Edward VIII—known formerly as a popular Prince of Wales before the death of King George V and his own coronation. He was a weak young man and a womanizer, known for his affairs with other men's wives. He was now caught in the scheming web of a twice-divorced American named Mrs. Simpson. One divorce was frowned upon by most people at that time, but two were considered entirely unacceptable and even suspicious. But evidently not by Edward, who was in a state of thrall by the divorcee. The nation was curious about her sexual power, but disdainful and untrusting. The prime minister judged public opinion to be against her, and it was made absolutely clear that the British nation would never accept her as their queen. When the new king abdicated rather than give her up, there was a general sigh of relief. She (and also, as it would turn out, he) had German Nazi connections that caused considerable embarrassment to the royal family. And they could be dangerous to Britain. He was given a post as governor of the Bahamas, in which he was a mere figurehead with no job description, but it kept them out of the way.

Even so, the former king remained a threat to Britain for years, while being willingly manipulated by German diplomats with the intention of reinstating him as a puppet king in England after they had invaded and conquered the British Isles and were able to pull his strings.

His abdication led to the coronation of King George VI, a man who had never been trained to be a monarch and thought himself unfit to serve, or even appear before the public, because of his severe stammer. He was afraid people might think he was an idiot. Nevertheless, he sincerely believed in serving his country, and he struggled to get control and speak with a commanding voice. Although not a warrior hero type, like Shakespeare's Henry V, he was, surprisingly, the ideal monarch to rule Britain in wartime, because he was so obviously genuine and sincere, despite his reserved personality.

Churchill became more alarmed at events in Germany, while the British government failed to respond in the same way. He continued to criticize the government's slow pace of rearmament. The war office moved at the snail's pace of the last war, whereas Hitler—a great admirer of Henry Ford— had encouraged German industry to greater productivity by more modern mass-production methods. Nevertheless, the difference now between Churchill and the government was one of degree rather than principle: both favored rearming and laid emphasis on the air force. Both worried about the darkening international situation. But the government was too slow, while Churchill was always conscious of the necessity of timing and attempted to push forward and place continual pressure on the cabinet.[2]

It was obvious that what Britain suffered from was a dearth of leadership. It seemed as if all the leaders had been lost on the battlefields in the last war. Churchill had openly called Prime Minister MacDonald "almost a mental case." Ramsay MacDonald, worn down by age and overwork, was being blackmailed because of letters he wrote to "a foreign tart," and was held to scorn by all.[3] MacDonald finally went to Buckingham Palace to hand in his resignation on June 7, 1935.

Prime Minister Baldwin retired in May 1937 after the coronation, making way for Neville Chamberlain as Britain's new prime minister.

Churchill described Chamberlain as "alert, businesslike, opinionated, and self-confident in a very high degree." As Chancellor of the Exchequer, he had kept a tight control on military expenditure. He was also a firm opponent of any emergency measures. That was largely because of Britain's poor economy since the Great Depression. His ambition was to leave a legacy as the Great Peacemaker, and he was prepared to keep the peace at any cost, even by groveling, as he would do, to Hitler. The public, who were generally disinterested in politics, and largely ignorant of it, would remember him only as he was at the end—a weak and frail figure bowed with ill-health and grief. But he was not the silly old fool with an umbrella who underrated Hitler as he was made out to be. Although he desperately wanted peace, he prepared for war. But he did so while trying to maintain a strong economy. His method, and Lord Halifax's, was diplomacy, which has been defined as war by other means.

But it was already too late. The damage had been done before Chamberlain took office as prime minister—he simply extended it. And he, too, would fail because he lacked imagination and an understanding of history and foreign affairs.

5

A THIN SLICE AT A TIME

WHEN CHURCHILL WAS STILL ONLY A private Member of Parliament and not yet in the cabinet, he was invited to a private meeting at the German embassy with the German ambassador to Britain. Ribbentrop told him he felt he should make the full case for an Anglo-German alliance. They spoke for two hours about Britain being willing to give Germany a free hand in Eastern Europe, because their expanding population needed more room in a Greater Germany. Ambassador von Ribbentrop showed him the areas they wanted on a wall map. Churchill responded that he was sure the British government would not agree. Ribbentrop turned away abruptly and said, "In that case, war is inevitable. There is no way out. The Führer is resolved. Nothing will stop him and nothing will stop us."

At which Churchill warned him not to underrate England.[1]

But Churchill knew that the Allies had only narrowly survived the previous war. He was also aware that Britain was threatened by the greatest danger and emergency in its entire history. For one of the major problems at that time was that it would take four years to set up munitions factories and manufacture armaments and other war materials to obtain parity with Germany. It would mean—if war commenced in 1938 (as H. G. Wells had predicted in his 1933 science fiction novel, *The Shape of Things to Come*)—Britain's forces would be at a disadvantage when fighting German and Italian troops for the first four years after the British government decided to transform existing factories and also find new ones to make war material. So how could Britain prevent itself from being invaded by much bigger and better-trained German forces?

It was already too late to count the cost of doing so in loss of lives. The cost of *not* going to war could have meant the annihilation of about 80 percent of the population of Britain and the continent of Europe. Those left alive would be used as slave labor until they dropped from malnutrition, disease, and exhaustion. And there was no doubt that the destruction and colonization of the United States would follow. It, as well as Russia, would be part of the Greater Germany that Hitler had always envisaged. Like the madman he was, he had candidly set out his plans in *Mein Kampf*—the bestseller that had made him rich but that hardly anyone seemed to have read. It had been aimed at making him popular with the German electorate, and it had succeeded.[2]

All of that had to be taken into consideration to form a judgment on policy by the new Prime Minister, Neville Chamberlain. Meanwhile, Churchill noted the deficiencies in 1938 when Britain had been rearming very slowly for three years; there was inefficiency and overlapping and waste. He remarked on all of them, big and small. For example, he asked why the Guards were drilling with flags instead of machine guns? Why the aircraft industry needed 90,000 men and produced only a half or a third of what Germany produced with a 110,000 men? And why was the government thinking in terms of hundreds of antiaircraft artillery when the Germans had thousands? [3]

Despite Churchill always showing courtesy and consideration toward Chamberlain, his private opinion was that the prime minister was "the narrowest, most ignorant, most ungenerous man."[4] And yet he had been educated at Rugby, one of the leading British public schools. Hoare had been a schoolboy at Harrow—the same prestigious private school as Churchill. Lord Halifax, whose family stemmed from Viking stock, was educated at Eton. So was Ambassador Nevile Henderson. Stanley Baldwin was another old Harrovian. Only Ramsay MacDonald (the illegitimate son of a laborer) had gone to a modest parish school at Drainie in Scotland. All the others were upper-class gentleman. We are left to wonder what it was they learned, with so little evidence to show for it in their highly rewarded political careers.

The Spanish Civil War

Meanwhile, a bitter civil war was being waged in Spain. It had begun in July 1936. There was a Communist conspiracy to destroy the government by a military coup, and also an anarchist plot to topple it. Instead, the army and the Church supported General Franco's military revolt. Spanish sailors killed their officers and a destructive civil war erupted with cold-blooded massacres of political opponents. The Communists seized power. And Franco's Fascist forces retaliated with equally ferocious violence.

In November 1936, Hitler's Condor Legion of army and air force troops supported General Franco and his Fascists when he overthrew the Republican Spanish government. It was a disaster for the masses, who had only recently been freed from oppression by the Church and the monarchists, whom the Fascists supported. The Luftwaffe learned the technique of carpet bombing. After that, Hitler proceeded to intimidate Germany's European neighbors.

Britain agreed to a policy of nonintervention in Spanish affairs. But both Nazi Germany and Communist Russia threw their forces into the struggle on opposite sides. Bombing civilians from the air by German pilots typified a new kind of "total war" to be waged from the air on old men, women, and children in small and vulnerable towns like Guernica. The objective was to demoralize the population.

It was an opportunity for Germany and Italy, and the Soviets, to rehearse military strategies and tactics and train their armed forces in all-out war in readiness for the far bigger world war to come. Piracy also returned with the outrages of several merchant ships being sunk in the Mediterranean by Italian submarines.

Yielding to Pressure

Meanwhile, in Austria, Chancellor Kurt Schuschnigg held off a German invasion for as long as he could, despite Hitler's warning and the assassination of his predecessor. But he knew he needed powerful allies if he wanted to prevent Hitler from annexing Austria. And Mussolini failed to continue to support him. He knew that Hitler intended to swallow up Austria, and that the dictator had planned his tactics in detail during the previous year of deceptions and obfuscation.

When Churchill considered Britain's obligations to Europe in those circumstances, he recognized two major questions that needed answering: whether decisive action by Britain and France would force Hitler to back down or even result in his overthrow by a military conspiracy—and whether the delays caused by attempting to satisfy Hitler and Mussolini's ambitions would place the Allies in a better or worse position, compared with Germany. The answer depended on who was asked.

Chamberlain grew despondent when Franco's Fascist armies drove deeper into the Communist-occupied part of Spain. Gazing at a wall map, he decided that Czechoslovakia would be Hitler's next target for invasion and annexation because of its German-speaking populations. But when he studied the map, he had to admit that Britain could do nothing to prevent the Germans from conquering it, too. As had happened in Austria, the German-speaking people in Czechoslovakia would welcome the Nazis. Who would be next? In the circumstances, Churchill was amazed that Chamberlain was prepared to give a guarantee of help and protection to Poland within a year. The British government proclaimed a formal treaty with Poland on August 25. As it would turn out:

> The declared objectives of the Nazi German government were two-fold—the absorption by the Reich of all German minorities living beyond her frontiers, and thereby the extension of her living space in the East. But the less publicized purpose of German policy was sound military tactics—it would prevent Czechoslovakia from becoming either a Russian air base or an Anglo-French military makeweight in the event of war. So, as early as June, 1937, Hitler had instructed the German General Staff to draft plans for the invasion and destruction of the Czechoslovak State.

Eliminating Opponents

Hitler's public justification for invading Czechoslovakia was made in a speech to the Reichstag at the beginning of 1938: "Over ten million Germans live in two of the states adjoining our frontier." He went on to say that it was Germany's duty to protect those fellow Germans and secure for them "general freedom, personal, political, and ideological." And—as if to reinforce his seemingly benevolent creed, Göring assured the Czech Minister in Berlin that Germany had "no evil intentions" toward Czechoslovakia.

As for Austria, on February 12, 1938, Hitler summoned the Austrian Chancellor Herr von Schuschnigg to Berchtesgaden. The following is taken from a record Schuschnigg made of their meeting.[5]

Hitler said, "You don't really believe you could hold me up for half an hour? After the troops will follow the S.A. and the Legion! No one will be able to hinder the vengeance, not even myself. Do you want to turn Austria into another Spain? All this I would like if possible to avoid."

"Naturally I realize you can march into Austria," Schuschnigg replied, "but Mr. Chancellor, whether we wish it or not, that would lead to the shedding of blood. We are not alone in the world. That probably means war."

"Will you take the responsibility for that, Herr Schuschnigg? Don't believe that anyone in the world will hinder me in my decisions! England? England will not lift a finger for Austria. . . . And for France it is now too late!"

Schuschnigg announced a referendum on Austria's independence on March 11. Hitler stated he would not accept it and sent him an ultimatum demanding he hand over all power to the Austrian Nazis. The next day, Hitler declared unification of Austria with Nazi Germany. Schuschnigg resigned. Austria was annexed by Hitler, and German troops marched into Austria the following day to cheering crowds.

The grim reality was that the strategic position in Central Europe had changed. And on March 14, although French Premier Blum announced that France would continue to honor its agreements with Czechoslovakia, the former French Foreign Minister Flandin was convinced that "there was no hope for France other than in an arrangement with Germany." No doubt he was well aware that although the French army was previously considered to be the biggest in Europe, it was in a shambles. When the Blum government fell, Daladier replaced him and bore the heavy responsibility of French policy from thereon, together with French Foreign Minister Bonnet, who replaced Flandin.

But the French, who were once masters of Europe, led by Napoleon, had never recovered from their crushing defeat in the Franco-Prussian War of 1870. Some said they had lost their pride in the French army after the defeat at Sedan and the Siege of Metz, followed by the fall of Paris and the collapse of France. And they had been demoralized by the previous world war. Despite the huge size of their army, they possessed no strong leaders and were too apathetic to fight.

6

THE MUNICH CRISIS

NEVILLE CHAMBERLAIN WAS NOW IN COMPLETE control of Britain's foreign policy, and he had not abandoned hopes of an arrangement with Germany. Halifax followed his guidance, although with increasing doubts. So did the cabinet. Now their eyes were focused on Czechoslovakia, where Hitler was convinced that neither Britain nor France would fight to protect the freedom of the Czechs. But Hitler's military advisers disagreed about the timing and the Allied strength, believing that using powerful invasion forces would leave too few reserve divisions to protect Germany's borders, since they feared an attack by Soviet Russian troops.

Whoever said Premier Blum wouldn't last was right—Daladier took over from him very shortly afterward. And it seemed at first that diplomats had been right about Hitler hesitating to invade Czechoslovakia for fear of a Russian attack. Then, on June 12, Daladier announced that France was pledged to the former premier's promise of support for Czechoslovakia—building up a war of nerves as to which tactics might trigger the wrong move.

Hitler's double agenda continued to confuse Britain while it provided time for Germany to prepare for its invasion of Czechoslovakia, by sending his personal aide to London to meet with Foreign Secretary Lord Halifax, suggesting further discussions with Chamberlain. Although negotiations broke down within fourteen days, Hitler's delaying tactics had served their purpose. He was a master of the art of deception. He overruled his advisers and ordered an attack on Czechoslovakia only six days later.

Even so, the threat of intervention by Soviet Russia persisted. Churchill wrote to Halifax to inform him that a French diplomat had called on Litvinov in Moscow to ask him what aid the Russians would give to Czechoslovakia in the event of a German attack. Litvinov responded by asking what the French intended to do and pointed out that the French had a direct obligation to act on behalf of the Czechs. The French diplomat received no direct reply except that the Soviet Union would fulfill its own obligations. Litvinov informed him that the Soviet Union was ready to join in conversations with France and Czechoslovakia on how to provide assistance to the Czechs. But both recognized the problems of Poland and Rumania, who were neutral. It posed a question of whether Russian troops and air forces would be allowed to pass through Rumanian territory.

Events followed swiftly when Daladier contacted Chamberlain late on the night/early morning of September 13–14, 1938, to inform him that his government wished to make a joint approach to Hitler personally. Instead, Chamberlain took his own initiative by telegraphing Hitler that he proposed to visit him. In reply, Hitler invited him to his headquarters at Berchtesgaden the same afternoon. The prime minister flew to Germany on September 15. But he had got it all wrong, since it turned out that the Czechs believed they had their situation under control. Chamberlain's trip merely gave the Germans an opportunity to increase their demands.

One thing Chamberlain recognized was that Hitler was in a fighting mood, whereas the French had no fight in them at all—they already looked defeated. So his only concern at that point was to obtain peace at any price. When Chamberlain's discussion with Hitler broke off, he was left kicking his heels and pacing the balcony of his hotel. Then he sent a written message to Hitler saying he was ready to convey new German proposals to the Czech government. After all, Britain had no treaty obligation with Czechoslovakia, and France was not prepared to go to war for the Czechs, so there was no point in resisting Hitler's demands.

As a result, the British and French proceeded to draft proposals, insisting that Britain and France (and Soviet Russia, whom they had not consulted) should guarantee the new Czech frontiers after Czechoslovakia had been partitioned in accordance with Hitler's threats. Churchill joined in the discussions. What he questioned was whether or not Hitler had grandiose Napoleonic ambitions. And, if they gave in to him and he succeeded in obtaining more territory, whether he'd go on demanding more and more.

Either way, they thought the Czech government had no choice other than to accept the Anglo-French proposals. But Churchill thought otherwise: to him it was "the complete surrender of the Western Democracies to the Nazi threat of force." He declared to the London press that it would not bring peace or security to England or France, who had been weakened by this more dangerous situation, since, in military terms, a neutralized Czechoslovakia would help Germany by freeing up twenty-five German divisions to threaten the Western Front. And it would give the Nazis access to the Black Sea.

Political tactics are often compared to a game of chess in which neither player knows what is in the enemy's mind. But Churchill's sense of history and geography, and his military experience, enabled him to visualize the whole picture of what was likely to happen if Britain made the wrong move.

Meanwhile, Litvinov warned the League of Nations that they intended to fulfill their obligations under the Pact and, together with France, afford assistance to Czechoslovakia by the ways open to them. Their war department was ready to participate immediately in a conference with representatives of the French and Czechoslovak war departments in order to discuss the appropriate measures.[1]

The naivety and inexperience in foreign affairs of Britain's prime minister would be confirmed years later in a letter he wrote to his sister after meeting Hitler at Berchtesgaden on September 15, 1938. "I got the impression that here was a man who could be relied upon when he had given his word."[2] He reported to the cabinet afterward that Hitler "would not deliberately deceive a man whom he respected with whom he had been in negotiation." In fact, Hitler had only contempt for Chamberlain's weakness when he saw how easily he could manipulate him.

Chamberlain was a decent and sincere man and completely unfit to be a head of state, because he seemed to believe that everyone else was, too. He lacked a sense of reality in a dangerous world from mixing only with his own sort of people. Nor did he possess the imagination to conceive of the type and extent of organized criminal evil and awfulness that others could perpetrate. It suggests also that he had no idea of history, since some knowledge of Tudor England alone—in which romance went hand in hand with extreme cruelty, deceit, and torture—should have opened his eyes to his fellow men.

When Chamberlain flew to Germany to meet Hitler again, he was told his proposals were unacceptable. Hitler told him they would be replaced with other proposals that he had not contemplated. All that the British prime minister obtained from Hitler was an extension of the dictator's assurances that he would not move his German troops, pending the results of negotiations. Chamberlain agreed to appeal to the Czech government to avoid any action that might provoke incidents. And Hitler ended by adding his pacifying mantra that "this was the last of his territorial ambitions." He assured Chamberlain that he wanted to be friends with England.

Chamberlain attempted to justify his acts to the House of Commons. But it was obvious that his limited experience of foreign affairs and his desire for peace had blinded him to the fact that he had been outmaneuvered and outwitted by Hitler. The dictator was merely using him as an errand boy to avoid having to move German troops to Czechoslovakia and make war to achieve his objective. The prime minister had also ignored the effects of his arrangements with Hitler on one of the greatest military powers in the world, as if it didn't exist. It was yet another blind spot. And his mark of disdain would not be forgotten by Soviet Russia.

Soon after Chamberlain returned to England, Hitler made an angry attack on Czechoslovakia and its premier, Benes, in Berlin, stating that the Czechs "must clear out of the Sudetenland by the twenty-sixth," adding, "This is the last territorial claim I have to make in Europe."

Chamberlain candidly admitted to the House that he was now aware that he was confronted by "a totally unexpected situation." And after discussions with Halifax and Churchill, a communiqué was drafted and issued, which included the following statement: "If, in spite of the efforts made by the British prime minister, a German attack is made on Czechoslovakia, the immediate result must be that France will be bound to come to her assistance, and Great Britain and Russia will certainly stand by France."

The Czechs Mobilize

Meanwhile, the Czechs mobilized their forces. "They had a million and a half men armed behind the strongest fortress line in Europe, and equipped by a highly organized and powerful industrial machine."[3] The French army was partly mobilized, and, albeit reluctantly, the French Ministers were prepared to honor their obligations to Czechoslovakia. Just before midnight on September 27, the warning telegram was sent out from the British Admiralty ordering the mobilization of the fleet for the following day. As an island, and without the protection of its fleet, Britain was not only vulnerable to invasion from the sea, but its population could also be starved to death by enemy blockades.

But contrary to Chamberlain's fears, the crisis in September scared the German generals even more than it did the British government, because thirty to forty Czech divisions were deployed on Germany's eastern frontier, in addition to the weight of the French army. So the odds were nearly eight to one against Germany succeeding if Hitler gave the order to attack. There was also a possibility that a hostile Russia might operate from Czech airfields, and Soviet armies might push their way forward through Poland or Rumania. So passions rose to fever pitch as Hitler wavered on the threshold of war.

Could Hitler take the plunge? Or should he retreat in the face of unfavorable public opinion? And anyway, could he afford to back down now, after all his threats? What he didn't know was that there had been a secret military plot to arrest him with Göring, Goebbels, and Himmler. It was a crucial point at which powerful actions by the Allies could have altered history, had they known about it.

"By the beginning of September," wrote German Chief of Staff General Halder, long afterward, "we had taken the necessary steps to immunize Germany from this madman."[4] But the action was deferred to await the outcome of Chamberlain's imminent meeting with Hitler at Berchtesgaden. The destiny of the civilized world was interspersed with such missed opportunities that might also be traps for the innocent and unwary.

Then, as Hitler hesitated, Prime Minister Neville Chamberlain broadcast to the British nation, "How horrible, fantastic, incredible, it is that we should be digging trenches and trying on gas masks here because of a quarrel in a faraway country." Soon after, he received a reply from Hitler to his letter offering to join in the guarantee of the new frontiers of Czechoslovakia. It changed nothing. But Chamberlain eagerly drafted a personal message to Hitler, saying, "I feel convinced that we could reach agreement in a week."

Chamberlain was speaking in the House when a message arrived from Hitler inviting him to Munich. He immediately conveyed the information to the government: "Herr Hitler has agreed to postpone mobilization for twenty-four hours. . . . That is not all. I have something further to say to the House yet. I have now been informed by Herr Hitler that he invites me to meet him at Munich tomorrow morning. He has also invited Signor Mussolini and Monsieur Daladier." But neither Soviet Russia nor any Czechs were included in the invitation.

"Churchill had called Chamberlain's flight to meet Hitler 'the stupidest thing that has ever been done.'"[5] But many people felt enormous relief at the news. And Chamberlain's followers would maintain that it bought another year for Britain to rearm.

Chamberlain's third meeting would be a memorable one. A memorandum was drafted and signed on September 30, which accepted that the Sudetenland would be evacuated in five stages beginning on October 1 and completed within ten days. Then the prime minister requested a private talk with Hitler. They met in Hitler's flat in Munich later that morning. Chamberlain brought with him a draft declaration he had prepared, and Hitler immediately signed it without comment. No doubt he saw that it didn't amount to much. And they left apparently on good terms.

The British prime minister should have known by now that Hitler's agreements meant nothing. And, in fact, a letter written by Mussolini to Hitler on June 26, 1940 reveals his real intentions:

Fuehrer,
Now that the time has come to thrash England, I remind you of what I said to you at Munich about the direct participation of Italy in the assault of the Isle. I am ready to take part in this with land and air forces, and you know how much I desire it. I pray you to reply in order that I can pass into the phase of action. Awaiting this day, I send you my salute of comradeship.
MUSSOLINI

When Chamberlain flew back to England and arrived at Heston Airport, where the press awaited him, he triumphantly waved in the air the joint declaration signed by Hitler. And in the car that drove him and Lord Halifax through cheering crowds, he confided to his colleague, "All this will be over in three months."

He waved his useless piece of paper again with a flourish from the window of 10 Downing Street, saying for the sake of the press corps, "This is the second time there has come back from Germany to Downing Street peace with honor. I believe it is peace in our time."

Prime Minister Chamberlain had signed away part of Czechoslovakia to the Nazis in an illusion that he had negotiated a peace settlement.

Hitler's assessment of Chamberlain and Halifax had been proved right again. Now we know in hindsight that if the Western powers had stood by Czechoslovakia instead of betraying it, Germany would have been unlikely to invade, because it was not strong enough militarily. Hitler had been bluffing all along. His generals were amazed at the outcome and so impressed by the success of his deception and the naivety of the British government that Churchill claimed it was the real moment when Hitler became the undisputed master of Germany.

7

THE PHONY WAR

A GRADUAL, BUT NEVERTHELESS EXTRAORDINARY CHANGE began taking place in England at this time. London, for example, appeared on the surface to be the same city as before, and yet it changed, little by little, with hardly anyone even noticing at first. Air-raid sirens began to be installed on some rooftops and other high places. Laborers dug trenches in some of the main public parks like Hyde Park and Regent's Park. But Londoners were unsure whether they would be dug deeper and reinforced with sandbags, for taking cover in the event of a land invasion, or if they were for growing vegetables in case Britain's food supplies were cut off by naval blockades. They soon became aware of workmen painting the tops of the bright red pillar boxes that stood on some sidewalks of major street corners for posting letters. A special yellow paint was applied that, according to the newspapers and the BBC, would change color in the event of a gas attack from the air or the ground if German armies invaded. Germany had used mustard gas in the First World War, which had blinded thousands of British and French troops, and crippled others by burning their lungs. It had killed thousands on the battlefronts. And now newspapers and BBC newscasters warned the public that the Italians had already used poison gas on civilians in Abyssinia.

One of the most noticed and talked-about changes occurred when workmen dismantled and removed all the railings around public parks. Rumors spread that they were to be melted down to make munitions. The newspapers confirmed it. But that change came much later. Some other changes took place in such a quiet and orderly fashion that many people were unaware of them for some time and then took them for granted.

Posters outside suburban schools and public halls announced where gas masks should be picked up in case of poison gas attacks. Volunteers who distributed them laughingly called them Mickey Mouse masks. Other black and sinister gas masks, with what looked like baby elephant trunks attached to a flat metal canister, somehow looked more serviceable; they were to be slung over the shoulders in army-issue side-packs, for air-raid wardens, the Fire Services, and other volunteers who appeared as if out of nowhere. The biggest gas mask being distributed without charge was designed for newborn babies to be slipped inside. It featured a hand pump for mothers to pump in filtered air.

The most common was the Mickey Mouse gas mask for the general public, which consisted of only three components that required assembling. There was the black rubber mask with two plastic windows and straps to keep it positioned. It had to be fixed to the canister containing wadding filters soaked in special chemicals—to prevent poison gas from being breathed in—by a strong rubber band, about an inch wide. Volunteers easily assembled them by using a special wooden machine on the trestle table, which stretched the powerful rubber open, so that the two larger components could be fitted tightly together without any possibility of gas leaking in. After someone showed them how the machine worked, adults of all ages, and schoolchildren, set to and made a mound of completed masks. Then they put each of them into a stiff cardboard box, with string in place of a shoulder strap, and handed one out to each member of the public who appeared in orderly lines.

Thousands of people volunteered to serve as air-raid wardens in the ARP (Air Raid Precautions). They read about it on government posters that were pasted outside public buildings and inside the school where gas masks were distributed to the public. Some ARP posts were set up in private houses, offices, and shops during the Munich crisis. Many of the wardens were veterans of the First World War. The war that was anticipated was first described by the government as "The People's War." It emphasized from the start how everyone would be involved.

It seemed, at first, that the biggest problem that ARP wardens had was enforcing new blackout regulations, which were intended to avoid any light leaking out from windows at night and signaling enemy aircraft pilots to their targets. Since lines of street lampposts would do that too, the public was warned that all streetlights would be automatically switched off in the event of war. And they were advised to buy flashlights with special blue filters to see their way at night. There was an immediate run on hardware stores. Meanwhile, different types of black curtains and stiff black paper, and rolls of adhesive tape, appeared in High Street stores. The public was also warned of the deadly effects of shafts or fragments of shattered glass that could mutilate bodies in bomb explosions, so all windowpanes in homes and offices had to be secured with strong adhesive tape. Gradually, shop windows, and those in homes and offices, were crisscrossed with broad strips of beige-colored tape that were soon commonplace. Windows in underground trains were protected by netting stuck onto the glass with a peephole left clear in the middle for passengers to see which stations they arrived at.

People frequently forgot to close their blackout curtains, not realizing how even the flame of a match could be seen from above, and argued with the wardens, who had to be strict. Wardens also had to register everyone in their district so that they would be able to help people into the newly created air-raid shelters when the air-raid sirens warned of enemy attacks. Havoc was expected when bombs fell from the skies, including smaller incendiaries that were designed to start fires and burn down entire office blocks, factories, warehouses, and homes. So Fire Guard messengers were needed as volunteers to carry messages by bicycle from one bombed or fired area to the next and help put out fires with red buckets of sand, as well as save people buried by falling masonry and remove corpses of anyone killed in the bomb blasts. They had to learn first aid to patch up wounded victims after the all clear sounded.

Except for assembling and distributing gas masks, none were spheres that schoolboys considered volunteering for, since they would soon have to go back to school or be evacuated to the countryside. It was just a temporary adventure for them.

Plans were broadcast by the BBC to evacuate mothers and children from major industrial cities, which would most likely be the main targets for German bombers aiming to destroy factories and warehouses, oil tankers and containers, industrial installations and shipping along the banks of the River Thames. Apart from bombing attacks by Zeppelins in the last war, the only experience of modern air warfare, so far, was the intermittent bombing of civilians in Spain and Abyssinia that the public in Britain read about. And it was expected to be much worse, with entire city blocks left desolate after the raids, and people buried beneath the rubble. So advance planning for orderly evacuation was considered far better than the possibility of panicked refugees blocking roads while escaping to the countryside and preventing British troops from dealing effectively with German invaders.

Most people in England knew little about history and almost nothing about politics, but there was a general sense that Britain had coped with the possibilities of invasions and actual attacks before, from the Normans (at least one enemy engagement that every schoolboy knew about) and the French, then the Spanish Armada, and Germany in the previous war. It created a sense of optimism that Britain could cope with this one and raised spirits to discourage anyone from panicking at the thought of an enemy attack.

There had been almost a sigh of relief at the sight of the preparations brought about by the emergency. The public seemed fed up with the anxiety of a waiting game. Britons wanted to get on with their lives, even if it meant waging war. In this they showed more spirit than the government. Nevertheless, the "plucky" Chamberlain was greeted with cheers from the public for his persistent efforts for peace. Most people did not realize his lack of understanding of the situation, nor the damage he might still do.

The Post-Edwardians

Wars change societies. Those of the British generation who survived the First World War were not the same as those who went into it. Nor would the ones in the 1930s be like them. For one thing, the result of the Education Act of 1870 was that, by about 1927, most Britons, for the very first time, were literate. It led to an abundance of popular magazines featuring short stories and serials by authors like H. G. Wells, Sir Arthur Conan Doyle, Rudyard Kipling, and P. G. Wodehouse, which provided the reading public with an escape from sad memories of the First World War and the present declining economy and joblessness. But in a population of 45.4 million (in 1927), only thirty-thousand went on to college. University classrooms were largely occupied by the privileged sons of the ruling classes and the clergy studying theology and Greek or Latin. And, of course, there were medical schools, and—as always—those specializing in teaching law for future lawyers.

Those statistics tell something of the weakness, not only in the army, but also in politics, and in the leadership at all levels in the British Empire where—if leading positions were held by boys from Eton or Harrow, Rugby, St. Paul's School, or Westminster—most of the middle management was likely to have been educated in minor public schools that emphasized games over learning, to emulate and compete with the top ten. The obsession with cricket in particular, but also football, rugby, boxing, and handball, shaped the minds of a multitude of dim young men employed all over the empire who were still immature boys at heart. Even worse, many of them were hired as school teachers and perpetuated a culture of ball games over hard thinking.[1] Novelist P. G. Wodehouse satirized them as "mentally negligible."

Satirist Evelyn Waugh depicted them as aimlessly occupied in boozing and whoring until expelled, rather than obtaining any semblance of an education. In his popular 1928 novel *Decline and Fall*, he has a porter at an Oxford university say to an undergraduate who has just been expelled, "I expect you'll become a schoolmaster, Sir. That's what most of the gentlemen does, Sir, that gets sent down for indecent behavior." First-class games were deemed essential for anyone applying for a job as a schoolteacher.

Senior civil servant and post-Edwardian political theorist Leonard Woolf (who was educated at St. Paul's School), explained in his memoirs that you got your education from school, not at university; university was for making lifelong friendships. He became a member of the homosexual or bisexual Cambridge Apostles (with economist Maynard Keynes and others) and was part of the Bloomsbury Group of intellectuals, and husband of author and feminist Virginia Woolf.

Meanwhile, women of all socioeconomic classes had been banding together since 1872 to insist on equality with men by means of the vote. Women over the age of twenty-one were granted the choice to vote only in 1928.

Gay or feminist or intellectual groups were the exception, since many of the very large middle classes, and the British working classes, were conservative in outlook, Calvinistic in morality, genteel, and still dedicated to a respectability left over from the Victorian era. Their culture involved an individual sense of responsible behavior, as if they imagined they were continually being judged, and approved or disapproved of, by a God or society that had already ceased to exist.

Despite the disappearance of Victorian and Edwardian values during the urbanization of England, with its huge impersonal cities and sprawling suburbs, Britons continued to believe in codes of morality and behavior that most people unconsciously summed up as "English Decency." Authors like George Orwell wrote about it as if it were something tangible he was afraid might be lost if we didn't guard it. It assumed that the English would behave with calm courtesy and consideration, fairness, and even compassion toward each other. Orwell worked for the BBC propaganda services during the war. To some people, his own personal life had come to represent that decency itself.[2] Orwell may have been the most Calvinistic, self-effacing, and ascetic of all the left-wing intellectuals. A former Etonian, that and his position in the colonial service as assistant district superintendent in the Burma police soured him against social injustice. He resigned from the colonial police force in 1927 to become a writer. One of his first short stories to be published was "A Hanging."

Those were the types of people who formed the backbone of Britain and its empire. They served their country, right or wrong, without question. But now that they saw all they had worked for and loved being threatened, they responded readily to Churchill's rhetoric about lack of willpower in government. Their own lives had been built on self-discipline, self-sacrifice, and willpower. And they could recognize its absence in others.[3] They were accustomed to prudence and saving and doing without what they could not afford to buy, because they were fundamentally unmaterialistic. But three million people were unemployed by the end of 1930, and the economy was in such poor shape that the government was reluctantly preparing to cut hard-won unemployment benefits by 10 percent.

Everyone had known by the 1930s that the effervescent days of imperialism were over—it was far too expensive and no longer of much purpose. What was wanted was more modest low-cost and democratic administration. It required a change in attitude. And there were plenty of people who questioned it, particularly left-wing intellectuals. They were a small but highly influential group of people in Britain who viewed the British government critically, like the sincere and talented Sidney and Beatrice Webb who founded the Fabian Society. They liked to think of themselves as a modern advance guard who planned ahead by leaning everyone they could toward socialism by gradual and unsensational means, known as "gradualism." Their biggest success was the irrepressible writer George Bernard Shaw. But the Fabians were not as advanced as they imagined or were viewed by others, since they were founded at the end of the nineteenth century.[4]

They and Shaw were more accustomed to mixing with cooperative British civil servants or municipal government, and they were bewildered by the pragmatic Communism of Soviet Russia, which was prepared to sacrifice millions of lives for a rigid ideology based on an unproven economic theory. But, like some other idealists of the well-educated intelligentsia, they knew of the appalling conditions under the former Tsarist Russian regime, which was the most oppressive in Europe. They would have read Maxim Gorky and seen Eisenstein's films, and wished to show their solidarity for a revolution that had apparently swept those inhuman conditions away. Consequently, Shaw, Bertrand Russell, and other intellectuals were happy to brush the Soviets' criminal misdeeds under the rug so that they wouldn't be seen, and continue to admire socialism. Only later would they discover they had been gulled, since—as Joseph Conrad warned—"only the names change at the top."[5]

British Communists were disillusioned by the three consecutive prime ministers, as well as more liberal and conservative individuals. So they, too, turned a blind eye to Russian pragmatism, hypocrisy, and brutality, since there seemed to be nowhere else to turn for help to redress the balance of power. Scientific journalist Arthur Koestler was more honest when he rejected his previous Communist affiliation and wrote *Darkness at Noon* in 1940 to expose it. His former comrades considered him a traitor. But as it would turn out, many would regret their own membership later on. As for typical Marxist expressions like "class struggle," they were more likely to be heard repeated in Manchester, where Marx and Engels wrote their *Communist Manifesto*, and in the industrial Midlands and the north.[6]

The "low dishonest decade" that W. H. Auden referred to had also alien-ated a number of Cambridge graduates, including the infamous "Cambridge Five." They were recruited to the Soviet Communist cause soon after graduating. The leader of the spy ring was Kim Philby, who was already working in secret as a Soviet spy while firmly established in MI6. The others were Donald Maclean, Guy Burgess, Anthony Blunt, and a suspected "Fifth Man," about whom there was much media speculation. Their spy ring passed secret information to Soviet Russia from the 1930s through the Second World War—when Russia was a major partner of the West—then during the Cold War with Stalin and Khrushchev, up to the time they were exposed around 1950. Military historian Sir Max Hastings described them as dysfunctional.

It began on a visit to Berlin in 1933, when the twenty-one-year-old Kim Philby witnessed Nazi brutality, close-up, at an anti-Jewish rally. He was prescient in understanding that anti-Semitism was not just a psychotic mental disease in a foreign country, but that the British establishment was already tainted by the Nazi sickness. It was a reality of life, and you had to choose which side you were on. He must have asked himself how could the Nazis be stopped, and realized that the only organized retaliation against Fascism was provided by the Soviet Union and the Communist Party.

Philby was born of an eccentric Edwardian father, the Arabist St. John Philby, who was ambitious for fame as a latter-day Sir Richard Burton or Lawrence of Arabia. Kim was self-confident enough to dedicate his own life to defeating the Fascists and Nazis. After all, his father had named him after Kipling's fictional British spy, who in Victorian times could pass as an Indian in the imperial "Great Game" against Tsarist Russian spies penetrating into British India through the Khyber Pass. Now Philby would pass as an urbane English womanizer and genial drinking companion with espionage agents and double agents and their handlers, whom he would gently pump dry of secrets to pass to the Soviets in order to defeat Germany, Italy, and Spain. It was "Kim's Game." He enjoyed the double life and would become the greatest spy of all time, sacrificing everyone in his path to achieve his goal.

Six Guilty Men

All of the Cambridge Five would have watched the three successive appeasing prime ministers of the British establishment with mixed emotions. They presided over Britannia while waiting patiently for her to expire, without the wits to revive her. Lord Halifax would have looked like their successor, or possibly one of the defeatists like Sir Samuel Hoare or Ambassador Nevile Henderson. It was impossible for eager young men of the political left, who were accustomed to energetic debate, to identify with them. They must have seen their rule as a sign of the end of England—a situation that very nearly happened.

It may be an inconclusive exercise to consider whether the Cambridge Five did more or less damage to Britain than the "Six Guilty Men." Or it may expand our thinking, since it seems that the Cambridge graduates recognized that Stalin's Russia could no longer be ignored even before Churchill did, when it was not politically correct to say so. Someone had to get up close to the Nazis and crush them in a brutal war on European soil. And no other nation had the capability at that time but Stalin's Russia. Meanwhile, Churchill collected facts and took his own time to make the same case. And President Roosevelt's thinking was as decisive as Churchill's when he agreed to provide Soviet Russia with tanks and other arms. But it is doubtful if the "Six Guilty Men" ever recognized reality, because their thinking was too narrow and their prejudices ran too deep—whereas it is a likely irony that the Cambridge Five may have even helped the Allied war effort to achieve victory.

Foreign Secretary Harold Macmillan was the Minister for MI6. An urbane old Etonian, he often looked faintly surprised at the inexplicable way people behaved, and found it hard to believe accusations raised about a Cambridge spy ring when it was exposed after the war was over in the 1950s. He became prime minister in 1957. None of the so-called Cambridge Five was prosecuted.[7] Evidently, as far as passing on state secrets was concerned, they did little harm, because Stalin didn't trust them or their information. In any case, he seemed to know Britain's and America's plans in advance and rarely looked surprised when they confided in him. The biggest danger was of the Ultra reports becoming known to the Germans, but that was not in Stalin's interest.

There were also enclaves of class discontent that could be seen surging in the columns of the *Daily Worker*, swirling around the actors and producers in the Unity Theatre in London, and even among the membership of Equity, the actors', stage managers', and models' trade union. But the class war that Marx and Engels had predicted would break out in England when they wrote their Manifesto didn't happen. However eagerly they encouraged the working classes to rise up and rebel for better working and living conditions, neither understood the resolve of the British people to deal with their own problems by gradual reforms and the willingness of others to accommodate them.

George Orwell, on the other hand, never sacrificed his integrity as a patriotic Englishmen, who nevertheless found much to criticize in England. He would attempt to reform it from within, and wrote *Animal Farm* (1945) and *1984* (in 1949) to show the effects of brainwashing and double-think—both warnings to his countrymen and women of what could happen if they were not vigilant. Working as a propagandist for the Ministry of Information, he understood the art and science of brainwashing and was one of the first to see though the false facade of Communist brainwashing to the brutal police state that sacrificed millions behind all the idealistic propaganda. If Churchill was the savior of civilization, Orwell was its conscience.

What most Britons had in common was the stubborn independence of an island race of hardy, seagoing people with perhaps a stronger strain of Viking stock than is generally credited to Britons.

As for the slow pace of rearmament, it was easy to blame Britain's poor economy for it. More to the point was that vacillating governments had left Britain vulnerable to attack when it should have been the government's priority to protect its population.

But it is important to emphasize again how different the times and the people were compared with the twenty-first century. The minds and attitudes of the "Appeasing Six" were fixed rigidly from their youth in the Victorian era, which was a patriarchal society. Today we understand those dysfunctional characteristics of men who won't consult experts for fear of showing their ignorance or ask women who might throw a different light on a subject, in case it is seen as a sign of weakness. TV sitcoms are replete with such dysfunctional characters and irrational situations today. But intellectuals, introverts, and nerds were not understood then, and therefore suspect. And women's opportunities were limited. Whereas today we search for different thinking in order to keep innovating and improving, the Victorian English became stuck in their rigid thinking around the middle of their era to produce stereotypes like the "Appeasing Six." It took Edwardian author Lytton Strachey to reveal their hypocrisies.[8] None of them were what they seemed. Strachey's intention was to deflate the pomposity of Victorian leaders who pretended to high ideals, morals, and ethics, when they were riddled with contradictions and flaws that made them weak and vulnerable like everyone else.

It was crowd psychologist Gustave Le Bon who first noted that although many historians had searched to find the real reasons for the French Revolution, they had studied only external events leading up to it and the Napoleonic Wars, and fallen short by not analyzing the minds of people who make history. It was the contradictory, irrational, and even psychotic minds of Britain's enemies that Prime Minister Neville Chamberlain had to deal with.[9]

Cheated

The crucial event that changed Chamberlain's attitude took place on March 15, when German forces occupied Bohemia at 6:00 a.m., and the Czech government ordered its population to show no resistance. Chamberlain's reaction was not what Churchill had expected. He appeared to have recognized the truth of his well-meant but misjudged trust in Hitler's words and shed his illusions. Evidently he suddenly realized he had been duped by Hitler. He explained that the guarantee he had given Czechoslovakia was now invalid because of Germany's military action and the Slovak government's declaration of the independence of Slovakia.

When he spoke in Birmingham two days later, he accused Hitler of a breach of faith about the Munich Agreement.[10] Hitler had seized Czech territory instead, claiming it had been necessitated by disorders, which the Nazis had actually fabricated themselves.[11]

"Is this the last attack upon a small state," Chamberlain asked rhetorically. "Or is it to be followed by another? Is this in fact a step in the direction of an attempt to dominate the world by force?"

It had become obvious that the next small state on Hitler's agenda was Poland. Two weeks later, Chamberlain announced in Parliament that His Majesty's Government had given the Polish government an assurance that if its independence was threatened, Britain would lend Poland all the support in its power. He added that the French government had made it clear it stood in the same position toward Poland. Now there could be little doubt that, with Hitler's ambitions to dominate Europe, Britain's guarantee to Poland could lead to a war that Chamberlain had done his best to avoid.

Although the Poles had a fair idea when and where the attack would come, they could have had little knowledge of blitzkrieg tactics, which had been only theorized by particular British and German military tacticians until now.[12] So they placed most of their troops close to the German border, which was 1,750 miles long—far longer than the Polish army could defend. According to German Intelligence Officer Major-General Frederick von Mellenthin, "they were lacking a sense of reality."[13]

Fear of war on two fronts, from British *and* Polish forces, meant Hitler had to protect his back. He tied up forty divisions to do it, but they were only second-rate units and had been given only three days' ammunition.[14] Hitler's "Plan White" assigned sixty divisions to conquer Poland, including five panzer divisions of three hundred tanks each.[15]

Hitler's Luftwaffe began the attack on Poland by bombing airfields, railway junctions, munition dumps, mobilization centers, roads, and cities like Warsaw, with Heinkels, Dorniers, and Junker 87 Stuka dive-bombers, before German troops moved in at sunrise on September 1.[16] A fusillade of shells from the *Schleswig Holstein* training ship hit the Polish garrison. The screaming of the sirens of the Stukas as they dived with their bomb loads was intended to terrorize the population below. Most of the Polish air force was destroyed on the ground to achieve German air superiority. General Heinz Guderian—a pioneer in blitzkrieg tactics—commanded two light divisions that raced ahead of the infantry troops. Chaos ensued when troop movements were hampered by fleeing refugees.

Britain now mobilized all its forces. Chamberlain invited Churchill to Downing Street and admitted he saw no hope of averting a war and intended forming a war cabinet. Although Churchill still considered an alliance with Soviet Russia, the Polish premier—Colonel Beck—assured Chamberlain that it would be dangerous to invite Russia to talks, since it was only interested in its own dominance in Europe. And the British cabinet mistrusted any Russian proposals, despite Churchill's feelings that a Russian alliance would make war less likely.

Then, on Good Friday, for good measure, the Italians invaded Albania.

But even after Chamberlain's guarantee to Poland, he continued to hope for permanent peace between Britain and Germany. Although there was a view that Chamberlain had finally abandoned appeasement after the Czech crisis, when he'd talked tough about Poland, he maintained that he was extremely obstinate and refused to change. Churchill was still considering war while Chamberlain was not. The difference in their attitudes seemed to be based on Churchill's convictions that Britain would be victorious, whereas Chamberlain apparently did not think so.

German Power

One of Churchill's errors in judgment was that the Germany army could not penetrate through the French Maginot Line with its state-of-the-art defenses. He felt that Chamberlain was defeatist, and so was the American ambassador, Joseph Kennedy. From the very beginning of the crisis, Churchill was convinced—with his pride in being half American on his mother's side—that the United States would come to Britain's aid because of the great heritage of the English-speaking peoples that was spelled out in a Charter of Human Rights in both the English *Magna Carta* and the American Declaration of Independence.[17] But Roosevelt pointed out, through his ambassador, that he could not provide material assistance as long as the British and French bowed to Nazi and Fascist aggressions: it prevented American public opinion from being aroused.

Churchill was also convinced that the will of the British people would be strong enough to endure any ordeal. Those two powerful beliefs sustained his own steely resolution. But in spite of a growing press campaign to recall Churchill to the cabinet, Chamberlain was unwilling to have him unless the crisis ended in war. He found him too difficult to deal with. Chamberlain asked him to join the cabinet when Germany invaded Poland on September 1. And the French were informed that if Germany did not withdraw from Poland by noon on the morrow, a state of war would be deemed to exist.

"There is no question of sparing Poland," Hitler told his chiefs of staff.

Poland will always be on the side of our adversaries. We are left with the decision to attack Poland at the first suitable opportunity. We cannot expect a repetition of the Czech affair. There will be war. Our task is to isolate Poland. . . . I doubt the possibility of a peaceful settlement with England. . . . England is, therefore, our enemy, and the conflict with England will be a life-and-death struggle.[18]

One of his officers remarked that France and Britain would declare war on the invasion of Poland. To which Hitler replied, "Yes, but will they fight?"

The British prime minister made an announcement to the nation at 11:00 a.m. on Sunday, September 3, that Britain was now at war. Everything had been done that was possible to avert it. And a new attitude prevailed. The French government reluctantly followed suit six hours later.[19]

Nevertheless, Britain was in a precarious position and at a tremendous disadvantage—they were facing better-armed, better-trained, better-indoctrinated, and better-motivated enemies from a traditionally paternalistic Prussian society devoted to obedience or death. Moreover, could Britain's economy sustain a war? He felt that Britain would be unable to win a short war because it was too far behind Germany in war potential, and it might be unable to sustain a long one with only a defeatist France as an ally. Whatever Britain's fate, the past was dead, and a new page was turned in British history.

As for Poland, even if France and Britain attacked the Siegfried Line immediately—where the French had eighty-five divisions—it would have been unlikely to have been saved in time.[20] As it happened, Hitler overestimated the French and feared a surprise attack on the German industrial area of the Ruhr and then a surprise landing by British forces that would attack the German north flank.[21]

But the Allies were unprepared for war and France was still mobilizing, so neither attack took place.[22] Hitler intended to seize Warsaw before the U.S. Congress meeting on September 21, in order to present the world with a fait accompli.[23]

That Polish troops could fight was shown by General Tadeusz Kutrzeba's forces that crossed the Bzura River in a magnificent attack against the flank of the German Eighth army. That attack launched the three-day battle of

Kutno, which almost destroyed an entire German division. But the Poles were outnumbered and out-armed, and they were finally pushed back by German panzers. The romantic myth that they heroically attacked German tanks on horseback with sabers raised is untrue. But it is true that their weapons were inferior to the German army's.

Why were the Germans so powerful? Most historians agree that their Prussian culture, in which civilians were treated almost like soldiers who were required to obey orders or die, was a powerful influence. "War was the national industry of Prussia."[24] And this was Germany's fifth war of aggression in seventy-five years, so they had plenty of practice. German civilians admired and deferred to officers in uniform. Germany had long been a paternalistic society in which commands were obeyed instantly with a nod of the head and a click of the heels. It was one of the reasons why blitzkrieg tactics worked so well for them: they required close cooperation and instant and disciplined reaction between all armed services.

Waiting for Britain

Mussolini waited to see what would happen before deciding whether to declare war on Britain. All his troops were in Libya and Abyssinia, and the British navy still dominated the Mediterranean. However, superior sea power could not prevent the consequences of a new war from the air. Churchill was worried about air raids. It brought a new dimension into the war that he had not experienced before. But, as one of the first pilots himself in 1913, he was aware of its dangers. Meanwhile, there was no sign of aggressive intent from Japan. And Britain's naval dominance at sea seemed to preclude a possibility that the British colony of Singapore would be threatened by Japan's fleet, since it was three thousand miles away.

As it turned out, Mussolini was not the only leader to watch which way the wind might blow. To everyone's astonishment, Britain's declarations of war were followed by a six-month lull and a long silence that was deceptive in that it gave an illusion of calm during the winter months, known as the "Phony War." But, in fact, there was plenty of activity going on behind the scenes.[25]

Poland was invaded and subjugated or destroyed in only a few weeks by Germany. However bravely the Poles fought, they were outnumbered and out-armed. They were too small an economy to possess powerful armed forces. Poland had long been the meat in a sandwich always in danger between two hungry jaws and about to be gobbled up by Germany on one side and Russia on the other.

Poland, the victim, endured firsthand the first successful demonstration of the new blitzkrieg technique by German panzers, while its Western allies were still preparing for war on traditional lines. Then, on September 17, the Soviet Union surprised everyone but Hitler by invading Poland, in accordance with a secret clause in the Nazi-Soviet Pact.[26] The Red Army advanced across Poland's eastern frontier. It was a blow to the back of the head that finished it off, since Poland had too few troops left to stand up to a second invasion.[27]

It took only a month to defeat Poland. Resistance ended by October 5. By the spring of 1940, the Soviet army had transported 4,100 Polish officers to a forest near Smolensk called Katyn. They had surrendered to the Russians according to the terms of the Geneva Convention, which entitled them to humane treatment as prisoners of war. Instead, each officer was murdered by being shot in the back of the head by the NKVD (The People's Commissariat for Internal Affairs, a law enforcement agency of the Soviet Union). It was not only the Nazis who were determined on a course of Total War. The total number of Polish soldiers executed by the Russians, there and elsewhere, was 21,857.[28]

Russia took 217,000 Polish soldiers as prisoners. Germany took 693,000. Fortunately for them and the Allies, ninety thousand to one hundred thousand escaped through Lithuania, Hungary, and Rumania, to join the Free Polish forces under General Sikorski, the Polish prime minister in exile. On the other hand, about a hundred thousand potential Polish leaders in the Russian sector were arrested by the NKVD and sent to concentration camps, from which virtually none returned.[29]

From the very beginning, this was a war to deliberately destroy other races than Germans, like Slavs and Jews, to make more room for the German master race in a Greater Germany. It was genocide on a huge scale never known before. And German troops were trained for "frightfulness" by shedding German blood, too. They were taught "the difference between real wars with live ammunition and peacetime maneuvers."[30]

"Take a good look around Warsaw," Hitler told war correspondents who witnessed the desolation of the lifeless city after its destruction. "That is how I can deal with any European city."[31]

Many German soldiers would claim to Allied intelligence officers at war's end, and to each other, that they had just obeyed orders from their superiors and knew nothing of the genocide against the Slavs and Jews, or had only heard rumors—but it was a lie.[32]

In total control of all activities in the Nazi Third Reich were the SS—which had already wiped out its Brownshirt rivals (the SA) in a bloodbath. The SS were specially chosen and trained to enjoy terrorizing people to quell any possibility of opposition. They were loyal directly to Hitler and enforced a doctrine of "Race and Blood," dedicated to the so-called "German Master Race." They dominated the police force, while the Waffen SS ran the concentration and extermination camps. They ruled the security services. They were a law unto themselves, separate from the German state. And they deliberately ruled by fear. They shot thousands of civilians at Dydgoszcz. They set fire to the Jewish district in Piotrkow. They shot nineteen Polish officers who surrendered at Mrocza. And they herded all Polish Jews into ghettos. The SS could be trusted by Hitler to place all allegiances to him ahead of morality. That old-fashioned tribal blood brotherhood was like a magical ritual.[33] Neither morality nor ethics existed any longer wherever the SS ruled.

The Nazi race policy was made clear as early as 1923 in Hitler's twenty-five-point program, that only pure-blood Germans could be part of the Greater German Nation. His supporters were mostly embittered ex-servicemen like himself. They included former officers who had previously been provided with a uniform, food, and a gun. They had been accustomed to giving orders and expecting them to be obeyed. But now they were vagrants like Hitler, or small and unsuccessful shopkeepers or businessmen failing to compete with harder-working and more experienced Jewish shopkeepers. The Nazi Party offered them power to eliminate their competitors. And Hitler soon took control of the German Workers Party.

Added to the lust for territorial expansion were the pent-up hatreds perpetuated throughout centuries of self-righteous religious wars between Roman

Catholicism, the Lutherans, and the Orthodox Church—as well as all sorts of superstitions about witches and terrifying hobgoblins and sinister tribal heroes of the forests—that had lain dormant under the rule of the more tolerant Habsburg Empire, and that the Grimm brothers would put to paper, and Wagner to music.

Hitler's almost instantaneous success with Poland as an almost defenseless victim must have given him comfort, since Germany's economy was stretched to the limit. So speed was essential. He had to launch an assault in the west to win the war. And there he would be met by the Allied Anglo-French armies at the Maginot Line that possessed more men, tanks, and aircraft than Hitler had at his disposal at the time.[34]

The Phony War occupied the six-month period after Poland's defeat in October 1939 and the German invasions of Denmark and Norway on April 9, 1940. Since it didn't appear to affect British or French civilians, they began to believe they were safe from attack, and life continued as usual in the civil service. Nevertheless, German U-boats were quietly surrounding the British Isles, waiting for instructions to act. And British shipping began to be torpedoed soon afterward.

Convoys

Convoys from Canada used the echo-sounding device called *Asdic* to track German U-boats. And the British navy began the war with only five aircraft carriers, one of which was sunk "by two torpedoes from a U-boat which had already dispatched three tankers."[35] The following month, another U-boat penetrated a fifty-foot gap in the defenses at Scapa Flow and fired several torpedoes at the twenty-nine-thousand-ton battleship HMS *Royal Oak*. Three torpedoes struck their targets and capsized the ship, killing 810 of the 1,224 crew in only thirteen minutes.

Another twenty-nine British ships were sunk by the end of November by magnetic mines that U-boats placed in the sea-lanes around the British Isles.

Britain's major victory at sea during the Phony War was to chase the German battleship *Admiral Graf Spee* and force it to scuttle itself in South American waters in the Battle of the River Plate on December 13. It sank at the entrance to Montevideo Harbor four days later. But it was a naval war of attrition on both sides with Britain losing a similar tonnage as the German navy.

The British Admiralty was convinced of it superiority in the Norwegian Sea and was shocked when the Germans landed troops and invaded Norway from the sea and by air with paratroops on April 9, using more than a thousand planes to the RAF's maximum of a hundred aircraft. British troops embarked for Norway were confused with changes of orders and supplies that excluded the right equipment. There was a sense of incompetent handling, with the British navy viewing the operation "through blinkers."[36] Nevertheless, nine German destroyers were sunk or put out of action by HMS *Warspite*.

The basic purpose of Churchill's ill-fated Norwegian Campaign was to prevent iron ore from being shipped to Germany from Narvik. What Hitler needed for his war effort was iron ore from Sweden and oil from Rumania and Russia. If Britain could cut off enough iron ore supplies, Germany's industries might come to a standstill. Churchill began by laying minefields in Norwegian waters.

In all the chaos, Denmark collapsed in under four hours. The general confusion between Britain's armed forces was blamed on Chamberlain's government.[37] Such a small British foothold in Norway was finally considered not worthwhile, and the Narvik forces were evacuated between June 2 and June 7, along with the Norwegian government and royal family. The Germans now ran Norway and Denmark.

Altogether, the Norwegian Campaign was a disaster for Britain. Its confusion and incompetence and delays allowed the Germans to invade Norway twenty-four hours ahead of the Allies. It was a serious setback, and it destroyed the Chamberlain government. The irony was that while it brought Winston Churchill into position as the potential leader of the Allies, his leadership of the Admiralty had made him more responsible than anyone else for the Norwegian fiasco.[38]

On June 8, the *Scharnhorst* and the *Gneisenau* sank the British aircraft carrier HMS *Glorious* with two aircraft squadrons and its two destroyer escorts. Before sinking with his ship, the skipper of one—the *Acasta*—sailed directly into the enemy and launched a torpedo that sank the *Scharnhorst*. The captain of the *Acasta* waved the British survivors good-bye and calmly lit a cigarette before going under.[39]

First Sea Lord

Churchill was appointed by the prime minister to his old job in the previous war, as First Lord of the Admiralty, and proceeded to dominate it by his quick wits and his tongue, and rarely took no for an answer. Eden accepted a position as dominions secretary, which effectively cut him off from major decisions and actions.

Meanwhile, a British antisubmarine convoy system was set up. In company with the French Admiralty, U-boat attacks on merchant ships were so far controlled by Anglo-French antisubmarine craft. And there was no doubt that the *Asdic* invention was effective. The British Admiralty was prepared to supply and install *Asdics* in all French antisubmarine craft, and it was hoped that the French Marines would increase the number of their *Asdic* vessels. Defeat of German U-boats would mean Allied mastery of the oceans. The fact that the enemy had no line of battle enabled the Allies to disperse their naval forces widely across the oceans with between seven and ten Anglo-French hunting units cruising the North Atlantic, the South Atlantic, and the Indian Oceans. Whether they would discourage Italy from entering the war against Britain and France remained to be seen.

Admiral Pound presented Churchill with a proposal to create a minefield barrage between Scotland and Norway. Nevertheless, nearly a dozen British merchant ships were sunk in September and October at the entrance to Britain's harbors, although they had been previously swept for mines. Six sank in the approach to the Thames. And Hitler claimed to be using a secret weapon that could not be countered. The Admiralty soon managed to recover a magnetic mine parachuted down from the air, which was sent to Portsmouth for examination; after which all British ships were demagnetized with lengths of electric cable.

Retaliation was considered by feeding large numbers of small floating mines—no bigger than footballs—into the Rhine, to deny the Germans the use of their important waterway.

The Baltic became another minor theater of war with other small countries, with the Nazi-Soviet Pact allowing Stalin a free hand in the north, where Latvia, Lithuania, and Estonia had been threatened into permitting the Red Army to be based on their territory.[40] With a far larger war on the horizon, Russia needed to annex more land to protect its northern border and Leningrad. Russia hastily installed the Red Army and Red Air Force in Estonia and set up an army garrison in Lithuania, barricading half of the Gulf of Finland to protect the Russian capital. Finland became a buffer zone between Russia and Germany. What Stalin wanted now was to lease the port of Hanko as a Russian naval base.

Stalin ordered the Finns to Moscow to hear his demands for the naval base, and also their frontier with Russia to be moved further back from Leningrad, which was only fifteen miles away. In return, he was willing to offer the Finns nearly double the territory they would lose. But the Finns, bravely but recklessly, refused. They decided to fight rather than submit. It would turn out to be a bad choice against such huge odds, since they had only courage and discipline on their side.[41] Stalin wasted no more time: Russia bombed Helsinki forty-eight hours later and mounted an unprovoked attack on Finland with 1.2 million troops at eight points along Finland's frontier.

The Finnish War

The small Finnish army of less than two thousand men showed extraordinary courage against its huge neighbor, with little chance of success, beating back Russian advances in white camouflage in the intense cold of snowy mountains, and using an improvised hand grenade, known as a Molotov cocktail, to defeat Russian tanks. The Finns were victorious by the end of the year.

Stalin had thought it would be a walkover and the Finns would rebel. But to his amazement, they were united behind their leader. "The Finns burnt their own farms and villages, booby-trapped farm animals, destroyed anything that could provide the Russians with food and shelter, and, equipped with skis and local knowledge, laid mines on tracks through the forests that were soon covered in snow."[42] Newsreels screened in Britain showed them wearing white camouflage coveralls that gave them a nickname that translated as "White Death."

Russian troops had no such camouflage in the snow-covered mountains and lacked warm winter clothes and felt boots. And the Finns knew what they were up to, because their troop communications were not sent in code. The icy-cold winter weather was as low as -58°F. The Russian army was soon freezing and starving, and their retreat was cut off by the Finns. Where Russian troops advanced on solid ice, the Finns sent aircraft to smash the ice, so that Russian tanks, with men, other vehicles, and the inevitable horses, fell into the freezing water and perished.[43] Russian troops sent to replace them became the Finns' next victims; some were machine-gunned from high up in the trees, from where they could easily be picked out against the snow in their darker uniforms.

"We don't let them rest," said a Finnish general. "We don't let them sleep. This is a war of numbers against brains."[44]

Much of the problem was that Stalin's 1937 blood purge of Red Army officers had weakened the Russian army. Stalin, holding on to power, had acted as Hitler had done with his own blood purge against the Brownshirts in order to destroy any possible opposition. They both knew that in order for a dictatorship to succeed in a police state there always has to be a plausible threat from an imagined enemy—what the Communists called an "enemy of the people."

But the defeat of the Finns was inevitable against such huge odds, and against Stalin's desperate intention of protecting Leningrad, which required the stubborn Finns to cooperate or be crushed ruthlessly. Finland's military collapse occurred on March 18 in the following year.

One result of the earlier successes of the Finns against the Russians was that both Hitler and Churchill thought that Soviet Russia must be much weaker than it really was.

In October, Hitler suavely offered Britain a negotiated peace in a belief that, when the German forces knocked out France, Britain would agree to a peace settlement.[45] But it was not believed to be sincere, just another ruse to give Germany more time to increase its armed strength. Chamberlain and Churchill were dining together while learning to work together and must have reacted sardonically to an offer from someone who could not be trusted. Even so, to judge from Hitler's admiration for the British Empire, he may have been sincere, but he was too tortured by envy.[46]

Of all the leaders of British Dominions, the Irish De Valera was the only one to stay neutral. There was a German connection there, with the Irish population caught between inflammatory IRA gunmen and the British army and police attempting to extinguish their fires.

The Shadowy Hero

Meanwhile, Churchill was acting more like a shadow prime minister giving directions to everyone. Chamberlain tolerated it because he hated war and knew he was no Minister of War himself.

As Churchill explained to Halifax in January 1940, he felt frustrated, as the machinery of war conduct seemed designed to prevent positive action. And unless they took action, they would lose the war. As he saw it, the problem was that war cannot be waged by a committee—particularly against a dictator who can change directions at will. Churchill wanted to seize the initiative with a significant campaign.

He was appointed chairman of the Military Coordinating Committee, but was given no more power, since Halifax's Undersecretary Rab Butler still hoped there could be a peaceful resolution to the war declared eleven months earlier. And neither Halifax nor Chamberlain had ruled out the possibility of concessions to Hitler to avoid all-out war between Germany and Britain.

But as far as the public was concerned, Churchill was, without any doubt, the most forceful Minister in the government, and the only one with a genuine purpose aimed at victory. So it was in the government's interest to encourage this positive appearance, particularly when so little appeared on the surface to be happening.[47]

8

BLITZKRIEG

THE FAILED ALLIED LANDING IN NARVIK, in Norway, on April 5, had been a particular campaign that Churchill wished to pursue. Chamberlain shared his view that the first phase of the war had strengthened the Allies and claimed that Hitler had "missed the bus." Churchill and the government, too, were in general agreement on that point. But rumors of the Norway campaign had spread to Admiral Raeder, the head of the German navy, who informed Hitler that the information seemed to be genuine. The result was that the Germans arrived in Narvik first.

Churchill would have to share some of the blame for stubbornly believing that ships could defend shorelines and fight forts, and that eight insufficiently equipped British battalions could deal with fifty-one German battalions. He had omitted the effects of enemy air power that had become the dominant force since the previous war, with the result that the Norwegian campaign ended in chaos. The concept was wrong and its execution was flawed.

The chiefs of staff recommended abandoning a direct assault on April 19 when the Germans were already in control of most of Norway. Churchill had overestimated what the British navy could do, and underestimated the Germans. But Prime Minister Chamberlain was the overall man in charge, so he bore the brunt of the criticism. It was ironic that the public, the media, and the House of Commons thought that Churchill should replace him as prime minister, when Churchill had been in charge of the Admiralty during the Norwegian fiasco. But Chamberlain's image was one of weakness, whereas Churchill knew how to present himself powerfully to the public.

The hugely popular Lloyd George—a former prime minister now viewed as an elder statesman—finished his speech at the cabinet debate on the Norwegian

Campaign by saying that the best sacrifice Chamberlain could make for victory would be to leave office as prime minister. And Churchill, although loyal to the government, gave such a persuasive speech in the House that it reinforced how much he was needed in a new government. When voting came, the government squeaked through but had lost most of its support, and the Labour members of the Coalition government refused to serve under Chamberlain.

Chamberlain called for national unity. And, after the Laborites turned him down as leader, he told Churchill and Halifax that he supposed he'd have to resign. But who should he recommend to the king as his successor?

Churchill's most powerful personal characteristic was his impatience. Everything he decided on had to be undertaken right away while he was energized. It was beguiling to some and annoying to others. It could also be dangerous. He had displayed impatience since childhood, as if he always knew there was a right time to strike or it would be too late. He was impatient with himself as well as with others. He was sixty-five years old, but still at the height of his intellect and his creativity, his energy, and his powers of persuasion by writing his own speeches and by his oratory in delivering them.

As historian Andrew Roberts would write, "His long years of largely unheeded warnings about the rise of Nazism had given him an unassailable moral right to the premiership during the parliamentary crisis that month, and he grasped it as soon as it became clear that Chamberlain could not carry on without the support of the Labour and Liberal parties and a small but growing band of Conservative rebels."[1] Churchill was impatient to take charge and took the opportunity by candidly stating that his rival, the Foreign Secretary Lord Halifax, could not lead the nation from the House of Lords.

As a Nazi blitzkrieg began on Holland and Belgium at dawn on May 10, Sir Howard Kingsley Wood told Chamberlain bluntly that—in view of the crisis on the Continent—he should go. The prime minister offered his resignation and saw the king. Winston Churchill was summoned to Buckingham Palace and asked to form a new government.

Churchill invited Halifax to join the war cabinet, although they disagreed on policy. There was a pragmatic method in his choice, since it is better to keep friends close, and best to keep enemies closer still.[2] Anthony Eden would go to the War Office. Churchill wanted Alexander to take charge of the Admiralty. Sir Archibald Sinclair was offered the Air Ministry. Churchill also assumed the responsibilities of the Ministry of Defense. And he invited Neville Chamberlain to lead the House of Commons. He sent the defeatist Sir Samuel Hoare to neutral Spain as Britain's ambassador to keep him out of the way.

At last, he told himself, he was dealing with facts. "Facts," he wrote, "are better than dreams."[3]

On June 4, 1940, Winston Churchill stated that he had complete confidence in defending Britain, even if necessary alone.[4] The idea of the "Lone Ranger" was not an American one. Churchill's idea of heroism was characterized by his own identity and the British people's. They could stand alone to confront any enemy, just as he would. It was one of his characteristics that caused some people to view him as a romantic dreamer. But he combined two personalities—perhaps from his English and his American ancestry—one imaginative and creative and the other hands-on and practical. Now, as soon as King George VI formally appointed him prime minister of Britain, he was ideally suited to what the British nation needed to lead them.

He became prime minister on the same day that Hitler's troops struck at the West and broke through their defenses. The tank commander Heinz Guderian's Panzer Corps crossed the River Meuse at Sedan only three days later. German tanks sped through the breach. It led to the collapse of France. Now Churchill and the British people were on their own.

The Shock of Arms

According the Churchill's postwar memoirs, four or five million men met each other in the shock of the most merciless of all wars on record. That was how he described the first contact of the Allies with massed German troops on the continent of Europe in the Second World War.[5]

But first he had to take the reins of Britain's new national coalition government in both hands and make sure he had their complete support as their new leader. He asked the House of Commons for a vote of confidence in the new administration on May 13 and got it. His colleagues in the coalition included Clement Attlee, Arthur Greenwood, Sir Archibald Sinclair, Ernest Bevin, who was secretary of the transport and General Workers' Union, and Lord Beaverbrook as Minister of Aircraft Production. Those in his small war cabinet with himself were Chamberlain, Attlee, Halifax, and Liberal Arthur Greenwood.

He had invited the former prime minister and Lord Halifax to join him in the Admiralty War Room two days earlier to study maps and discuss events. The Belgians were fighting well and the Dutch were making a stubborn resistance in the "awful little battle" that was going on across the Channel.[6] If only the size of their armed forces counted, then France should have been the master of Europe. But size only creates an illusion of power. Readiness is all. And Germany was ready for war. Britain, despite the huge size of its empire, was unprepared.

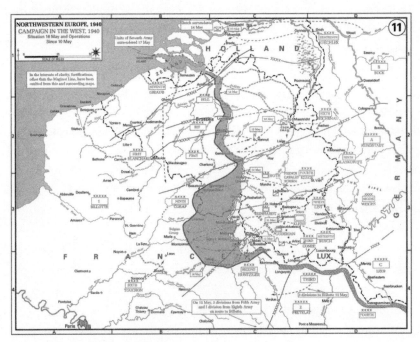

German invasion of Europe and the fall of France. May 1940. Code-named "Sickle Cut."

As for France, Hitler had only recently approved a plan by Erich von Manstein to destroy France. Manstein was General von Runstedt's chief of staff. It was called "Sickle Cut." It replaced a previous plan that they thought might have fallen into Allied hands. This one featured seven panzer divisions that would be taken from the right flank and placed in the center with German Army Group A, keeping the left flank weak. It relied on the Allies moving into Holland and Belgium to meet a prearranged German attack by Army Group B. Then, at the crucial moment, Army Group A would burst out of the Ardennes Forest and strike at the point of maximum effect—the *Schwerpunkt*—in the Allied line. They would pierce it and race fast toward the English Channel, thereby cutting off a third of the Allied forces from the rest. Field Marshal Keitel attributed the plan to Hitler, who had claimed credit for it, because Keitel thought Hitler was a genius and frequently told him so.[7]

Keitel considered the *Schwerpunkt* to be a fifty-mile-wide portion of the River Meuse (between Danant and Sedan). Speed was, of course, vital to the enterprise, as in every blitzkrieg. And there would have to be close cooperation between the Luftwaffe and the panzer units racing ahead of the other German troops. They would be grouped tightly together and strike the point like lightning.

The plan involved specific risks since the Ardennes is a heavily wooded forest with mountainous terrain, consisting of roads so narrow that they were thought to be almost impassable by heavily armored vehicles. There were also a few bridges over the river that had to be captured swiftly. Army Group C would be open to attack by forty French divisions from the Maginot Line. But few people had a high opinion of the famous Maginot Line except for the French politicians. It was more of a metaphor for the French state of mind than an impregnable fortress, since it should have been extended further along the Belgian border and was incomplete.

In fact, the Allied plans did include moving into Holland and Belgium. But despite France and Britain's powerful armed forces, "this campaign was to prove once again how much more important psychology, morale, surprise, leadership, movement, concentration of effort, and retention of the initiative are in warfare than mere numbers of men and machines and quality of equipment." The German idea of mission-oriented leadership would inspire a victorious outcome as much as any tanks or weapons they used.[8]

The French and British military staffs had agreed to General Gamelin's Plan D, which had been in action since dawn on the previous day. The Allied plan made great progress by the following morning. General Giraud's Seventh French Army had already begun its dash into Holland. The British Twelfth Lancers were in the center with their armored cars patrolling the banks of the River Dyle. And General Billotte's First Group of Armies hastened to the River Meuse. There were also twenty-two divisions of the Belgian army beside ten of the Dutch army. Churchill waited patiently for the outcome of the initial shock, as if he were back in the thick of the action himself.

The German army had grown in strength and battle experience, and it possessed more powerful armor than when Plan D had been drawn up in 1939. And the French army had deteriorated after a chilling winter on the front. Belgium had trusted Hitler's respect for its neutrality and had not therefore coordinated its tactics with the Allied forces. Consequently, anti-tank obstacles and other defenses on the Namur-Louvain front were not adequate and not finished. Meanwhile, the Germans had made good use of the eight months since destroying Poland by arming, equipping, and training about 155 divisions, ten of them being armored "panzer" divisions.

Hitler had come to an agreement with Stalin that left him free to strike at France with 126 divisions and ten panzer divisions, involving three thousand armored vehicles, including at least a thousand heavy tanks. The divisions were deployed from the North Sea to Switzerland. Their spearhead was the almost cannon-proof tank and dive-bombing aircraft that had already successfully obliterated Poland. Germany's fighter aircraft were much better than the French and superior in numbers.[9]

The French deployed about 2,300 tanks, which were mostly light, while Britain had only just trained its first armored division of 328 tanks—but they were still in England. And neither the English nor the French had equipped themselves with dive-bombers. So Germany had overall superiority in the arms that mattered most.

German aircraft attacked airfields, communications, headquarters, and munition magazines during the night and early morning of May 9–10. Then

German armed troops sprang out of the darkness toward France, trampling underfoot the frontiers of Belgium, Holland, and Luxembourg with complete surprise in their eagerness to reach and crush France, which had imposed on them the humiliating terms of the Versailles Treaty that had impoverished them. The hundred and fifty–mile battlefront was in flames long before dawn.

Plan D

General Gamelin ordered Plan D to commence at 6:45 a.m. on May 10, 1940. The Allies leapt into the fray. Nevertheless, the German infantry broke through everywhere, bridging canals and capturing locks and control of the water. All outer lines of the Dutch defenses were taken over in a day. And German Luftwaffe bombers used their explosive powers on a defenseless country.

Belgium was another unready small state. Its army had just doubled the length of monthly leave. And many of France's frontline troops were still on leave, in spite of the war entering its ninth month. General Proux, who commanded the cavalry, was fifty miles behind the lines practicing target shooting on a range. And the Belgians held up Allied troops for an hour because they had neglected to remove their road blocks. Nor were there any trains on hand to transport French troops and equipment to the front.[10]

The Belgian government had for some time anxiously watched France's political and military weakness and also the indecision of the British government and its pacifism. So instead of allying themselves with France and Britain, they chose neutrality, even after the French and British had entered the war. As for strategy and tactics, Belgium simply placed 90 percent of its troops on the frontier with Germany instead of coordinating activities with the Allies. The result was that the Allies and neutral Belgium were taken by surprise at the blitzkrieg launched by German forces.

"All the Belgians seem to be in a panic from the higher command downwards," claimed General Gort's chief of staff.[11]

German troops under General Bock launched a spectacular attack on Belgium and Holland, according to plan, and destroyed Dutch and Belgian aircraft in their hangars.[12] Dutch resistance allowed Queen Wilhelmina and the government to escape capture by the Germans, while paratroops took airfields and other strategic areas close to Rotterdam and The Hague. It took only eighty-five German paratroopers to destroy the fortress's guns.

Field Marshal von Mellenthin was delighted to see the Allies reacting to the German offensive exactly as von Manstein's plan had predicted. In fact, some Allied generals had been unhappy with Plan D, but General Gamelin had prevailed.[13]

France had lost close to 1.5 million soldiers in the previous war and carried the weight of the battle on land in this one. And yet they had thought that their concrete bunkers and forts on the Maginot Line by the River Rhine were the best answer to attack, without considering to acknowledge that the German enemy could simply go around them. The concrete fortress was the epitome of the French military's purely defensive attitude to the German enemy.

Now the Allies in the north sped to rescue Belgium. The French assault was so fast it outran its ammunition supplies. The superiority of the smaller number of British aircraft became apparent. There was no reason to imagine that the Allied operations would not succeed as intense fighting took place along the whole front. But bad news began arriving on May 14. The Germans had broken through at Sedan and the French were met by an irresistible combination of tank fire and dive-bombing. The French generals were not fast enough. They had been taken by surprise at the rapid rate of the German advance and were calling for ten more squadrons. One German Group had already broken through the lines by destroying or scattering all French troops ahead of them.

According to military historian Liddell Hart, "The French had based their plans on the assumption that an assault on the Meuse would not come before the ninth day. That was the same timescale the German chiefs had in mind originally, before Guderian intervened. When it was upset, worse was to follow. The French commanders, trained in the slow motion methods of 1918, were mentally unfitted to cope with panzer pace, and it produced a spreading paralysis amongst them."[14]

It was while the Allies were pushing forward into Belgium to meet the Germans' assault that the mass of the German tanks—seven panzer divisions—advanced on them through the hilly and wooded Ardennes, a forest the Allies had thought was impenetrable by tanks. General Manstein was one of Germany's brightest officers. He had conceived a new plan of tank attack through the Ardennes, where—as military historian Liddell Hart explained—the French had left the gap opposite the Ardennes poorly fortified and guarded. The German armored forces were on a scale never known in war before this. They broke the center of the French line of armor and armies, and in forty-eight hours they threatened to cut off all the northern Allied Armies from their communications in the south and from the sea. According to Liddell Hart, the French High Command should have given orders to those armies by the fourteenth to make a general retreat at full speed. Instead, confusion reigned.[15]

The attack of General Wilhelm List's Twelfth Army through the Ardennes was a masterpiece of staff-work of the OKW (German Armed Forces High Command). The Panzer Corps arrived at Sedan and Montherm on the Meuse on May 13, at the perfect time and place to effect the *Schwerpunkt* against General André Corap's Ninth Army, when a far heavier concentration of German armor and aircraft broke the French force.[16]

That, at least, is how some historians viewed the situation. But, according to military historian Antony Beevor, what was erroneously described as a blitzkrieg strategy, "was to a large degree improvised on the ground," when Guderian "sensed that the French were in chaos."[17] According to his account, the German forces were already exhausted and stretched to the limit. They were short of ammunition, and the Luftwaffe had only enough bombs for fourteen more days of combat. It suggests that if the French forces had been better trained, less defeatist, and had more aggressive officers who were not wedded to purely defensive tactics, they might conceivably have been able to hold out long enough to beat the German forces.

Instead, the Allied armies barely managed to escape as the Germans broke through and followed them back toward the coast—then halted. That the Allies escaped from the German forces was due to Hitler's hesitation. He held back his generals just as the British Expeditionary Force (BEF) and some of their French allies were about to sweep into the last remaining escape route, which was the port of Dunkirk. The surrender of the Belgians increased the danger that the BEF would be cut off before it could escape by sea.[18] Many of the French failed to retreat to Dunkirk as a consequence of General Weygand's plan, and had no other choice but to surrender on the thirty-first. But their resistance over the following three days helped the others to escape.

Nobody knows to this day the real reason why Hitler prevented his troops from slaughtering the Allies before they could be rescued. Perhaps he hoped to make Britain another peace offer in order to keep his forces intact, since he had found that his empty words had given him time to prepare in the past. Wars come at a cost, and Germany's economy was stretched at a time when his main objective was to invade Russia. Even after the British and French retreat across the Channel, the remaining French armies were incapable of withstanding the German divisions. Hitler's lack of action not only saved some of the Allied forces, it also gave a boost to the morale of the British people that enabled them to carry on the war to the end.

On May 11, Winston Churchill wrote that he felt as if he were walking with destiny, and that all his past life had been a preparation for this moment and this trial.

Evacuation

The first troops to be evacuated from Dunkirk were brought back to England at night on May 26. The first heavy German dive-bombing attack on Dunkirk Harbor came in the evening of the twenty-ninth. Fortunately, the vital channel was not blocked by sinking ships.

It was anticipated that no more than another forty-five thousand Allied troops could be saved from strafing by German planes dive-bombing the exposed Dunkirk beaches. But emergency measures were taken to find small serviceable craft as well as bigger boats in boatyards on the Thames and the coast. Tugs and yachts, barges, fishing boats, and pleasure boats were rounded up and taken to channel ports, and then across the sea to the British Expeditionary Force at Dunkirk.

A spontaneous movement by the public added to the numbers of small craft, as everyone with a boat made for the Normandy beach where two-thirds of the troops were stranded with no other hope of escape. Nearly four hundred boats played a role in the rescue of troops under continual attack by German Stukas designed with an intimidating siren that screamed as they dived down to attack. French troops who had become isolated from their divisions were also rescued, with the help of the Royal Air Force, and bundled into the boats to be brought to the safety of England.

They were fortunate that Hitler had made a mistake in halting his tanks and troops, who would otherwise have massacred them all. General Kleist's panzers were only eighteen miles from Dunkirk when they were stopped. Hitler personally ordered him to withdraw.[19] And General Wilhelm von Thoma's tanks halted near Bergues, which looked down on Dunkirk. When he sent messages to headquarters for orders to push on and was refused, he said of Hitler, "You can never talk to a fool. Hitler spoilt the chance of victory."[20] But Hitler distrusted his generals.[21] And von Thoma made that remark after the war, when the fool was dead. General Halder wrote that the Führer was afraid to take any more chances of falling into an Allied trap, since large forces of French troops still remained free. And Hitler was apparently convinced he had thrashed the British and they would not return to the Continent.[22]

"It was the first example of very many cardinal errors that were to cost Germany the Second World War," wrote historian Andrew Roberts.[23] And military historian Sir Max Hastings scornfully described Hitler as "the Allies' best friend," because of his wooden-headedness and general incompetence.[24]

The German panzer columns were led by tank commander General Guderian, who was a swashbuckling advocate of high-speed warfare, one of the first to study and put into effect the mobility of tanks, which had been conceived two decades earlier by British military theorists of this type of integrated warfare at lightning speed.[25] He reached the unseasoned British troops as quickly as possible to cut them off before they were prepared or reinforcements might arrive. But Hitler was caught by surprise at Guderian's speed and ordered him to stop while he considered the next move. Hitler had been so successful at hoodwinking the British government with threats and lies that he may even have thought he could achieve victory by using more words instead of wasting bullets.[26]

In fact, Hitler was seen to be edgy and anxious about the ease and speed of his victory, as if he suspected that something more must be coming. But he didn't know what and needed time to think about it. So the order was given that Dunkirk should be left to the Luftwaffe.[27] Hence the halt order to give him time to consider if new tactics might be needed.

The result of his hesitation was that over 250,000 British soldiers and about 88,226 French were saved and brought to England. But although the British War Office and media made much of the incident, it could hardly be called a victory, particularly as they left behind most of their guns and equipment, amounting to 7,000 tons of ammunition, 90,000 rifles, 2,300 guns, 120,000 vehicles, 8,000 Bren guns, and 400 antitank rifles. And out of a total of 693 antiaircraft cruisers, destroyers, gunboats, minesweepers, and other craft attempting the rescue of the troops, 226 were sunk by the Luftwaffe.

Hitler's second mistake was the number of German airmen who would be slaughtered. British Fighter Command maintained continual patrols over the area, taking a heavy toll on fighters and bombers. And German aircraft were apparently shot down in scores.[28] Hitler's Halt Order was finally changed on May 27.

One result of Germany's victory against the British and French forces on the Continent was Mussolini's decision to declare war with Britain on June 10. Another was General Weygand's view that he could see no possibility of the French continuing to fight. So he and Marshal Pétain decided to seek peace with Hitler before France could be systematically destroyed by the Germans. It seemed that only the young and energetic General de Gaulle favored carrying on by means of guerrilla warfare.

The net result of the Allied defeat at Dunkirk was that Britain lost its only ally. Now its cities were in the range of the German Luftwaffe, and the British army was too small and unarmed to prevent an invasion of the

British Isles. Germany, on the other hand, had Italy and Russia as allies, and new coastal bases in Europe, as well as all the resources they had captured. "To most observers, Britain's position seemed hopeless."[29] Despite that, the attitude of many of the British toward the French surrender was, "Thank heavens—now we can get on with the war!" The vague and defeatist French generals had been an encumbrance from the beginning.

A journalist in *The New Yorker* of June 29 wrote, "It would be difficult for an impartial observer to decide today whether the British are the bravest or merely the most stupid people in the world."[30]

But Churchill knew that Britain must continue the fight and not seek peace terms. He warned the British cabinet that it was impossible to negotiate with Hitler because the Germans would demand the Royal Navy, use its bases, and disarm the British forces, and Britain would become a slave state led by one of Hitler's puppets. He maintained that Britain could get much better terms if it was prepared to fight for them. Britain's overall strategy would still be to wear down Germany's strength and morale in a war of attrition.

Nevertheless, Britain was still limited to the defensive until it could build up its war chest of weapons. Churchill told the war cabinet that only bombers provided the means to retard and destroy Germany's industries. He confessed he could see no other way. But those were long-term plans. In the short run, there was the simple matter of survival. Influencing Britain's survival in June 1940 was a question of who would use the modern French fleet. Churchill warned that it must not fall into enemy hands, or the balance of power would go to Britain's enemies.

Now that the Dunkirk episode was over, Britain knew that Germany would follow up on Hitler's military errors by invading the British Isles as soon as possible, and despite Hitler's long-term plans for the enslavement of Russia, Hitler and Stalin were still working together. Churchill admitted he had no illusions about Marshal Stalin, and that he understood the future better than Britain's enemies. When he addressed himself for the first time to Stalin, it turned out that he understood their dangers and their interests better than they did themselves—since Stalin had allied himself with Hitler, whereas Churchill recoiled from supping with the devil.[31]

Meanwhile, Germany's Admiralty staff had begun preparing a study for the invasion of Britain shortly after September 3, 1939, when war broke out. They decided the best way to attack would be to cross the English Channel. They never considered any other option. Fortunately for Britain, it was the best-defended coastline, with all its ports fortified. And, later on, most of Britain's airfields and air-control stations were based there to defend London. Britain would become a fortress, with the English Channel as its defensive moat, and no drawbridge to let the Germans in.

9

THE BATTLE OF BRITAIN

AFTER HITLER'S VICTORIOUS 1940 OFFENSIVE IN Europe, the question in everyone's mind in the West was what did he intend to do next? He was not a traditional military leader trained in strategies and tactics in a military academy like Napoleon had been. But he evidently had similar delusions of grandeur and similar goals. He had been captivated by stories in a book when he was an unemployed vagrant in his youth about the so-called Aryan race, which had, supposedly, sprung out of the north and conquered nations all over the world. True or not, it gave him a purpose in life when he had been floundering and living in cheap workingmen's hostels until the First World War broke out in 1914. Then, as he wrote, he'd gotten down on his knees and thanked God, since now he would not be alone anymore with his dreams— he would have a purpose.

Hitler's wartime experience as a corporal carrying messages at the front during poison gas attacks had evidently affected his mind, and he had become a bitter and discontented rebel. But whatever reservations he may have had before becoming Chancellor of Germany, the brilliance of some of his generals with their high-speed blitzkriegs—the combined effects of integrated dive-bombing and tank warfare that defeated and destroyed countries in an instant—had given him enormous self-confidence. But how would it influence his delusions? And where would they turn to next?

The British war cabinet fully expected that Britain would soon be bombed and invaded in a similar fashion as Poland and Belgium. Although they were small nations, the German army had now shown the effects of its military tactics and might on France, the country previously considered to possess the biggest and most powerful military force in Europe. So evidently Britain, as her main ally, would be next on Hitler's revenge list.

Britain's war cabinet met for five days, from May 24 to 28, to discuss possible peace negotiations with Hitler, perhaps even through Mussolini.[1] But Churchill insisted publicly on continuing the fight. Foreign Secretary Halifax claimed he was against sacrificing national sovereignty or the Royal Navy. And Churchill maintained that any accommodation with Hitler would legitimize Germany's conquests and destroy British morale. All agreed on one point—that after German victory in Soviet Russia, Hitler would likely turn against Britain to settle the score anyway.

Instead of simply attempting to negotiate from weakness, the War Office had the Ministry of Information and the Ministry of Home Security distribute a leaflet advising the British public, "If the Invader Comes: What to Do—and How to Do It." It declared boldly that the Germans—if they arrived—will be driven out by our armed forces. To avoid clogging the roads, the public was advised to stay put. They were told not to believe rumors and not to spread them.

Even when he had been chosen as prime minister, Churchill had to deal patiently and cautiously with Halifax's continual proposals of new ways to approach Hitler for a peace settlement by appearing to consider each of them as a reasonable alternative. He knew that if he didn't, circumstances might conspire to replace him, with Lord Halifax leading the appeasers. It took seven months for him to feel secure enough to get rid of Halifax by sending him to the United States as Britain's ambassador—not an ideal choice, since he was a cold and aloof man who could never engage convivially with the Americans. "I have never liked the Americans," Halifax admitted to Baldwin. It is likely that the irony was not lost on Churchill. But at least he was out of the way.

The Home Guard

Britain had already begun to prepare for an invasion. The south and part of the southeast coast of England was protected with coils of barbed wire, concrete tank traps, and pillbox emplacements in strategic positions facing the

Channel and at selected crossroads. Some beaches were mined. Iron girders protruded from the seabed with their sharp ends ready to tear out the hulls of invading naval craft, like commando landing barges.

A uniformed "Home Guard," as Churchill called it, was suggested by Eden, and at first known as the LDV or Local Defense Volunteer, a name Churchill thought too bureaucratic and unfriendly. It was being organized with men who had fought in the last war and were too old to enlist in regular armed forces in this one. There were more than a million by August. So far, they had only wooden rifles to practice with, since the real ones left behind in the Dunkirk retreat had added to the problems of defending the British Isles. They were replaced by the real things from America, still covered in protective grease from the previous war. Then came handheld machine guns.[2]

One fear that occupied Churchill's mind was German tanks being landed ashore, because the idea of sending tanks across the Channel had appealed to him, so he was convinced the Germans had thought about it, too. And Britain had very few antitank guns or even ammunition. Nor, he complained, even basic field artillery.[3] The shortage was so acute that it was difficult to decide whether to let the men fire a single round for practice, or keep it for the invasion. Fortunately, in this time of extreme shortages, British ingenuity usually found a way to produce effective results economically. That was partly why Churchill had decided to keep close control of the Ministry of Defense and its experimental establishment, since he was always full of innovative ideas himself and able to inspire other backroom boys to be inventive, too. He was not averse to picking Professor Lindemann's brains as his scientific adviser. He harvested other people's ideas too; becoming engrossed at one time with the idea of making a "sticky" hand grenade that even civilians could toss into the opening of a tank or attach to the outside—no doubt influenced by the explosive Molotov cocktail that the Finns had used so effectively against their Russian invaders.

He wrote a memo to the Ministry of Information, telling them that all news media should be directed to handle air raids calmly and on what he called a diminishing tone of public interest. In other words, all facts should be expressed without unnecessary prominence or dramatic headlines. In his opinion, the public should be led to treat air raids as normal routine.[4] It should be business as usual with typical British decorum.

Self-dramatization by getting excited or hysterical was frowned upon in Victorian and Edwardian times when Churchill grew up. And it was still considered impolite, inconsiderate, thoughtless, and even vulgar to show emotions in England. Anyone who drew attention to themselves was suspected of being shallow and unreliable. Emotional behavior was neither ladylike nor what was expected of gentlemen. It was what untrustworthy foreigners did. Fortunately, Britons had so far been protected from it by the English Channel. Certainly it was taken for granted that people in the armed forces who had no self-discipline evidently possessed no moral fiber.

One of Churchill's other anxieties was how soon the Germans would take over factories in their newly occupied territories on the Continent and use them for air production and other military equipment to be aimed at Britain in the coming invasion. It was one more reason for the RAF to bomb the Germans' newly acquired plants, so he asked for any spare production capacity for the air force to focus on it immediately.

When he received a message from the Vatican about peace proposals, he warned the foreign secretary to make it clear to the nuncio that "we do not wish to hear any inquiries regarding peace terms with Hitler." Everyone was forbidden even to consider such suggestions.[5] He was not prepared to allow defeatism from anyone. In a speech to the House of Commons on October 5, 1938, he made it clear that a vague idea of peaceful coexistence with a belligerent Germany was out of the question, since Germany had rejected Christian values and reverted to barbaric aggression, conquest, and paganism. He was the only leader with the imagination to understand that complying with Hitler's wishes would mean the destruction of civilization.[6]

The month of June passed on the edge of a possible invasion at any moment, which everyone felt. Churchill reminded General Ismay to study the charts of tides and state of the moon to ascertain on which days' conditions might be most favorable for a seaborne landing on the English coast. And he was aware that a German landing from the air in Ireland could be like a knife in the back. He was conscious that for the first time in 125 years a powerful enemy was preparing to invade Britain's shores.

Booby Traps

The Territorial army had to create and man a secret and elaborate system of defenses with a series of booby-trapped concrete bunkers all along the shortest route from the Channel to London. The commander in chief of Home Forces, Field Marshal Sir Edmund Ironside, shared his plans with the chiefs of staff. They consisted of an entrenched "crust" on the most likely invasion beaches, where defenders would fight where they stood to the last man, supported by mobile reserves who would counterattack, then a "line of anti-tank obstacles manned by the Home Guard, running down the east-center of England and protecting London and the great industrial centers from inroads by armored vehicles." The main reserves would be concealed behind that line for major counter-offensive action. Some of the innocent-looking shops and offices and homes in villages and towns on the route to London were equipped for a last stand against invading troops. They would be manned by suicide volunteers who would delay the German army from reaching the capital city, which was the center of strategic power at General Headquarters in London. They were supported by hidden gun emplacements nearby. Other measures were designed to harass the enemy's rear.

That was what Churchill meant when he made his famous speech: "We shall fight on the beaches, we shall fight on the landing grounds, we shall fight in the fields, and in the streets, we shall fight in the hills; we shall never surrender." Preparations were made for that eventuality exactly as he claimed. Zones of defense were created in a spider's web of corps zones and command zones in a system as deep as a hundred miles or more. And behind them were major antitank obstacles that ran across the southern part of England and north into the county of Nottinghamshire. To cap it all, any resources useful to the enemy were to be blown up in case of capture. The question of whether Britain should fight on alone was never tabled in the wartime cabinet agenda. After the fiasco in France, Belgium, and Luxembourg, the British felt more confident in not having to depend on allies who might turn out to be unreliable. England had always been independent.

Food supplies had already been organized and controlled and rationed. And a Women's Land Army had its members scattered throughout the countryside and in urban city allotments and on formerly private estates to grow food and advise farmers what crops were needed to be grown and how to increase productivity.

Domestic servants had already begun to leave their employers, with the heavy demand for men and women in the forces and munitions factories. Chauffeurs now drove army trucks, armored cars, or tanks. Women had as wide a choice as men, chauffeuring officers, nursing the wounded, driving ambulances at the front, or flying newly made aircraft from U.S. assembly lines to England. The glamour of the Royal Navy appealed to young women who liked the chic and flattering uniform of the Wrens, the adventure it provided, and the promise of a social life. It was thought unlikely that there would be any more domestic service after the war. It also resulted in the appeal of smaller houses that could be managed without servants and the division of larger ones into a number of separate apartments.

Populations of major cities that were likely to be targets for the Luftwaffe's bombs, and residents of coastal resorts on the Channel, like Dover, Folkstone, Brighton, and Hastings, were advised to leave for the countryside. Some children were evacuated to the Dominions and the United States, although Churchill thought that running away from challenges created an impression of defeat.

Code Breakers of Bletchley Park

Another secret enterprise was the breaking of German military and naval codes at the National Codes and Cypher Center in Bletchley Park. These were the codes used by the Nazis to give orders and instructions to German officers in command. Bletchley was another example of low-cost British ingenuity. It became one of Churchill's special interests because of the millions of lives it saved by warning the War Office where and when Hitler planned to strike next, and for its usefulness in creating new strategies or tactics based on the knowledge of hard and up-to-the-minute intelligence.

The project was triggered by the discovery of the Enigma code by the Poles in 1932. It began with a group of MI6 secret agents who arrived at a mansion called Bletchley Park in Buckinghamshire after Poland was threatened with destruction in 1938. Their mission was to decide how to crack the Nazi codes, which were changed at least once every day. They returned in 1939 to begin work by recruiting the most suitable talent.

A number of brilliant intellectuals were hired to decode German military secrets in order for Britain to win the war. Key personnel who were recruited included mathematicians, cryptanalysts, historians, and chess and crossword-puzzle champions. At the peak of its activities, it employed up to nine thousand personnel, most of them women. All were sworn to secrecy by signing the Official Secrets Act (1939). It may have encouraged the wartime phrase "Careless Talk Costs Lives," which was reproduced all over wartime Britain on posters, in buses, on subways, and in underground trains.

The "ultra" intelligence obtained at Bletchley Park is alleged to have shortened the war by at least two years. Once the cyphers were broken, the discovery had to be kept secret to prevent the Germans from using it to pass false information to the British. Meanwhile, decrypts of secret German military and naval signals were delivered daily to Churchill from 1940 on and helped him to formulate strategic plans and tactics. After one visit to Bletchley, he wrote to the head of British Intelligence, "Make sure they have all they want on extreme priority."[7]

How Hitler Planned to Invade Britain

For all his wild claims to enlarge Germany by invading and annexing surrounding territory and attacking any nation in his way, Hitler had never made detailed plans of how to do it or how he would deal with opposition from Britain. Even when France fell to his panzer divisions—apparently as much a surprise to him as to everyone else—he appeared to have the idea that Britain would have no choice but to agree to a peace settlement, enabling him to free his forces to invade Russia for its huge territory, its oil, and its potentially massive supply of slave labor. In his racist mind, Poles and Slavs were an inferior species and good for nothing but working in German industries until they dropped.[8] But Germany was dependent on oil. About 85 percent of Germany's oil supplies had to be imported, and this could make it vulnerable in war."[9]

Ever a liar and a bluffer himself, Hitler assumed that Churchill and the British government were bluffing, too. He was confident that Britain would finally recognize that Germany's war potential was unbeatable and it would be politically wise to compromise with Germany's territorial objectives. It was only on July 2 that he ordered a serious study made of how to overcome Britain by invasion. And he ordered it to be carried out two weeks later. The proposed military campaign was named "Operation Sea Lion." It was to be ready by the middle of August.

Nevertheless, he was far more immersed in plans to turn and attack Soviet Russia in the autumn. Britain was only a small island, a walkover that appeared in his mind as a mere sideshow in comparison with the vast plains and massive peasant population of Russia. So General Guderian was sent back to Berlin to plan how to use the panzer forces in a Russian campaign, and Field Marshal von Rundstedt was given the responsibility for the invasion of Britain.

It was considered so easy that it was not seriously studied by military staff officers. Nor were his troops trained in seaborne and landing operations.

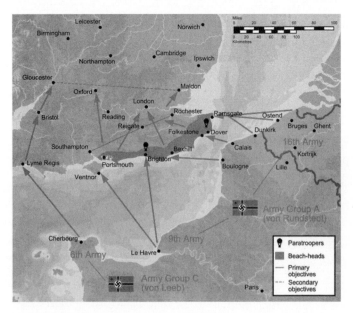

Planned German invasion of England in 1940 code-named Operation Sea Lion.

It was simply a matter of collecting shipping and bringing barges from Germany and the Netherlands to the Channel ports. They had already seen how vulnerable the British Expeditionary Force had been when it had been strafed on the open Dunkirk beaches by gunfire from Göring's Stuka dive-bombers.

Rundstedt would command Army Group A and employ General Busch's Sixteenth Army and General Strauss's Ninth Army. The German forces would be shipped to the southeast coast of England between Folkstone and Brighton. Meanwhile, an airborne division planned to capture the heights of the white cliffs in the area of Dover to Folkstone. A first wave of ten divisions was expected to land and establish a wide bridgehead over four days.[10] The main advance inland would begin a week later. Its objective was to gain the high ground in a curve from the Thames estuary to Portsmouth.[11] London would then to be isolated from the west of England.

A subsidiary operation, with three divisions in the first wave, would be mounted by Field Marshal von Reichenau, to set sail from Cherbourg and land at Lyme Bay for a push north. A second wave of invasion was planned to exploit the mobility and speed of six armored and three motorized divisions in three corps. It would be followed by a third wave. Cross-channel ships were to include 155 transports, including over 3,000 smaller craft, 1,720 barges, 470 tugs, and 1,160 motorboats.[12]

The timing for the launch of "Operation Sea Lion" was scheduled for no sooner than mid-September (despite Hitler's original target date for mid-August). But then the German naval staff recommended a postponement until spring 1941. As that date came closer to being a reality, the German generals became more anxious about keeping their passage clear for the Channel crossing and recommended a wider invasion front to distract British defensive forces. They also became nervous about resistance from the British naval fleet and insisted on a narrow mine-protected corridor for the invasion. Moreover, Admiral Raeder demanded the protection of air superiority by the Luftwaffe. Göring assured everyone that his air force could prevent any interference by the British navy as well as drive the British from the skies.[13]

Britain was at bay. And the struggle for air dominance was to become the main feature of the Battle of Britain.

10

FRANCE FALLS

CHURCHILL CONTINUED TO OFFER AID TO France as its military collapsed. One of the problems of the French collapse was the very real possibility that Germany would take possession of the entire French naval fleet as part of a peace agreement.

Meanwhile, the President of the United States could not commit himself to military participation in Europe under the U.S. Constitution, even if he wanted to. And he was always suspicious of England with its empire, since he and many Americans were conscious of having once been one of England's colonies. But he had persuaded Congress to appropriate $50 million to supply food and clothing for civilian refugees in France. In order to support any arguments he might have with Congress, Churchill warned him of the danger to the United States if Europe fell and Britain failed to prevent a German invasion of the British Isles.

French armies were still fighting the enemy, but their disarray deteriorated from bad to worse. Paris fell on the fourteenth and the French armies were scattered. The much vaunted Maginot Line was penetrated on the same day. Two days later, the Germans cut off the French retreat and nearly half a million French troops were forced to surrender since their position was hopeless. The huge and disorganized battle for France was over.

Like all the previous German blitzkriegs, the war to crush France had been fast and short and deadly. Everyone was shocked at the speed with which France fell, since the French were believed to have the biggest and most powerful armed forces in Europe. And although de Gaulle called for resistance, General Weygand told him he was talking nonsense—that in three weeks England would have her neck wrung like a chicken.

Churchill, seldom downhearted in public and always able to quip, made a speech to the Canadian Parliament in Ottawa after visiting the U.S. President for a week. He warned that the Canadian army might be engaged in one of the most frightful battles the world had ever seen, and he informed Parliament that Britain's objective was the final extirpation of its enemies. Then he took the opportunity to recount how he had told the French that Britain would fight on, and how the generals warned that England would have its neck wrung like a chicken. Churchill proudly inflated his chest and called out, "Some chicken—some neck!" The Canadian parliamentarians cheered.

Evacuations of what remained of the British Expeditionary Force—a Canadian division—the French 157th Brigade, and over twenty thousand Polish troops from the Continent continued at Brest, Cherbourg, St. Malo, and St. Nazaire. It was a repetition on a much larger scale of the retreat from Dunkirk, with heavy German air attacks on the transport. A liner evacuating five thousand men was set on fire by the bombing and some three thousand men were killed. On the following day, Marshal Pétain ordered all French forces to stop fighting and asked the Germans for an armistice.

The French government's intention was to split itself in two and establish the authority of a French government-in-exile across the sea and move the French fleet out of reach of the Germans. Some hoped to continue the war from Africa. General Weygand adamantly refused to surrender personally to the Germans as a matter of honor, leaving it to the politicians to do business with Hitler. One of them was French Foreign Minister Pierre Laval, who had withdrawn to Bordeaux. He was convinced that not only should France make peace with Germany but she must change sides and abandon Britain. It was the only way to save French territory and her interests. On the other hand, Churchill had discussed with the British government a proposal that France and Britain would not continue as separate nations, but as a Franco-British Union instead. General de Gaulle eagerly called for an immediate proclamation of unity with the Allies.

As soon as a Declaration of Union was drafted, de Gaulle read it enthusiastically over the telephone to Premier Reynaud in Bordeaux. The French premier read the document to the cabinet and told them he was in favor of it, but he was met with hostility. Still agitated by defeat and confused about their options, the French cabinet was divided and largely defeatist. One section refused to discuss it, since it seemed to place France in a position whereby the British would take possession of France's empire, and France would become a mere Dominion. Arguments ensued at the prospect of the French being citizens of the British Empire and not of Britain, whereas the British would be citizens of France. Moreover, General Weygand persuaded Pétain that, in any case, England was finished.

In the end, the proposal of an Anglo-French Union collapsed, and Pierre Reynaud resigned. The whole mood was now deflated by hopeless resignation. Weygand seemed to have abandoned all hope, and Pétain was even more depressed than before. After visiting them, Churchill described Pétain as "senile, uninspiring, and defeatist."[1] Reynaud was "tired and emotionally drained." The result was that the French government capitulated only three weeks after Dunkirk.

The Fate of the French Fleet

It has been remarked that nowhere but in France did such a significant part of the political class agree to do the bidding of what they thought would be the winning side.[2] Apparently French politicians and generals still had an antiquated idea that "you just exchanged a couple of provinces, paid a certain amount of millions, and then called it a day and started off the next time hoping you would be more lucky."[3]

Meanwhile, urgent discussion continued about placing the French fleet beyond German control. The British ambassador asked for it to be sent to British ports. It was vitally important that it not be used against Britain. And there was still the problem of extricating Polish, Belgian, and Czech troops who had been fighting beside the British and French armies.

Churchill sent a personal message to Pétain on the seventeenth declaring that he wished to repeat his deep conviction that "the illustrious Marshal

Pétain and the famous General Weygand"—whom he took care to describe as "our comrades in two great wars against the Germans"—would not inflict injuries on their friends by delivering the French fleet to the enemy. He tactfully suggested that it could be sailed safely to British or American ports—thereby providing hope for the future and for the restoration of France's honor.[4] After that, personal contact was made with Admiral Darlan and others to ensure that the French fleet would not fall into German hands.

On June 18, Churchill made one of his most stirring speeches in the House of Commons to prevent panic before news of the French armistice was made public: "Let us therefore brace ourselves to our duties, and so bear ourselves that, if the British Empire and its Commonwealth last for a thousand years, men will still say, 'This was their finest hour.'"

In the meantime, French Foreign Minister Daladier planned to set up a French resistance administration in North Africa with himself as premier. Churchill had a similar idea to enable any French who wished to continue fighting to travel to various ports where the British Admiralty and air force would offer them support, with the cooperation of General de Gaulle and his Free-French committee. And Churchill still continued to seek an Anglo-French Union. He wanted to tell the French leaders to go to French Africa and invite them to continue fighting the war together.[5]

It took a while for Churchill and de Gaulle to realize they had made the same mistake. While they had believed that most of the French shared their vision and desire to fight on, it turned out that the French preferred to get on with their own lives.[6]

"It was a period of decay," explained General Beaufre afterward, "caused by the excess of the effort during World War I. I think we suffered from an illness, which is not peculiar to France, that of having been victorious and believing that we were right and very clever."[7] It was the tragedy of the First World War, in which France lost more men in proportion to their population than any other nation, that explained France's fate in 1940. They had lost their will.

As a result, the fate of France was harsh and humiliating.[8] Particularly so for French Jews. The new Vichy-French client state, set up in the Midi and the Massif Central of France, was so eager to obey the anti-Jewish

German laws that it implemented them even before the French were asked to by Berlin.*

After the collapse of France, the question on everyone's mind was, "Would Britain surrender, too?" Britain might have been forced to surrender if the entire French fleet was used by the Germans.

When Admiral Darlan became Minister of Marine, he could have ordered the French fleet to a colonial harbor, but he did not. What he did do, at least, was ensure the French navy was not manned by Germans, because he hated Germany. But it turned out that he was also one of those brave Frenchman who hated England, because his great-grandfather had fought for Napoleon and was killed by the British at the Battle of Trafalgar.

The position of the French fleet was now imperative. British Vice-Admiral Sommerville sent a communication to the French admiral on July 2 to explain that it was impossible for their former allies to allow French ships to fall into the hands of the enemy and be used against them, and that the allies were determined to fight to the end. He spelled out four options for the French navy: to fight on with Britain, to sail to British ports to prevent the fleet falling into German hands, to sail to a French port in the West Indies, or to be demilitarized or scuttled.

Negotiations continued between British and French admirals, with the British war cabinet determined to prevent the French navy from increasing Germany's strength and endangering Britain. A final signal was sent to Captain Holland at 6:26 p.m. the next day: "French ships must comply with our terms or sink themselves or be sunk by you before dark."

Admiral Sommerville finally opened fire on the French fleet, although it was protected by its shore batteries, and reported he was heavily engaged at 6:00 p.m. The bombardment lasted for about ten minutes. It was followed by heavy attacks from British naval aircraft that were launched from the *Ark Royal*. The French battleship *Bretagne* was blown up. The *Dunkerque* ran aground. The battleship *Provence* was beached. The *Strasbourg* was attacked and damaged by torpedoes, but escaped. It reached Toulon. So did the cruisers from Algiers. French Admiral Godfroy agreed to discharge his oil fuel at Alexandria, remove important parts of his gun mechanisms, and repatriate some of his crew. Meanwhile, the aircraft carrier HMS *Hermes* attacked the battleship *Richelieu*.

Winston Churchill declared afterward to the House of Commons that the destruction of the French navy was a vital factor that required violent action to produce a profound and sobering impression everywhere. Parliament grew silent as he described the incident. According to Churchill, the action made plain to everyone that the British war cabinet was afraid of no one and would stop at nothing.[9]

---

* The self-imposed subjugation of the French to Germany resulted in many humiliations, hardships, and deaths for the French people. The following are only a few of them: A total of seventy-seven thousand French Jews were murdered in the French Holocaust. The Vichy government sent non-French Jews to death camps, like Auschwitz.[10] French Police rounded up French Jews and non-French Jews to two transit camps, then on to French trains to their ultimate deaths. Four thousand Jewish children under the age of twelve were separated from their parents by French police and starved for a week.[11] About thirty thousand French non-Jews were shot as hostages and resisters, and sixty thousand were sent to concentration camps. One and a half million French prisoners of war were sent to work abroad, mostly in German factories.[12] Death squads of the Vichy-French paramilitary police, called the Milice, tortured and murdered members of the French Resistance.[13] Six hundred fifty thousand French workers were drafted to work in German factories in 1943.[14]

Three to four hundred thousand French enrolled in German military organizations and fascist movements.[15] The passivity of the French enabled only about thirty thousand German troops to control France initially, while millions of French learned to coexist with the German-occupying forces, who considered themselves superior to Mediterranean and Latin races like the French. "Germany requisitioned half of all the food produced by France between 1940 and 1944. . . . Around 80 percent of the meat that came into Paris was effectively confiscated."[16] Many French were starving toward the end since the Germans commandeered much of the food. "We who have not known hunger have no idea how empty bellies debilitate and dominate."[17] There were plenty of collaborators and few heroes: some French betrayed their country for sex or food, others for money. "Patriotism . . . had lost much of its magic."[18]

Looking for someone to blame for their defeat, the French military and government targeted socialists and intellectuals, trade unionists, schoolteachers, Protestants, and Jews. But the real cause of their defeat was an inept military and government who couldn't be bothered to take the trouble to learn the lessons of modern mechanized warfare.[19]

11

ANGLO-SAXON ATTITUDES

BRITAIN STILL POSSESSED AN EMPIRE, WHICH had been gradually becoming more of a partnership or commonwealth of nations. But the British Isles had only themselves to rely on for their defense. Fortunately, President Roosevelt was largely responsible for rearming the British forces after Dunkirk. And he encouraged Churchill through his closest adviser, Harry Hopkins.[1]

Even so, the American President was somewhat leery about the British Empire, since the United States had been a British colony before achieving liberty in the American War of Independence. And yet, his reaction and that of other Americans showed how sentiment played a large role in the wartime relationship between the two leading democratic nations.

Since so few people now know what old-fashioned England or the much-maligned British Empire was like in the 1930s and early 1940s, it is enlightening to examine three artifacts of British culture of that time. The first is a poem that portrays a sentimental American concept of "Little England." It was written as a novel in verse by a New Yorker named Alice Duer Miller in 1940.

I have loved England, dearly and deeply,
Since that first morning, shining and pure,
The white cliffs of Dover I saw rising steeply
Out of the sea that made her secure.

Those were her opening lines. She ended her lengthy and dramatic story with the following ones:

I am American bred,
I have seen much to hate here—much to forgive,
But in a world where England is finished and dead,
I do not wish to live.

She was farsighted in realizing that only England stood as a barrier to protect the hard-won principles of America's Declaration of Independence, drafted by President Thomas Jefferson and edited by a committee of five before being adopted by the U.S. Congress. It states, "We hold these truths to be self-evident, that all men are created equal, that they are endowed by the Creator with certain inalienable Rights; that among these are Life, Liberty and the pursuit of Happiness." That was what Hitler's Nazis were intent on destroying, and Winston Churchill was determined to protect.

Her story stirred the sentiments of many Americans with English, Scottish, or Welsh ancestry, who were united in being a part of the English-speaking peoples.

The second cultural artifact of that time was a romantic black-and-white American wartime film made in 1942, entitled *Mrs. Miniver*. It starred the very English Greer Garson and Walter Pidgeon. It was based on a 1937 novel, written as a series for *The Times*.[2] And at its core was the same sentimental love for all that England stood for, as defined in "The White Cliffs of Dover." Mrs. Miniver's husband is the hero of the story—a solid and dependable, pipe-smoking Englishman. The pipe was a stage prop, since men in self-confident patriarchal societies imagined that puffing tobacco solemnly in a pipe conveyed an image of deep thoughtfulness and dependability.

Mrs. Miniver was a romantic story, but hardly a soap opera, since its English hero and heroine always restrain their emotions. Wearing one's heart on one's sleeve was foreign to English people at that time, since it might be interpreted as lack of self-control, and that was unthinkable. Imperial English men and women were supposed always to be in control, decidedly cool and polite, and philosophically distant or objective. They were, after all, in positions that required them to set a moral example, since the British Empire was the most powerful ever known in history, and they were naturally proud of it. Mutual respect and regard for personal privacy were considered more important than shows of love, affection, or romanticism, which were thought to be insincere sentiments more suited to the poorer sort of melodramatic Hollywood movies than to sensible and responsible people like the English.

In 1930s England, men and women did not draw attention to themselves, or boast, or show off their knowledge or skills, since it would be considered vulgar. Instead, even the most brilliant pretended to be amateurs. They venerated the amateur who was doing it simply for the love of the sport or pastime, whatever it was—certainly never for money; that would have been considered crass. And not even for the goal of winning, but merely for taking part and encouraging the others.

The film of *Mrs. Miniver* fairly accurately mirrors how English people of different social classes behaved at that time. They were strong and silent, brave, decent, modestly heroic, and always polite and considerate— if a little dim or bewildered about deeper issues like money, politics, sex, or religion. They knew little or nothing about them. Fortunately, those subjects were taboo in polite society. All they wanted, it seemed, was a picturesque but modest house in the countryside to shelter their family in privacy, and to be left alone by tiresome foreigners. Respecting each other's privacy was almost as ritualistic as in Japan. Nevertheless, one had to be tolerant of people who didn't know any better, out of politeness and human decency. They preferred to be regarded as comfortably dull, and they favored simple common sense over all sorts of different opinions and ideologies coming from France or Germany or anywhere else. And yet they were a truly extraordinary generation to whom we all owe our lives. We shall never know their like again.

We see in the film the difficulty that the hero has in coming to terms with the beastly German aviator who virtually drops into his backyard. Mr. Miniver is caught between natural gentlemanly courtesy and unwanted heroics, since he cannot conceive of a new breed of Hun that considers itself racially superior to everyone else and is prepared to kill anyone as a consequence of an irrational and erroneous theory about different human races.

The British Empire

As for their sentiments about the British Empire, the third artifact is a black-and-white film made in England in 1935, before the invention of Technicolor, called *Sanders of the River*.[3] It told the story of a modest and self-sacrificing district commissioner in a British colony somewhere in Africa. Sanders is known familiarly as Sandy and played by a popular leading man named Leslie Banks with typically English modesty and self-assurance—a trick that apparently only the English could pull off successfully. Sandy patiently and conscientiously looks after the welfare of the natives in his allotted district of some insalubrious and far-flung outpost of the British Empire. He suffers from malaria without complaint. Regarded more as a genial uncle (the British Empire itself being both mother and father to its colonial populations), Sandy might today be one of those doctors without borders, those altruistic volunteers who work for a pittance, providing humanitarian aid and emergency care all over the world by treating the sick in third-world countries. Humble British colonial district commissioners like Sandy were their forerunners. They were pioneers, since doctors were scarce on the ground in the jungles of Africa.

The film featured the first dark-skinned man that most British people had ever seen at the time. Audiences were enthralled by him. He was a famous American actor named Paul Robeson—magnificently built and handsome, with a deep warm voice, and a genuinely modest personality. His theme song, which was chanted as they canoe down an almost endless and swift-running river, conveyed the very spirit of the British Empire—at least as most British people liked to envisage it at the time.

Sandy the strong
Sandy the wise
Righter of wrong
Hater of lies
Laughed as he fought
Worked as he played
As he has taught
Let it be made

Away you go
Yae guh deh
And make it so
Yae guh deh
Together all
The paddles fall
In tune and time
For life is the burden of labor
When each bends his back with his neighbor
So each for all
We stand or fall
And all for each
Until we reach
The journey's end

The lyrics—particularly the final verse—portrayed what most British people believed at that time about Britain's role in the world. Of course it was paternalism. But what was wrong with that, if you loved the country and the people and wanted to help them? Sandy and the Minivers shared a code in common with most British people in prewar Britain. It was a code of honor, decency, courage, and moderation in all things. Although Britain was still a class-conscious society, the First World War had drawn the social classes closer together in a spirit of comradeship where each respected the virtues and problems of the others. And, though there was some upward mobility from class to class, it came about very slowly and cautiously, with people preferring to enjoy what they already had rather than change it for something that might bring unintended consequences with it.

Wartime Propaganda

Films produced or directed by the Hungarian brothers Zoltan and Alexander Korda were not only engrossing and thrilling; to English audiences who had never been overseas, they revealed new vistas, geographically and from other people's attitudes. Few suspected they might be purposeful propaganda, designed to instill patriotism and courage for the conflict with Germany. In 1937 came *Elephant Boy. Drum* was released in 1938. And in 1939, two films from Alexander Korda appeared to warn cinema audiences of Britain's fate. They were *The Four Feathers*, about an imperial war in Africa in Victorian times, and *The Lion Has Wings*. Both extolled patriotism and heroism. The latter documentary-style film was a contemporary call to arms about Britain's air force. It warned audiences of possibly imminent Nazi domination if they didn't do something about it. In view of Alexander Korda's personal relationship with Winston Churchill, it is easy to imagine that Churchill might have inspired it as wartime propaganda to recruit the necessary aircrews.

Less promoted, but nevertheless influential as war propaganda in 1937, was *Dark Journey*, about spies and double agents in World War I, with Vivien Leigh and Conrad Veidt. There was also *The Spy in Black* in 1939, and *Contraband* about merchant ships and their vulnerable crews in 1940, in which audiences could see how the unarmed merchant navy was targeted by German U-boats, dive-bombed by enemy Stukas, or blown up by German mines. All shared one particular ingredient in common—a call to the adventurous spirit in young men and women.

War films were all the rage beginning in 1935, when Mussolini's troops invaded Abyssinia using modern weapons and poison gas against a half-naked native population whose only defensive weapons were spears. British public opinion was outraged on hearing the reports of the war on BBC radio and seeing current Pathé and Movietone News on the silver screen. The nation overwhelmingly thought that Mussolini and his Fascists were primitive savages, and not the Abyssinian natives who should rather be left in peace. Britons considered that administering an empire was an altruistic responsibility and not a landgrab or for the use of natives as slave labor, like in the Belgian Congo and German South-West Africa. Prewar audiences saw nothing wrong with benign paternalism if it helped to develop African economies and improve the standard of living in third-world countries.

Alfred Hitchcock's film called *The 39 Steps* was released at the same time as Italian troops attacked Abyssinia in 1935. It was a thriller about a German spy ring operating in Britain. So was *The Lady Vanishes*, which Hitchcock made in 1938. Neither was an antiwar film; rather, they were stories of adventure in wartime. What they appealed to was boys' powerful desire to be heroes. So that, in that sense, they too were war propaganda films.

In 1939, an unusual play called *Thunder Rock* appeared on Broadway.[4] But America was too cut off from Europe to care about the subject. However, it struck a chord with London audiences when it was tried out at a tiny theater in Kensington.[5] It was funded by His Majesty's Treasury to transfer to the West End at the Globe Theatre, because it suggested that people were not paying enough attention to the rise of the Nazis on the other side of the Channel and for fear of a looming possibility of a German invasion of Britain.

The story portrays a lighthouse keeper who has fled from the banality of a world in which people are absorbed in their own self-indulgence and fail to realize that they will be crushed by a world war unless they pay attention to reality. There he learns of a heroic sea voyage by passengers and crew of an old-time sailing ship fleeing the brutality of religious wars in Europe to escape to America. The hero of the story is persuaded to return to civilization in order to help a troubled world. The objective of the play was to wake Britons up out of their complacent dreams to the reality of the threat from across the Channel.

The 1942 film of the play had the advantage of being able to use flashbacks of the sea journey that ended in shipwreck on Thunder Rock as well as montages of cinema audiences shown to be not in the least bit interested in the latest news films on the screen of the threat of a rising armed and belligerent Germany, but so occupied in laughing at the Mickey Mouse cartoons in fantasy-land as to be oblivious to the very real threat on their own doorstep. Its message too was "Britain Awake!"

Preserving Dignity

The national anthem would strike up at the end of each performance of a film and at every other public gathering, when the audience would rise and sing "God Save the King" (or Queen). If available, a gramophone or orchestra would play the familiar tune. This was obligatory under the Royal Proclamation Act of Parliament, which was intended to remind groups of people not to conspire against the Constitution and to show their loyalty to the Crown. The Royal Family were very conscious of their German ancestry, which embarrassed them during the First World War, when they Anglicized their German surname to Windsor. The Russian Revolution and assassination of their complacent, incompetent, and oppressive cousin the Tsar had taken place not long afterward.[6]

But everyone in England—including Winston Churchill—loved the Royals, who were important role models. They were the biggest celebrities Britain possessed. The Windsors were a reflection of themselves, or an idealized version of what they would like to be. The King and Queen and Princess Elizabeth, on the other hand, were remarkably modest and even shy or apprehensive of the role they were obliged to play. But that was one of the endearing features that was approved of in a nation that had been taught to be self-effacing and considerate to the less fortunate.

Preserving their dignity was a cultural feature of the British in wartime. Many would not want to reveal any fear by rushing to an air-raid shelter when the warning sirens sounded or throwing themselves to the ground when bombs fell. Instead, they tended to stand and stare with curiosity up at any aircraft overhead, as if watching a trapeze act in a circus performance. Women did not become hysterical and men did not cry in public at their bereavement, since they all faced the same situations together. The traditional custom of wearing a black tie or a black armband in respect for their dead soon disappeared as they shrank from drawing attention to their own personal problems.

Whatever tragedy occurred was accepted stoically as a hazard of war. And the death of a loved one might be met with a cryptic remark like, "Oh, what bad luck!"

Perhaps one of the most noticeable differences between people then and now was caused by the absence of television. Sets didn't appear in large numbers until well after the war was over. It meant that most people reacted naturally and calmly to events; whereas once TV cameras became commonplace after 1945, people who liked to have their picture taken and be in the limelight began to act and overreact in front of the TV camera lens, as if they imagined they were playing a role in a TV sitcom and looking for applause. British people did not dramatize themselves in wartime any more than they had done before. But the prevalence of popular movies on the cinema screen, with suave heroes and scintillating heroines, made audiences more dress conscious after the war and generally more elegant or fashionable, like their role models. Those earlier black-and-white films reveal the differences very clearly.

During the war, and the years of austerity that followed, the British looked shabby. They hardly noticed it themselves, because it was so commonplace. And they were not materialistic (that would change with the next generation in the 1960s). The shortage of razor blades meant that men's faces were often shadowed in gray. Some returned to using a straight razor and were clumsy with it, so that the effects of cuts could frequently be seen. Men's shirts were generally threadbare at the collar and cuffs. Buttons were often missing. Some women were ingenious in using alternatives for cosmetics, even painting a thin line down the back of their legs to simulate silk stockings that were no longer available. Britons were determined to preserve their dignity and carry on with their lives as much as possible as they had been before the war. Women's nylons only arrived in England as part of the extraordinarily varied inventory of the American army's PX stores that catered to young American GIs training for the invasion of the continent of Europe. Consumer goods in PX stores made American GIs very attractive to British girls accustomed to shortages.

Antiwar Films

After the 1914–1918 World War, a Swedish author named Ernst Johannsen wrote an influential antiwar novel that was filmed with the title of *Westfront 1918*. It was directed by the famous German filmmaker Pabst. Its author's intention was to reveal the grim realities of war and banish any illusions created by previous patriarchal societies about glory and heroism and self-sacrifice on the battlefields. His point was that "the paths of glory lead but to the grave."[7]

The novelist also wanted to eliminate nationalism, which induced young men to sacrifice themselves as martyrs for what was only a delusion. Paternalism or nationalism subdued women's personalities by turning them into domestic drudges, sex slaves, and nonentities. It restricted society by preventing people from asserting their own individual personalities and skills and potential.

Most typical of that state of mind had been Bismarck's Prussia, in which society was based on the Prussian army, where commands were given and had to be obeyed. Since everyone obeyed the same rules and regulations, there were not meant to be any individuals with minds of their own. And with no individuals, there was no discussion and no progress. Everyone simply did what they were told. The punishment for disobedience might even be death. That attitude was generally justified by religious authority. Sociologist Max Weber described the military state as a rigid iron cage with a steel-hard casing. German domestic life was similarly ironbound, with the father or husband as a dictator in the home.

Remains of that type of society lingered on in Europe, even more so in Germany and Japan, where everyone knew their appointed place and what they could wear, and they obeyed orders like robots. It laid the groundwork for the Nazi ideology. It was also part of the samurai tradition.

By the time Hitler rose to political power with the Nazis, the book and film of *Westfront 1918* were banned. Pacifism was not an outlook that Hitler wanted in Germany since he aimed to turn it back to the brutal past of the Germanic tribes where the strong took whatever they wanted from the weak. To do so he had to whitewash violence, brutality, and mass murders, and conceal them behind more seductive symbols of glory and self-sacrifice for the Fatherland.

Way back in a previous century, it was considered that there were only three main reasons for war: gain, safety, and glory.[8] The Kaiser's Germany started World War I for *safety*, under a delusion that they might be encircled by France and Britain. Hitler initiated World War II for *gain*, beginning by stealing all Jewish property in Germany and all the territory he conquered, and concealing his true intentions under the guise of *glory*.

For the eighteenth-century philosopher Rousseau, human beings were solitary, timid, fearful, and more likely to flee from one another than fight. Hitler knew that, and relied on it by building up an intimidating power base—armed and dressed in menacing black, with death-head symbols that encouraged a heart of darkness in its wearers.

But when, in 1929, a German author named Erich Maria von Remarque wrote his antiwar novel to discourage any possible future wars—as, no doubt, he envisioned would erupt with the rise of the Nazis—it seemed to confirm publicly what Hitler thought, that soldiers might break disciplined ranks and run away if they all knew the dreadful truth about wars. *All Quiet on the Western Front* was so popular that it sold 2.5 million copies in twenty-two languages in the first eighteen months after publication. Remarque's intention was to show the real horrors of war, as opposed to the typical romantic fantasies that perpetuated Prussian warlord ideology, in which the strong survive by crushing the weak. He depicted schoolmasters brainwashing their inexperienced students into believing in the adventure and glory of going to war, while showing that the truth of mass murders on battlefields is horribly different from all the fictional propaganda.

Since Hitler intended to wage war even more brutally and ruthlessly than in the past, in order to steal territories for a Greater Germany, the Nazis banned and burned Remarque's books in public on a pile of other antiwar and anti-Nazi literature, and the author fled to America to avoid being sent to a death camp by Hitler.

Burned on the same pile of banned books was a 1933 psychological study of Fascism by one of the leading psychiatrists of the time. Wilhelm Reich was considered a genius at the age of only twenty-three when he managed Sigmund Freud's public psychiatric clinic in Vienna. His book was a character analysis called *The Mass Psychology of Fascism*. But Hitler did not want anyone to read a book by an accomplished psychiatrist who described the collective delusions of the Nazis. As a result of Hitler's anger at the revelations of the Nazis' sick minds, Reich also fled for his life to America.

Hitler had spent years weaving a tapestry of lies and illusions to seduce his followers and provide him with an army of millions of other discontented rebels who would do whatever he wanted, including throwing away their lives for him. He needed propaganda to perpetuate the myth that war was glorious and courageous and that all good Germans must sacrifice themselves and their families as martyrs for the Nazi cause. He indoctrinated them in the Hitler Youth movement. And his Minister of Propaganda, Joseph Goebbels, was brilliant at creating illusions as a veneer to conceal the sordid realities of the brutal crimes they planned to commit on a global scale.

Triumph of the Will

Leni Riefenstahl worked closely with Hitler to make her propaganda films, which served two purposes. The most important one was to glorify Hitler as a savior of the German people. The other was to persuade German schoolgirls that their destiny was to breed a so-called "master race." Her masterpiece was her documentary of the 1934 Nazi Nuremberg Rally called *Triumph of the Will*.

But the war story that captured the imagination of most movie audiences in Britain and the United States was called *The Dawn Patrol*. It took place in a Royal Flying Corps airfield in 1915. The RFC was the forerunner of the Royal Air Force, or RAF. It starts with the commander of the squadron and his adjutant waiting anxiously for the return of the dawn patrol—to find out how many German planes they'd shot down and how many British pilots were missing. Major Brand, the commander, has already lost sixteen pilots in the past two weeks, all young volunteers straight out of school, with not enough experience to compete against seasoned German veterans. He is ordered to send up another batch in the air the following morning at dawn and is under pressure because of the hopelessness of the situation of using untrained young men straight out of school. But this is war, in which you either kill or are killed. And Brand knows it will be yet another suicide mission.

The two seasoned pilots, Courtney and Scott, return after losing two beginners in their squadron. One of the inexperienced replacements who returns with them is a youngster named Hollister, who is in shock after witnessing his best friend being shot down. They retire to the bar to drink with fatalistic bravado. Courtney attempts to cheer Hollister up. But the young man breaks down in tearful grief.

When Brand announces the names of tomorrow's dawn patrol, Courtney objects angrily that there aren't enough experienced men. Brand tells him that four replacements are scheduled to arrive imminently. As soon as they turn up, he chooses two with the most flying hours to their credit. But flying experience and combat experience are two different skills, and neither of the two rookies return from the mission. Nor does Scott, who is shot down attempting to save Hollister from a German pilot who swoops down from out of the sun with blazing machine guns.

Not long afterward, British soldiers bring in the German pilot who shot down Scott. Hauptman von Mueller is now a prisoner of war but seems philosophical about it, since enemy officers in those days were treated like gentlemen. Courtney gets angry at first when Brand tells von Mueller that he was the officer who shot him down. The German fighter pilot acknowledges him with good grace. But the others have to prevent Hollister from attacking the enemy flyer.

A scruffy British officer appears afterward. He turns out to be Scott, who survived the crash after his plane went into a tailspin.

The next day, another flight limps back to the airfield with its wounded leader warning the squadron that a formidable air ace named von Richter was encountered during their air battle. And Richter flies low over the airfield soon afterward in order to drop a pair of trench boots with a note to warn them they'd be safer to remain on the ground. When the excitable pilots express their anger at the insult, Brand warns them that getting emotional will only harm their combat skills at a time when they should instead keep cool heads. He forbids anyone to fly off in an angry attempt to retaliate. But emotions run high, and so does the alcohol. Courtney and Scott take off in the misty dawn to return the boots and avenge their lost comrades.

They fly to von Richter's airfield. Seeing the German fighter aircraft lined up on a field with engines running, ready to take off for the next battle, they swoop down and strafe them on the ground with their machine guns, drop a few bombs, and manage to shoot down two German pilots who attempt to take off, as they destroy the rest. Then Courtney swoops down to return the boots. Von Richter comes out of a hangar to pick them up and impotently shakes his fist at the retreating British planes.

On the return trip home, Courtney's plane is shot down in a field. Scott manages to land and rescue him. But after taking to the air, Scott's plane is struck by antiaircraft fire, and oil leaking from the engine is swept back in the slipstream to blind him. Courtney has to talk him down to crash-land in a trench behind their own lines.

Major Brand has been fuming at their disobedience in the face of his orders. But his reaction changes when he receives a call from headquarters to congratulate him on the success of the dawn patrol. He is promoted to wing commander and released from his current responsibilities. Before he leaves, Brand makes a point of choosing Courtney to replace him. From now on, Courtney—who had previously criticized Brand for his hard-hearted ruthlessness—will have the dubious responsibility of sending inexperienced pilots to their deaths. To do so, Courtney will be obliged to adopt the very same ruthless and coldhearted qualities in order to carry the war to the enemy, day after day, sacrificing one young and untested pilot after another.

Although it showed the bleak and pointless side of war when the original film was made, society had changed with the rise of the Nazis since then, and there were a number of flaws in the story that failed to ring true in the Second World War. First there were the gentlemanly sentiments portrayed in the film that were true of the First World War in 1914–1918, but already untrue of the 1940s. Hitler's war was a Total War. And it was not fought by gentlemen. Instead, it was dedicated to the extermination of everyone else, including any Germans who disobeyed orders. The second flaw was the lack of recognition that young men seeking adventure and excitement will go to war rather than be bored with domestic inactivity at home. It was the reason why audiences were drawn to the film. The third flaw was the emotional breakdown of the young and inexperienced pilot, Hollister—since young men in Britain were brought up to believe that "Englishmen don't cry."

This Happy Breed

The only people unlikely to laugh at the film today would probably be romantic adolescents who are alive to adventure and innocent about the realities of human nature, even ignorant of what death means. What Hitler taught the Nazis, on the other hand, was limitless brute force. As one of his secretaries would remark years later when interviewed on TV, he stole the German conscience.[9]

When we consider the characteristics of the British at the time of the Second World War and wonder how it came about through a tribal mixture of Celtic

Britons, Danes, Vikings, Romans, Saxons, and Normans (generally described in shorthand as White Anglo-Saxon Protestants or WASPs), we find that it was very largely William Shakespeare who formulated England and the English character from its imagined history and the stark realities of King Henry VIII's time, and also from the reigns of the first Queen Elizabeth and King James. He wrote the following sentiments for Elizabethan and Jacobean theater audiences. And, although most of the British involved in World War II would not have known the words, the picture he conjured up of the British Isles and its breed of men was very much how the British visualized Britain and themselves in the 1940s.

This royal throne of kings, this sceptered isle,
This earth of majesty, this seat of Mars,
This other Eden, demi-paradise,
This fortress built by Nature for herself
Against infection and the hand of war,
This happy breed of men, this little world,
This precious stone set in the silver sea,
Which serves it in the office of a wall
Or as a moat defensive to a house,
Against the envy of less happier lands—
This blessed plot, this earth, this realm, this England.

Those sentiments were featured in several other wartime films, which were brought up-to-date for modern audiences to identify with them. Two popular Technicolor ones exemplify those characteristics: *In Which We Serve* (1942) and *This Happy Breed* (1944). Both were written by Noel Coward. The first one was made with the assistance of the Ministry of Information.[10] They were successful because British audiences, and particularly servicemen and women, could easily identify with the characters and situations, both of which possessed a realistic 1940s wartime flavor. What they and *Mrs. Miniver* reveal is the matter-of-factness of the English character of the times, which took everything in its stride as it came along, without complaint.

If the polite middle classes were the ones who patronized the shops and theaters and kept the economy going, it was the Cockney working classes who were the backbone of Britain. With their cheerful irreverent spirit, they could never take Hitler or the Nazis seriously. The men were skeptical of strangers, foreigners, and employers who might take advantage of them. The women were cheeky, good-natured, and warmhearted. One of the first books written about Hitler's planned invasion of England includes two photos that reveal more than anything else why wartime Londoners were indestructible.[11] The first is a picture of four working-class women wearing aprons over their floral frocks and reading in amazement a Nazi leaflet offering peace terms, which was dropped by German aircraft. Its heading is A LAST APPEAL TO REASON BY ADOLF HITLER. All four women are laughing at Hitler. We can easily imagine them saying, "Cheeky devil!" Another picture shows the deck of a ship on which thousands of soldiers are returning to England after the defeat at Dunkirk. They are all laughing. The book was published in 1956 when the author, who served in the war, was closer to it than later writers who did not experience it and had to take a theoretical or academic approach instead of relying on firsthand observations.

The great difference between those last two or three films and Remarque's *All Quiet on the Western Front* and *The Dawn Patrol*—apart from the fact that they mirrored a different society with different values—was that the days of antiwar novels and films were gone by the Second World War, because it was an all-out total war that had to be fought, or its heroes and their families would become victims of the most ruthless and deadly criminals in the history of the world.

Nazi Germany was not only equipped and trained to slaughter millions of victims, it was out to destroy a civilization that the English-speaking peoples and leading European nations had fought to create for centuries, until they had established the human rights of life, liberty, equality, and the pursuit of happiness that all free-thinking people had since taken for granted; it would all be snatched away in an instant if the war was lost. That was what had been done in Germany with Hitler's 1933 decree to suspend civil liberties.

There was no choice but for the British people to face up to the challenges of war and hope that their armed forces and leaders were ready to meet and overcome them.

WAR IN THE AIR

PRESIDENT ROOSEVELT'S LEND-LEASE ACT WAS NARROWLY approved by the United States Congress in March 1941, and the first fifty destroyers were made available to the British navy. Roosevelt, who had to justify his actions to a government and electorate that preferred to be isolated from the European mess, made it public in June that it would save American boys from enlisting or being conscripted into the armed forces. At the same time it enabled America to be involved without going to war. Rifles, revolvers, mortars, machine guns, ammunition, light bombers, and dive-bombers followed. Weapons supplied by the United States in the previous year had been largely out-of-date, even obsolete, for which they had demanded cash. Only when Britain's gold bullion, cash reserves, and foreign assets ran dry did the United States consider credit. America's primary intention was still to surpass Britain as a trading power. And it triggered America's economic boom by increasing the average American family income by about 50 percent.[1]

But back in England, after the catastrophe of Dunkirk, serious questions began to be asked about a possibly hopeless situation if invading German troops became so firmly established in England that Churchill's famous speech about fighting them on the beaches and never giving in would turn out to be only empty threats. Britain's politicians required confirmation from the army whether it would actually be possible, and whether the morale of the troops had suffered as a consequence of the retreat of the British Expeditionary Force from the exposed Dunkirk beaches. Should the British government and the armed forces withdraw to Canada?

In the end, the doubts about British morale made it even more vital to resist a German invasion on the beaches or even in the English Channel.

Meanwhile, the British government refused Hitler's latest peace offer, which he sent by air in the form of a leaflet in July 1940, entitled "A Last Appeal to Reason." It appeared that Hitler still hoped to avoid invading England with troops and aircraft, which he wanted to preserve for an invasion of Soviet Russia, by sweet talking the British government once again.

A remarkable feature of the projected invasion was that the British were efficient, whereas the Germans muddled through without plan or coordination toward only vague objectives.[2] That was because the Nazis couldn't seem to justify it logically. After all, they had invaded Poland for reasons of racial extermination, France for revenge against the Treaty of Versailles, and they intended to invade Russia for more German living space. Hitler's mind seemed to falter when it came to the prospect of invading Britain. In fact, "he showed little interest in the plans."[3]

But the Nazis did have a revenge list of 2,820 Britons and European exiles they intended to arrest after the invasion. It included Winston Churchill, journalist Rebecca West who had written against the Fascists, H. G. Wells, E. M. Forster, Vera Brittain, and the modern poet Stephen Spender. Sigmund Freud and Lytton Strachey were dead by the time the Black Book was printed.[4]

Meanwhile, the Nazis were cautious for all sorts of different reasons. Modern historian Andrew Roberts points out further errors on Hitler's part: Hitler should have developed long-range heavy bombers when he came to power in 1933. He should have built more fighters than he did and trained the German army for amphibious operations; he should not have dissipated German naval forces by invading Norway. And he should have attacked Britain earlier to take advantage of months of better weather in the Channel.[5] Instead, he wasted time in self-indulgent sightseeing of the battlefields of the First World War and visiting Paris. Then he retired to Berchtesgaden as if he had lost interest. It even suggested he might have suffered from a short attention span.

Nevertheless, Hitler crowed to Major-General Jodl that "the British have lost the war, but they don't know it." He still seemed to think that they would come around to his peace offer. Meanwhile, Lord Beaverbrook, as Minister of Aircraft Production, trebled the rate of aircraft coming out of the factories in 1940, whereas Germany only doubled their production rate.[6]

Air Superiority

Churchill wrote afterward that Britain's fate depended on victory in the air. He urged the need for air superiority in the coming Battle of Britain. Göring's Luftwaffe possessed 2,669 operational aircraft, consisting of 1,015 bombers, 346 dive-bombers, 933 fighters, and 375 heavy fighters.[7] And Göring was proud of what his air force had already achieved on the Continent. Now, still with the "Operation Sea Lion" beachhead landing in mind, he targeted Kent and the Channel coastline, which were well within their fuel capacity. But he found that the area occupied most of his fighter squadrons. A few weeks later, he decided to make daylight raids on industrial cities north of Norfolk. Since it was a distance too far for fighter planes to reach with their limited fuel capacity, he used bombers escorted by Messerschmitt 110s.

RAF assessments, compared with the Luftwaffe, showed them to be fairly evenly matched in the designs of fighter aircraft and in the combat skills and bravery of their young pilots. How long Britain could resist heavy bombing would depend on leadership, strategy, and tactics on both sides. Fortunately for the British air force, Göring was not a strategic planner. He was a conceited braggart who had no idea of strategy or tactics. He had flown as a celebrated air ace in the First World War and now gave his pilots instructions to cruise around the south of England dropping bombs haphazardly as he had done then. They were only pinpricks that scared no one. But his vague start-up may have been because Hitler still hoped for victory without actually wasting his resources: he needed aircraft, pilots, and bombs for his planned onslaught on Russia.[8]

The anticipated battles with the Luftwaffe over England began in earnest on July 10, when they bombed naval port installations and merchant ships. The order changed six days later to eliminating the RAF so that it could not provide opposition to the proposed invasion forces of "Operation Sea Lion" that would consist of twenty German divisions to be landed between Ramsgate and Lyme Regis. The question of how to transport German troops, horses, and artillery across the Channel had not yet been addressed. Historian Andrew Roberts listed a further failure on Hitler's part: he had not grasped "the fundamental principles of air warfare," to which he attributes the defeat of the Luftwaffe in the Battle of Britain. In short, Hitler's thinking was land-based—he understood neither water nor air.[9]

Evidently Göring was just as bad. Although in complete charge of the Luftwaffe, according to Roberts, he spent most of the time of the air battles at his country house in Prussia, 735 miles away from the action. He "also regularly displayed ignorance of the details of logistics, strategy, technology, and the capabilities of aircraft."[10]

An essential prelude to invasion by sea was minesweeping and minelaying by the German navy. Raeder informed Hitler on July 31 that it had begun. After sweeping away British mines, millions of new German mines had to be laid from the French coast to the south coast of England, leaving lanes for German ships. It had not been achieved by September 10—eleven days before the planned invasion by sea. Suitable weather was essential. So was German air superiority. Göring and General Halder expected to destroy the RAF defenders in four days and the remainder of the British air force in four weeks.[11]

But the Nazis had only vague and limited ideas of what was going on in England. Their naivety has since been attributed to misleading information by the head of German Intelligence (the *Abwehr*). Spymaster Admiral Canaris had no time for Hitler or the Nazis and was apparently often in touch with the Allies in attempts to stop the war.[12]

Nevertheless, the invasion of England was an essential part of Hitler's plan when he said, "We can oppose Russia only when we are at peace with the West."[13] It was a tactical necessity that turned out to be impossible—particularly as the Germans were not just buying a one-way ticket, but a pass to go back and forth at will. While they worried about weather conditions for a sea landing, they pinned more hope in Göring's air force softening up the British first.

The Battle of Britain

The Luftwaffe was split into three air fleets, totaling 1,800 bombers and 900 fighters, with a defensive reserve. Fortunately for Britain, the air attacks were not properly coordinated. Against them, the British commander in chief of

Fighter Command, Air Chief Marshal Sir Hugh Dowding, initially commanded a total force of less than 700 fighters distributed between fifty-two squadrons.[14] He was fortunate to no longer have any commitments to use them on the Continent since the fall of France.

Göring sent over about a hundred bombers on August 15, escorted by forty ME 110s, to target Tyneside in the north and, simultaneously, more than eight hundred planes to pin down British forces in the south. But now they met Air Chief Marshal Dowding's Fighter Command with seven Hurricane or Spitfire squadrons ready to intercept them in the air. The RAF shot down thirty German planes—mostly Heinkel heavy bombers—including 120 German aircrew. Those German losses compared with British losses of only two injured pilots. It was an example of fine British leadership, strategy, tactics, and skills. As a result, Göring never again risked a daylight raid outside the range of fighter protection.

The second stage of the battle came on August 8 with continual Luftwaffe strikes over a front of 500 miles. There were 1,485 sorties on that day alone. They rose to 1,786 daily a week later. Fortunately, Britain was prepared for them by its ring of radar stations that passed mostly accurate information on invading Luftwaffe planes. It sent their positions and numbers, with their height and directions, to RAF control stations. Women's Auxiliary Air Force (WAAF) personnel displayed them on huge table maps at each control station, so that RAF squadrons could be scrambled within minutes to intercept enemy aircraft. Updates came, and were sent, through radio-telephone, to keep pilots apprised of almost instantaneous changes. They continued to do so throughout the battle.

The Luftwaffe lost seventy-six aircrew in battles in the south, compared with thirty-four British losses, in addition to those in the north.

Air Chief Marshal Dowding was nicknamed "Stuffy." His job was to maximize the effectiveness of every single RAF pilot and aircraft available to him, and he did so brilliantly. Due to the limited number at his disposal, he was the one man of the war who could "lose it in an afternoon."[15] Realizing British air superiority, Hitler sent out a directive in August, which stated that the Luftwaffe must overcome the RAF in the shortest possible time. Attacks should focus on the aircraft, the ground organization of the RAF Brigade, their suppliers, and the British aircraft industry.

Hunters and Hunted

As the German Colonel Galland of one of the Luftwaffe's "hunting groups," said, "The first rule of all air combat is to see the opponent first." But he complained that, on the German side, it took three hours to obtain information of what was going on, by which time it was useless, whereas the British had instantaneous information.

"Radar really won the Battle of Britain—we wasted no petrol, no energy, no time."[16] That claim was, of course, simply excited hyperbole, since it is the caliber of people who win or lose wars, with whatever technology they use. But similar claims were made about the designs of aircraft. The superior designs of British planes like the Spitfire fighter and the Hurricane gave considerable advantages to RAF pilots in climbing, diving, and making tight turns. By comparison, the ME-109 had only enough fuel for about an hour, and twenty minutes of that had to be spent in crossing and recrossing the Channel. The ME-110 suffered from less maneuverability. Colonel Galland compared the limitations of the ME-109 to a fighting dog chained to its kennel and restricted by the chain's length from reaching its intended victims.

As a result, much of the air activity over England took place in an area that came to be known as "Hellfire Corner," in the south of Kent, at Folkestone, Dover, or Lympne, because they are closer to France.[17] That was where most fighter pilots died in heroic single-combat battles, watched by civilians gazing up at them from the ground below.[18]

Despite enormous affection, even love, by pilots for the classic design of the Spitfire, it was pilots of the Hurricanes who shot down more German planes in battle "than all other RAF planes combined."[19] The Hurricane was the first fighter to exceed 300 mph in level flight.[20] It was also sturdier than the Spitfire, and more easily repaired.

Nevertheless, as excitement mounted in the chase and frenzy of battle, fatigue deadened feelings and numbed the spirit, so that life and death lost their importance somewhere beneath the main objective, which was to grab hold of the enemy and destroy him.[21]

Hitler had been right to fear the RAF and offer peace terms to forestall the day of confrontation. On August 13 when the Luftwaffe struck at Britain with 1,485 sorties, they lost forty-six planes, whereas the RAF lost only thirteen (from which six pilots survived). On the following day, twenty-six German planes were destroyed, compared with only eleven lost by the RAF. It was beginning to be a costly war for Germany. Many German planes and pilots ended up in the waters of the English Channel with only about forty seconds to escape from the cockpit before drowning.

Even so, the Germans tended to overestimate their gains and underestimate their losses. Whether it was a result of incompetence in calculations or wishful thinking is impossible to determine. Either way, it made them overconfident of winning. Nor did they realize that their every move was intercepted either by British radar, or by the British government's Code and Cypher School at Bletchley Park. In addition, British Bomber Command listened in to their traffic on German telegraph lines. German Luftwaffe officers were unaware that just about every bombing raid during the battle was intercepted by the British.[22]

The Third and Fourth Stages

When the Lufwaffe began targeting RAF air bases further inland, in the third stage, their raids were often undertaken by eighty to one hundred bombers escorted by one hundred fighters. The result was that a number of RAF bases were damaged or put out of action. British Fighter Command lost thirty-nine fighters on August 31. Now, marginally more British pilots were being killed than could be replaced by newly trained ones. "Some RAF pilots were being sent up with only twenty hours training."[23] Victory or defeat hung in the balance.[24]

Fortunately, the Germans made another significant mistake—this time of changing the *Schwerpunkt* from British air bases to the cities. It gave the RAF valuable time for repairs—gained by a trap that Churchill contrived to set for them after a solitary bombing of London by a lone Heinkel-111 that might have lost its way on August 24 and made an error of judgment. The RAF retaliated instantly by bombing Berlin on August 25, 28, and 29, first with eighty bombers. Hitler had promised to protect the German capital;

now his words were seen to be a lie. Angry at the strike on Berlin, he promised the German public in September that the Luftwaffe would eradicate British cities. According to historian Andrew Roberts, his tactical error was as self-defeating as when he had mistakenly halted his panzer divisions before they could push the British and the French into the sea at Dunkirk.

The fourth stage of the Battle of Britain began on the morning of September 7 with a heavy strike on London's docks in the Port of London, with its stretch of shipping along Britain's trading lifeline, the River Thames, and the warehouses, office buildings, shops, and homes in the biggest city in the world.

"On the afternoon of [September] the 7th," wrote historian Liddell Hart, "an air armada of about a thousand aircraft of Luftflotte 2—over 300 bombers escorted by 648 fighters—set out for London, watched by Göring and Kesselring from the cliffs at Cap Blanc Nez, between Calais and Wissant. It was echeloned upward in solid layers at between 13,500 and 19,500 feet, flying in close-knit formations and in two waves. The German fighter screen adopted new tactics, one escort flying well ahead at a height of 24,000 to 30,000 feet, while another escort gave the bombers close cover on all sides, at a distance of only about 300 yards."[25]

Their bombs and incendiaries set the Thames afire and turned it into an inferno of petrol, sugar, and rum from damaged warehouses on the bank of the river. Fires burning furiously in the East End became guiding beacons for the night attack that came afterward. It continued from 8:00 p.m. until nearly 5:00 a.m. Göring telephoned his wife to tell her triumphantly, "London is in flames!"[26] And the British government issued a warning of the numbers of German invasion barges increasingly arriving in the Channel, since it could be a prelude to a land invasion.

It was the worst attack in a continuous stream of blitzes on London that would last for eight months. "It caused more damage than the Great Fire of London of 1666."[27] The Luftwaffe returned in the afternoon with 247 aircraft that dropped 440 incendiary bombs and high explosives. The London Docks began to burn. Firemen and bomb disposal units were hurriedly called. The Home Guard was convinced that it was a signal for a German invasion to commence and that one was now under way. It was the heaviest bombing raid Britain had ever received, and it was concentrated on London.

Even so, RAF Fighter Command inflicted a loss of forty-one German aircraft, while losing only twenty-eight planes itself.

Meanwhile, in the countryside, damage to the airfields by the Luftwaffe was filled in or repaired, communications were restored, and the most important RAF bases were fully returned to operations. "The RAF had more fighters operational at the end of the Battle of Britain—despite the high attrition rates—than at the beginning."[28]

Bombs began to fall on London's West End in mid-September. The City suffered heavily, and so did Whitehall, Downing Street, Buckingham Palace, and the Law Courts. Most windows were shattered at ARP headquarters and civil service office buildings. But the damage in the East End was more severe, particularly in Docklands and Whitechapel. What was extraordinary was that no one complained. It was a characteristic of the well-known attitude of the English "stiff upper lip," which was particularly evident among the Cockneys of the East End. Another sign of high British morale was that 60 percent of those who stayed in London continued to sleep in their own beds at night rather than go to an air-raid shelter.[29]

Watchers of the skies, like Civil Defense volunteers, were struck by the grim and menacing beauty of the illuminated scene in the air that looked as artificial as a theater stage set, with flashes of unrealistic explosions reflected back from the underbellies of cloud formations, as sharply aimed searchlights probed the sky for enemy bombers. Even ARP wardens felt the excitement of the chase as the searchlights hunted down invaders in the air and caught them in a net of crisscrossed beams like inescapable spiderwebs, in which attacking aircraft were doomed to destruction.

Another example of morale was the reaction of an army officer returning home to England after the defeat at Dunkirk. He said, "Well, we'll get them next time."[30] A research organization asked Londoners in 1941 what had depressed them most during the previous winter. Most cited the weather, not the bombing raids.[31]

There were seventy-one major bombing attacks on London between September 7, 1940, and May 16, 1941. Other bombing raids took place on Liverpool, Birmingham, and Plymouth. The Luftwaffe targeted major ports and the biggest industrial cities, like Bristol, Glasgow, Southampton, and

Portsmouth. But ARP units were so well organized that death tolls rarely exceeded 250 at any one time. (The number of deaths would be far greater when the RAF began to retaliate with incendiaries on German cities.)

One surprise of the German blitz on London was that "more bombers were lost to flying accidents than to antiaircraft fire or night-fighters."[32] Nevertheless, Hitler claimed in a conference to his underlings on September 14 that, "Successful landing followed by occupation would end war in short order." Britain would starve to death.[33]

One result of the conflagrations in major British cities was the realization by Hitler and Göring that clusters of incendiary bombs created far more damage than high explosives that just made a huge hole, because fires spread and could destroy an entire city (as would happen when the RAF retaliated on Hamburg in 1943). Britain's bombing attacks stemmed largely as retaliation for the German bombing of Coventry Cathedral with five hundred bombers on November 4, which destroyed much of the city center. It became a symbol of Nazi ruthlessness and disdain for others.

The Battle of Britain reached its peak on September 15 with a heavy raid on London by one hundred bombers and four hundred fighters. Fifty-six German planes were shot down with a cost of twenty-six RAF planes.

Losses of RAF bombers were another story, however, since bombers needed fighter escorts for protection—as Göring provided his air force with—whereas Britain needed all its fighters to defend the British Isles. The result was that British bombing raids on Germany cost far greater losses of aircrews.

Even so, Göring and his supporters were convinced that their heavy attacks were inflicting considerable damage to British squadrons and airfields, reducing the strength of the RAF and, in particular, making inroads into the British aircraft industry. In fact, Lord Beaverbrook had organized the British aircraft industry so that the numbers of aircraft produced exceeded the losses. And Britain's productivity continued to overtake Germany's.

The German navy was particularly attentive to ensuring air superiority before attempting to launch an invasion by sea. The results of Göring's alleged successes, however, had convinced Hitler that the decisive battles of the war with Britain would be fought in the air over London, since the British fleet controlled the Channel between Germany and Britain.

Counting the Cost

Nevertheless, a great deal of damage had been done to five forward airfields of Britain's Number Eleven Fighter Group and six others. Some were bombed night and day and so damaged as to be unfit for operations for several days, even up to a week. If the Luftwaffe attacks continued, the operation of RAF Fighter Command could break down. But Göring made the mistake of switching his bombing attacks to London on September 7, instead of continuing to damage airfields.[34]

Meanwhile, the period of August 24 to September 6 had effectively drained British Fighter Command. In those two weeks alone, 466 Spitfires and Hurricanes were destroyed or seriously damaged, with 103 pilots dead and 128 seriously wounded.

Field Marshal Kesselring launched another big air attack on the morning of Sunday, September 15. According to Churchill, it was the culminating date of the Luftwaffe's attacks on Britain, and "one of the decisive battles of the war." Although there were two heavy attacks the day before, this was the greatest concentrated bombing of London.[35]

The German air armada was attacked all the way from the Channel, alternately by twenty-two RAF squadrons in all. And although 148 bombers broke through to London, they were prevented from dropping their bombs accurately because they were too scattered. Then, as they turned to fly back home, they were attacked again by sixty RAF fighters from East Anglia.

In spite of that, an even larger number of German bombers returned to London on a cloudless afternoon to inflict heavy damage on the city, particularly in the East End. About a quarter of the aircraft were put out of action during the day. Many more were damaged and returned to their airfields with dead and wounded aircrews to demoralize the German ground crews who had to carry out, scrape out, or hose out the remains of the bodies.

RAF Operational Command

Since Churchill considered the weather particularly suitable for an enemy bombing raid, he drove to Group Headquarters at Uxbridge to see for himself what might happen. As he wrote, "Number 11 Group comprised no fewer than twenty-five squadrons covering the whole of Essex, Kent, Sussex, and Hampshire, and all the approaches across them to London." This was the group, Churchill claimed, "on which our fate largely depended."[36]

All was quiet in the Group Operations Room, where they looked down on a large-scale map table from a gallery, around which twenty air-raid plotters waited with telephone assistants for electric lightbulbs to signal that RAF squadrons were "standing by" for action at two minutes' notice. The glow of a lower row of bulbs showed that various squadrons were standing by in readiness. Then, suddenly, a succession of signals were displayed to warn that a serious air battle was imminent as aircraft filled the skies.

Each battle lasted little more than an hour. But the size of the Luftwaffe allowed Göring to send out new attacking waves. And however effective the RAF pilots were in scattering or downing enemy aircraft, they had to refuel after seventy or eighty minutes. And they had to land to rearm after a five-minute air battle. Whenever they did so, they were vulnerable to being destroyed on the ground by German aircraft. In the meantime, the Luftwaffe was able to arrive with fresh pilots in freshly serviced planes.

The red bulbs warned that most of the RAF squadrons were engaged, and busy plotters pushed their discs about on the map table, according to instructions phoned from the battle lines. Air Vice-Marshal Park, who had accompanied Churchill, gave directions for the fighters. Those directions were transformed into more detailed orders to each fighter station by a young RAF officer beside him. By that time, all the RAF fighters were airborne, except for only one reserve squadron needed to protect London.

All was calm in the Operations Room as the plotters followed their usual routines of smoothly pushing their discs across the map table according to telephoned directions, while orders were murmured in cool, low monotones, and a row of bulbs soon showed that the reserve squadron was now in the air with the other RAF fighters. At that moment, there were no more squadrons left to hold back in reserve. It was the "crux" of the Battle of Britain.

Although enemy losses were only fifty-six, Britain's defensive squadrons had prevented the Germans from achieving their objective of destroying Britain's capital city and demoralizing the population.

That night, Britain's offensive Bomber Command attacked enemy shipping in ports across the other side of the Channel, from Boulogne to Antwerp, where heavy losses were inflicted. And, within forty-eight hours, Hitler postponed the "Operation Sea Lion" invasion of England indefinitely. But it was not before September 27 that Göring completely lost any hope of the Luftwaffe defeating Britain. His small-scale attacks continued into the first days of November, but his concentrated efforts gave way to dispersion. Even so, London was still his main objective.

An average of two hundred German bombers attacked London every night from September 7 to November 3. There were only ninety-two anti-aircraft guns in position at the beginning, since it was considered better to leave defensive action clear for the RAF fighter pilots. But within forty-eight hours, General Pile had doubled the number by moving them from else-where. Londoners had sheltered in their houses or their shelters and stoically put up with what seemed to be unchallenged enemy attacks for several days. Then suddenly, on September 10, a whole barrage of British antiaircraft fire opened up with blazing searchlights. In reality, this roaring and blazing spec-tacle did little damage to the enemy, but it gave a great boost to the morale of Londoners. Everyone felt heartened that the British forces were hitting the enemy. And the score of successes on German raiders slowly increased.[37]

The actual figures of aircraft losses from July 10 to October were 915 RAF fighters lost, to 1,733 Luftwaffe aircraft destroyed.[38] Churchill described it as one of the decisive battles of the world. It involved trial and error by the Germans and continual changes of plans. But their plans were never fully accomplished, because of the bravery of a handful of British fighter pilots, who were largely young men straight out of school. Part of the reason for their skills and their courage was a sense of purpose from knowing how much they were appreciated and admired.

Leaving Group Headquarters on that day of his visit, Churchill was greatly moved by the experience. He turned to Major General Hastings Ismay in the car and confided in tones of admiration, "Never have so many owed so much to so few." He elaborated thoughtfully on his words before he decided to inform the House of Commons and the public what they all owed to the bravery of the young RAF fighter pilots: "Never *in the field of human conflict was so much owed by so many to so few.*" A poster was displayed with his words.

The morale of the Luftwaffe sank after that; they had achieved no noticeable success. German Command mismanaged the situation, and orders were continually changed. There was lack of purpose, and unjustified accusations. German fighter pilots, who were already suffering from physical and mental strain, were demoralized. Comrades had vanished from their squadrons. As well as complaining about leadership, they felt dissatisfied with themselves.[39]

By comparison, the British public—certainly Londoners—were drawn out into the streets to gaze expectantly up at the sky for more Nazi "entertainment." The German Nazis were viewed by most Britons as a farcical music hall novelty act, or as hilariously incompetent "Keystone Cops" out of a comic Hollywood movie. But at that point, the Luftwaffe began to drop delayed-action bombs. British bombers retaliated by attacking the bases they came from, and soon the French docks and waterfront were set ablaze.

"Operation Sea Lion" was postponed after the end of September. Hitler seemed to have lost interest in England, while German forces prepared to launch "Operation Barbarossa" on Soviet Russia.

Churchill noted that, at the end of 1940, Hitler had realized he could not destroy Britain by direct air assault, and that neither the British nation nor the government had been cowed by the bombing.[40] Hitler and Göring's air force had wasted time, money, and lives in attempting to destroy Britain's capital city and its major industrial cities and ports, since the Stuka dive bomber was only fit for short-duration blitzkrieg-style attacks in which they supported ground troops and tanks. And it was an easy target for Hurricanes and Spitfires. Fortunately for Britain, Germany did not possess any efficient long-range bombers.[41]

The German Colonel Galland freely admitted that the bravery of the RAF pilots "undoubtedly saved their country at this crucial hour." Nevertheless, 43,000 British civilians had been killed and 51,000 seriously injured; a quarter of a million Britons were now homeless; 16,000 houses were destroyed, 60,000 uninhabitable, and 130,000 damaged. And yet the morale of the British people had not been broken. On the contrary, they were more eager than ever to show their contempt for the Germans and how they would bounce back and destroy Hitler and the Nazis. So was Winston Churchill, who remarked with satisfaction that it was Hitler's first defeat.[42]

Public Ignorance

Churchill knew that the biggest threat, now that the possibility of invasion had been fought off, was complacency. If the British army was left with nothing to do, its discipline—such as it was—would deteriorate. And if the British public saw nothing happening, they would become restless and complain of no victories. After all the drama of the bombings by the Luftwaffe, they were avid for more excitement, more "theater of war." But the public had no idea that Britain did not possess the overwhelming force necessary for an invasion of Germany. They would lose heart at what they perceived to be inertia. And the momentum of courage and belligerence that Churchill had built up would falter and collapse. Worse, they might lose interest and begin to question whether perhaps a peace settlement with Germany might enable them to return to their old lives.

Meanwhile, the United States appeared to be even further away from coming to Britain's aid. Churchill received a personal letter from Averell Harriman in Washington: "People are wondering why you don't do something offensively."[43]

When Lord Louis Mountbatten became chief adviser to Combined Operations, Churchill told him, "Your whole attention is to be concentrated on the offensive." But with what? It required a great deal of courage for Churchill to continue to resist demands for a Second Front in France or Germany when the American military and President Roosevelt were pressing heavily for it, as well as the British public and the news media. Only the war cabinet and the Americans were aware that the entire land force they urged him to send to Europe—mostly British—would be sacrificed to battle-hardened German troops with state-of-the-art tanks and weapons. But Churchill could not explain publicly that an untrained and ill-equipped British invasion force would be going to their deaths: it would invite defeat by the enemy.

One of the problems that Churchill inherited was a shortage of military leaders, since the professional British army was riddled with young officers who had been unfit for management in the private sector and sought security without responsibilities in the military establishment. They were largely concerned with irrelevant mess room rituals—not only in Hong Kong, Singapore, and Malaya, but also in administrative offices in Cairo and elsewhere in the British Empire. Between the wars, neither government nor the military establishment had thought to attract imaginative and clever young men to their ranks.

That military culture still persisted in its suspicion of cleverness from an old guard who were equally dim, "a bit wooden," or "mentally negligible," as P. G. Wodehouse would have called them. When Churchill decided to sack General Sir John Dill as CIGS because of his pessimism, it was difficult to find an experienced, intelligent, and zealous replacement. Despite the urgency of the war, there was still a sentimental culture of sympathy for losers. The War Office was, similarly, unable to match the quality of tanks being made by the Germans and Americans, because imagination, creativity, and innovation were scarce in the wooden British army culture.[44]

Whether or not the cabinet members were aware that Soviet and German ground forces fought better than British soldiers because they had a pistol held to their heads if they hesitated or failed, Churchill had no doubt that the famous execution of Admiral Sir John Byng in 1757 for not trying hard enough to fight the French enemy had galvanized the British navy ever since.[45] But now that Britain was a democracy, it was limited in how best to treat lack of effort in its ground forces or malingering by noncombatants.[46]

It was not only the officer class that suffered from lack of zeal, or indifference to the war effort; a similar culture of avoiding work existed among civilian workers in the coal mines, at the docks, and in munitions factories—despite being paid more than ever before, often double—with their continual disputes and strikes and loss of working days from absenteeism. European dictatorships ensured that trade unions were banned in wartime, whereas in Britain, "slackness and difficulty in controlling shop stewards" resulted in a loss of 1.8 million working days at De Havilland alone in 1943, as a consequence of 1,785 disputes. By that time, the slacking off occurred from a perception that victory was now certain and it was back to the peacetime work-shy ethic of "working to rule," which meant applying minimum effort.[47]

Meanwhile, optimistic news from Russia rocketed membership in Britain's Communist Party from only twelve thousand to fifty-six thousand by the end of 1942. And new public demands for a Second Front on the continent of Europe to help the Soviets attracted crowds of British supporters. It was yet another example of the popular ignorance of what was really going on—not only by the British public but also by the Americans, who seemed to imagine that the British army could launch an attack on the ground without trained soldiers, tanks, or landing craft, when as much equipment as possible was sent to help Russia. Nevertheless, Churchill had to find a way to win the war despite all the factors mitigating against success.

SECRET SERVICE

CHURCHILL'S EUPHORIA, AND THAT OF THE media and the British public at the victory over Germany in the air and the end of the air raids, would be deflated soon after war spread to the North African desert. Churchill knew from personal experience that wars cannot be won without ground troops taking possession of enemy territory. And Mussolini had 215,000 Italian troops in the North African coastal strip and garrisons in Abyssinia, Eritrea, and Somaliland, which were not all that far away from British Egypt.

At the same time, Churchill also had work to do on the home front. It had to be managed efficiently in order to survive. He introduced a new section to the 18B Act, which enabled him to intern pro-Fascists for the duration of the war without trial, although he didn't like it—as he told the Socialist Home Secretary Herbert Morrison when it came to deciding what to do with Britain's Fascist Leader Sir Oswald Mosley. Morrison would have been happy to put Mosley behind bars for life. But Churchill said, "Just because we find him odious is no reason to put him in prison." But about two thousand Britons had been openly pro-German before the war, and there was always the possibility of a pro-Nazi fifth column undermining the war effort in England, and even committing violence.

As for the scary rumors of armed German parachutists dropping on England from the skies and saboteurs giving signals to the enemy, they amounted to nothing more than a few bungled attempts to drop fairly ignorant German spies behind British lines, like the fifty-year-old Lieutenant Hermann Görtz of the Luftwaffe. He had already been imprisoned in Maidstone on his first attempt at espionage in 1936 when he'd met up with the IRA. In 1940 he parachuted into Ireland. He was dropped in the wrong place, wearing full German uniform. His military identity documents were in a false name. After land-ing, he forgot to recover his parachute, wireless set, and other equipment. He lost his invisible ink while swimming across the River Boyne. He had no Irish money and didn't know he could use English currency. In his pocket were his First World War medals. He was arrested a year later by the Irish police after achieving nothing. When told, after the war, that he would be repatriated to Germany, he took poison instead. It was thought he was part of the plan for the "Operation Sea Lion" invasion. A whole group of spies arrived in Britain from fishing boats in September and were promptly arrested. Three were hanged in Pentonville Prison after their trial.[1]

The case of the American traitor Tyler Kent, a cypher clerk in the U.S. embassy, and his contact with a small subversive and anti-Semitic group called the "Right Club" was somewhat different. Headed by an Old Etonian named Captain Ramsay and run by Anna Wolkoff, it possessed patologi-cal and utterly ridiculous invented ideas about a Jewish conspiracy with the Freemasons. Kent and Wolkoff were arrested and imprisoned, and Ramsay was interned for the duration of the war to keep him out of mischief.

Altogether, German intelligence was remarkably ineffective for a nation previously considered to be efficient. But "the Luftwaffe's intelligence depart-ment misjudged every aspect of the Battle of Britain, from respective aircraft strengths and losses to target selection."[2]

Wartime Economy

Since Britain still imported 70 percent of its food, Churchill's "Dig for Victory" campaign was intended to reduce imports and relieve Merchant Navy seamen from the dangers of convoys (30,589 would be killed in the war). The amount of land for farming was increased by 13 percent, adding seven million acres for plowing and planting. Food rationing was introduced and food wastage abolished. The number of allotments for growing food was increased by 1.7 million. And Churchill introduced subsidized canteens for the public to eat in, which were called British Restaurants, where two substantial courses—a main course and a dessert—were provided for only eight pence.

Little had been done before this to organize and manage a wartime economy. More than a million Britons were unemployed and women were now volunteering for work. Eighty thousand women joined the Women's Land Army, and twice that number replaced men who had joined the armed forces. It changed British society. "By June 1944, of the total of 16 million women aged between fourteen and fifty-nine in Britain, 7.1 million had been mobilized for war work in some form, including the auxiliary services, Civil Defense and the munitions industries, and 1.64 million were engaged in 'essential war work' which freed up men for the forces or heavy industry."[3]

By the end of the war, 1.75 million men had served in the Home Guard, and another 1.75 million more in Civil Defense. Others were on Fire Guard duties.

More than a million children were removed by the State from the bombing dangers of major cities and transported to the greater safety of the countryside. Carrying a gas mask was compulsory. So was the evening ritual of closing blackout curtains.

Since more than half of Britain's industrial production switched to making arms and equipment for war, which kept a great many of the population from productive commercial or profitable industrial employment, the economy shrank and tax revenues fell. Churchill's government risked bankruptcy to keep Britain fighting the war effectively.

Other nations tried to preserve their economies by declaring neutrality in the war. Churchill summed up the situation in a radio broadcast in which he declared, "Each one hopes that if he feeds the crocodile enough, the crocodile will eat him last. All of them hope that the storm will pass before their time comes to be devoured."[4]

The Meaning of Neutrality

One problem with neutrality in a world war was that it allowed the enemy to observe and plot on neutral territories, so that noncombatant nations like Spain, Portugal, and its colonies were at the cutting edge of an espionage war where large-scale German intelligence operations were launched. Britain's MI6 expanded its own Iberian department where Section V was involved in counterintelligence. They had the advantage of the code breakers in Bletchley Park who intercepted German wireless messages that provided insights into German intelligence. Kim Philby would become the head of the Iberian department in 1941. He had long been an undetected double agent sending allied secrets to his handler for analysis in Soviet Russia.

Switzerland and some other countries like Ireland and Turkey were breeding grounds for spying and secret agents who sought to buy and sell military secrets. Gestapo officers in plainclothes hoped to turn agents and obtain useful information or pounce on refugees or their Swiss bank accounts. The Swiss government allowed German and Italian military supply trains to pass through their country. A "Swiss state-subsidized timber company had built the German concentration camp of Dachau, with the contract for thirteen million Swiss francs being negotiated by the son of the then Swiss Commander-in-Chief, Henri Guisan."[5] It seemed that the spread of Fascism had lowered standards of honesty, morality, and ethics right across Europe. Corruption was rife.

Switzerland would not accept Jewish refugees seeking asylum after escaping from Vichy militia roundups during 1942–43.[6] "Some committed suicide in front of the Swiss border guards."[7] They knew they would be sent to the Nazi gas chambers otherwise.

Jewish emigration from Europe was banned in October 1941 and Jews were deported from the Reich to death camps or to mobile gas vans that killed them almost as efficiently. "You could look inside the lorry through a peephole or window. The interior was lit. Then they opened the lorry. Some of the bodies fell out, others were unloaded by prisoners. As we technicians confirmed, the bodies had that pinkish-red hue which is typical of people who have died [of carbon-monoxide poisoning]." Sometimes they were shot instead. By the end of 1941 the SS were using Zyklon B gas—a preparation of prussic acid that killed much quicker and with greater certainty. It was also used to kill Russian prisoners of war.[8]

When German mass production methods got under way with greater efficiency and effectiveness in the Nazi death camps, they found it more economical to use Zyklon B gas in packed rooms. The victims "were terrified. Mothers held their children tight. . . . They were embarrassed. . . . Some of them cried out of shame and fear. They were very, very afraid. The children behaved like children. They looked for their parents' hands, hugged their parents. What did they know? They didn't know a thing."[9]

In other chambers where the gas collected on the floor and rose upward, the stronger people climbed on top of weaker ones in a vain attempt to avoid choking to death—it took about thirty minutes. "The people there knew that the end was approaching and tried to climb as high as they could to avoid the gas. . . . Sometimes all the skin on the bodies peeled due to the effects of the gas. The victims clawed on the doors and walls, and their screaming and weeping could be heard even through the thick metal airtight doors."[10]

Sweden accommodated the Nazis early on.[11] They made plenty of money by exporting to Germany. As for Eire, the Irish leader de Valera refused to denounce Hitler or the Nazis. (On the contrary, he would pay his respects by personally expressing his condolences at the German legation on Hitler's death, even though the Nazi death camps and their genocide had been revealed by then.) Neutrality was an easy way to avoid responsibility while exploiting the vulnerability and pain of others and stealing their property.

Most of the spying in Turkey took place in Istanbul. "In 1942 some seventeen different intelligence organizations converged on Istanbul to mix and mingle, bribe, seduce, and betray, and with them came a vast and motley host of agents and double agents, smugglers, blackmailers, arms dealers, drug runners, refugees, deserters, black marketers, pimps, forgers, hookers, and con artists." Most knew each other by sight."[12]

Special Operations

Churchill's adventurous spirit tended to conceal his overdeveloped sense of responsibility and his compassion. His imagination was always unrolling, considering all the ways he could help finish off the war and release everyone from its horrors. He organized a Special Operations Executive (SOE) "to coordinate all actions by way of subversion and sabotage against the enemy overseas."[13] He appointed Labour Minister Hugh Dalton to run it. Its purpose was to create social chaos behind enemy lines by irregular warfare, and to link for that purpose with local resistance movements to distract and hold down or harass the enemy. It involved assassinations of enemies and destroying lines of enemy communications. Dalton enjoyed it but was hopeless at it.

Knowing that the Germans took reprisals—the Germans retaliated on the Continent by taking innocent local hostages at random and murdering them, sometimes slaughtering entire villages—British auxiliary units were set up in 1940 on the home front. Their function was to protect Britain by retaliating against any German occupying forces, and they took great care to ensure their hideouts were unknown by local inhabitants, in case they were betrayed.[14]

Hugh Sinclair was already preparing for war against German invaders by expanding the Secret Service (SIS) and buying a war station at Bletchley Park. Section VII of SIS set up a network of stay-behind agents across Britain who would form the basis for an intelligence network in case the Germans invaded. It recruited people who would play a key role after an invasion, like "doctors, dentists, chemists, bakers, and small shopkeepers." "Section VIII under Richard Gambier-Parry, who was recruited from Philco (where he was general sales manager), would produce up-to-date wireless transceivers and set up radio networks to ensure reports from both officers and agents abroad arrived in time to have any effect."[15] Section IX was a sabotage unit run by Lieutenant Colonel Laurence Grand of the Royal Engineers. During the Munich crisis in September, "they established a sabotage network in the Skoda armaments factories in Czechoslovakia, intending to sabotage German access to oil in the Balkans and disrupt railway supplies in Germany."[16]

SIS began reporting in early 1939 that Hitler was planning to invade Czechoslovakia, and MI5 confirmed it from another source. Spying and sabotage were frowned on by some bureaucrats and politicians, and even by some army officers who found it disreputable or unpalatable. But despite Churchill's "grand alliance" of Britain, which included the United States and Russia, their three leaders possessed entirely different goals. Churchill's was to protect Britain and liberty by winning the war, whereas Roosevelt's was to score against monarchies and imperialists to the economic benefit of the United States. Stalin was different. He too planned to defend his country, but he was also intent on spreading his form of totalitarianism across Europe. Although he'd had a Soviet agent assassinate his main competitor, Trotsky, while in exile in Mexico, he had not abandoned the goal of international communism, starting with the United States.[17]

British intelligence officer Guy Liddell headed the Irish section of MI5 in 1942. According to him, "There is no doubt that the Russians are far better in the matter of espionage than any other country in the world."[18]

As Sir Max Hastings explained, "hundreds of impeccably middle-class British and American men and women . . . did indeed betray their countries to the Soviet Union, while a handful of British Fascist sympathizers, and many more European ones, lent their services to the Nazis."[19] The Cambridge Five were merely a handful of a much larger variety of similar thinking pro-Communists who came to light much later on. The reasonableness of many British-thinking men and women, and intellectuals—in their gentlemanly and ladylike ways—caused them to consider communism thoughtfully as one possible form of society, without having any clear idea of its brutal consequences. English people growing up in a more orderly and just society than most (although certainly imperfect), were famously insular, with a broad protective ocean between their cozy theories and the harsh realities of life led by the underdogs on the continent of Europe. Respectable intellectuals, like the Fabians, with their gradualism, spread their revolutionary ideas as subtly and slyly and effectively as they had intended. For others infected by its gradualism, communism became a religion—an escape from the sordid injustices of an authoritarian society in which the working classes were crushed or marginalized and treated almost like slave labor.

Some other intelligent young people, like Philby, were shocked by the Nazi rallies and Hitler's hate-filled tirades and threats. The main question requiring a practical answer seemed simple to them: who possessed the power and drive and motivation to stop Nazi Germany? Obviously not the appeasers in government, but Soviet Russia.

Many British people in the 1930s possessed a compassionate attitude toward oppressed segments of society, such as women, gays, prostitutes, homeless people, and some ethnic minorities, but not the authoritarian establishment or the upper socioeconomic group who were more intent on holding on to what they had inherited or accumulated themselves with little concern for anyone else. They regarded the rising masses as dangerous competitors for resources who would outlive and replace them if given any encouragement.

Fortunately, the British were saved from having to make violent choices, unlike the underground partisans across the English Channel, by the reluctance of Hitler and his generals to cross the English Channel. That did not mean that Operation Sea Lion had been scuttled, but it remained stalled because they didn't have the stomach for it.

A danger to General Wavell's eastern flank was Iraqi troops that attacked RAF air bases on the fringe of Baghdad on April 30. Churchill and Eden agreed that Iraq must be seized to prevent a preemptive strike by German troops. This was done in short order. But German forces began to appear in Vichy French–controlled Syria on May 20. Again, Churchill decreed that the British army must go in. Ironically, the Vichy French army fought the British with more determination than they had fought the German enemy in France.[2] Nevertheless, Syria too was pacified.

Wavell was a brave soldier and a sportsman with a brilliant career. Although taciturn, he was a considerable linguist. He had served on the Northwest frontier and in the Boer War and saw action in the First World War in Turkey and Palestine. He was probably the most literary and philosophical of the British generals.[3] But Churchill thought he was too conventional and cautious. He preferred generals who took risks and triumphed. That was not Wavell's way (even though he later supported the more unconventional styles of General Ord Wingate in the Burmese jungle and Ralph Bagnold in the North African desert). He and Churchill were wary of each other. Wavell's reserved manner made him inarticulate when confronted by the forceful Churchill, who was curt when cross-examining him. Churchill lacked patience with people who could not stand up to him, and their mutual dislike continued to smolder.[4]

On the other hand, Anthony Eden would find Wavell's account of the battles in North Africa in 1940 masterly. The Italian Tenth Army planned to invade Egypt along the coast with five divisions. After taking Sidi Barrani, Marshal Graziani stopped seventy-five miles from the British troops at Mersa Matruh, where both armies were reinforced. But the British troops were reinforced with dummy tanks and guns that created an impression—at least from the air—of size and strength. The dummies were even moved around a few miles away from time to time to confuse the enemy. It was the same as on the Canal Zone, where "every other anti-tank gun was a wooden one."[5]

The British forces protecting the internal security of Egypt comprised an armored division, much of an Indian division, and about a third of a New Zealand division. There were also two regiments of the Royal Artillery, amounting, in all, to only about fifty thousand men. The Italian army was more than four times that size and with a great deal of modern equipment.

Mussolini was preparing to launch an invasion to take Egypt with a growing army by the autumn, increasing his odds of winning to five to one.[6]

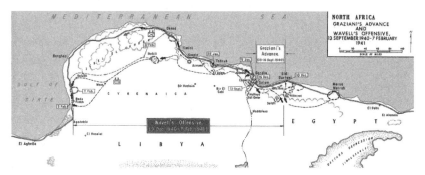

Britain's North African offensive by General Wavell against Graziani's Italian forces. Code-named "Operation Compass."

Britain's forward position was a railhead at Mersa Matruh, with a reasonably decent road running west to Sidi Barani. Churchill considered they were some of the finest troops, including the Seventh Hussars with light tanks, the Eleventh Hussars with armored cars, two motor battalions, and two regiments of Royal Horse Artillery. They were ordered to attack Italian positions as soon as the Italian dictator declared war on Britain.

The Italians were unaware that Mussolini had just declared war on June 10, 1940, and were taken by surprise when British troops attacked and took prisoners. They achieved a similar success during the next few days, destroying enemy tanks and taking another 220 prisoners.

More Italian forces advanced from the west in mid-July. Italian casualties during the first three months of engagement were about 3,500, whereas British losses were as few as 150 men. So the favorable results of the opening phase of the war gave the British government and the public cause for optimism. But emotions swung up and down and back again as their fortunes and misfortunes fluctuated in the following months.

Meanwhile, General Wavell awaited the shock of the main Italian forces near the fortifications at Mersa Matruh. And Churchill decided that Wavell could be supported by dormant British troops from less endangered quarters, like South Africa and Kenya. There was also an Australian division in Singapore, a Polish brigade, and the Egyptian army. Churchill arranged meetings with Wavell in Britain, where he also met Eden and various staff officers. That was when he described the battle situation in North Africa, Egypt, and Somaliland.

As a result of their meetings, the War Office arranged the immediate transport of 52 tanks, a light tank regiment with another 52 tanks, and an infantry tank battalion of 50 tanks, with 48 antitank guns, 28 Bofors light antiaircraft guns, 48 twenty-five-pounder field guns, 500 Bren guns, and 250 antitank rifles, with ammunition. Churchill also ordered alternative defenses for areas he denuded of troops and equipment for the imminent battle for Egypt. They included fighter planes and antiaircraft guns from cities in Britain, now destined for Malta and Egypt.

About four heavy bombing squadrons would be based in Greece, in order to maintain the British army in Egypt and attack the Italian fleet in the Mediterranean.[7]

The main Italian army, led by Marshal Graziani, began its advance across the Egyptian border on September 13. Every column comprised hundreds of vehicles, accompanied by tanks, antitank guns, and artillery at the front. The Italian infantry was transported in trucks in the center. They reached Sidi Barrani and attacked the British forces on the seventeenth. The British Coldstream Guards fell back tactically, "inflicting severe punishment as they went."[8]

Graziani was now confronted by British, New Zealand, and Indian troops guarding Egypt. And instead of remaining on the defense, General Wavell now thrust part of his armored division (General Creagh's Seventh Armoured Division, the "Desert Rats") forward in the desert. He followed up with an aggressive advance with surprising effect. His victory at Beda Famm, where twenty-thousand Italian prisoners were taken, was all the more remarkable in that the British force consisted of only three thousand men, but they used similar mobile tank tactics of the kind that had inspired Guderian's panzer divisions against the Allies in France.

On December 8, Lieutenant-General O'Connor, who commanded the Western Desert Force with only thirty-one thousand men and 275 tanks against four times as many troops, opened up "Operation Compass" with the support of the navy and the RAF. The coast road that straddled North Africa was within reach of British naval guns in the Mediterranean, and air superiority was even more necessary in the open desert with little ground cover. The RAF dominated the Italian air force in short order. O'Connor's forces swept the Italians out of Egypt by mid-December and took thirty-eight thousand prisoners. Bardia fell to the British on January 5, and the Desert Rats captured the port of Tobruk on January 22, 1941. The destruction of Graziani's army opened up a clear corridor to Tripoli, which was their next destination.

The Greece Fiasco

But—like Hitler's hesitancy at Dunkirk—Churchill suddenly changed plans to send fifty thousand of Wavell's troops immediately to Greece instead of capturing Tripoli. He reasoned that the opportunity presented by the Greek prime minister's sudden death, and his replacement by a leader who might be more accommodating by allowing British troops in Greece, could enable Britain to dominate the Mediterranean as well as the Aegean Sea.

When German troops invaded Greece on April 6, the British had to mount another "Dunkirk retreat," forcing them to evacuate and leave their tanks and other equipment behind, and leave twelve thousand British troops in German hands.

Churchill was, almost simultaneously, attempting to support General de Gaulle to form a Free-French outpost at Dakar in Africa. But it was thwarted by the arrival of a Vichy-French fleet. The French ships were warned off, but escaped and sped south of Casablanca toward Dakar, resulting in a postponement of the plan in order to avoid General de Gaulle shedding the blood of the Fascist Vichy-French, since he was sure that Dakar would be defended to the last man.[9]

Meanwhile, Hitler reacted to Lieutenant-General O'Connor's victory in the desert by providing support for Mussolini in North Africa. He sent five hundred aircraft from Norway to bomb Benghazi, so that O'Connor was prevented from using the port. Left without the troops who had been sent to Greece, the Western Desert Force was now too weak and vulnerable to be effective.

And now a new factor appeared, which would complicate and lengthen the North African Campaign. It was a German general named Erwin Rommel, a hero of the panzer divisions in the fall of France. He was personally summoned by Hitler to rescue the Italians and make sure that Britain's campaign in North Africa failed. He flew immediately to Tripoli on February 12. Rommel was a risk taker whose audacious tactics would be a continual challenge to General Wavell. He was also what was known as a "lucky" general.

The difference between Churchill's belief in the influence on history of great men and Wavell's more pragmatic military approach was that Churchill took the view that wars are won by superior willpower. He was determined to reject the self-destructive tradition of being on the defensive. On the other hand, General Wavell believed that wars were won by superior armor, firepower and armaments, which was what he lacked. They were at loggerheads. Churchill thought Wavell was too careful, whereas Wavell thought Churchill was too impetuous—particularly after he had been prevented by him from making a clear run to Tripoli by the fiasco in Greece, when Churchill and Eden had cornered him into agreeing to it only after accusing him of being too cautious.[10]

The Lucky General

The British tank regiment of the Fifth Light Division arrived in Tripoli on March 11, and surprised Rommel by not engaging with his much smaller tank force. They probably thought it was bigger because of the dummy tanks that Rommel mounted on Volkswagen cars to deceive British air surveillance. The Desert Rats had been sent to Egypt for rest and refitting and had been replaced by an inexperienced armored division. Two other divisions had been sent to Greece, and another was short of equipment and trained men. The experienced tank commander O'Connor had been relieved by an untried commander named Neame.

And Wavell later admitted that he'd given no credit to reports of an impending attack. Rommel was blessed with luck again.*

Rommel immediately took the initiative by launching an offensive against the British with fifty tanks on March 24, followed by two new Italian divisions. Wavell was unable to restrain the Africa Korps in Cyrenaica since his forces were now spread too thinly across Greece, Crete, East Africa, Syria, Iraq, Palestine, Ethiopia, and Egypt.[11] The result of Rommel's unexpected and audacious attack was that the British forces fell back in confusion. A British armored brigade lost most of its tanks in the retreat. And they evacuated Benghazi on April 3.

Lieutenant-General O'Connor was hurriedly sent back to advise General Neame in an unescorted vehicle. Their car ran into German troops and they were taken prisoner. On the next day, the Second Armored Division was surrounded and forced to surrender. The British were pushed out of Cyrenaica and Egypt, except for a small force trapped in the fortified port of Tobruk.

The cost of not exploiting the golden opportunity to make for Tripoli was that the British had to refit and begin all over again—and Churchill prompted Wavell to do so. But although the British forces were larger than Rommel's, they lacked technical and tactical quality. Wavell was not prepared to attack until they were ready. He was not about to sacrifice himself or his troops for the greater glory of politicians. His instructions to his forces now were to fall back and fight a delaying action. Meanwhile, Rommel kept the British tank commanders under constant pressure as they continued to retreat as far as four hundred miles back in less than a week. Most of their tanks broke down and were lost or ran out of fuel.

Churchill telegraphed Wavell to indicate that he could surely hold Tobruk with its Italian defenses. But Wavell explained that the situation had greatly deteriorated.

Rommel attacked on Good Friday and made his main thrust on Easter Monday, nine miles from the port of Tobruk, breaking through the thin defenses. His leading battalion drove on for two miles but was held back by defensive artillery and lost sixteen tanks out of the original thirty-eight, revealing how thin Rommel's strength really was. Meanwhile, nearly a thousand Italians surrendered in a counterattack by Australian troops.

General Paulus was sent to the front "to head off this soldier gone stark mad."[12] Rommel—like Guderian—was disliked by more conservative generals for his dashing celebrity. Such leaders were viewed as too smart and ambitious, and too eager for the limelight. And there was always a practical fear of overextended supply lines that might fail to bring up water, food, fuel, ammunition, and replacements. Nevertheless, Paulus agreed to another attack on Tobruk.

It was launched with reinforcements on April 30. German infantry opened up a breach more than a mile wide for the leading wave of tanks that drove the ten miles toward Tobruk. But they ran onto a newly laid minefield, and seventeen tanks out of forty were disabled. The second wave of tanks and infantry swung southeast to roll up the defenses, but was finally checked by artillery fire from behind the minefield, and by a counterattack from twenty British tanks, then resistance from several Australian posts they had failed to subdue.[13]

By the following day, only half of the seventy German tanks were fit for action, and the attack was suspended. Paulus vetoed any further attempt to renew the attack and returned home.

Tobruk remained under siege, and Wavell asked for—and got—reinforcements. Rommel would remain, alternately, a scourge and a spur to Wavell and the two other professional generals who followed him in the desert. But the Axis decision to open a Mediterranean front "was a critical strategic mistake that the Allies would have been foolish not to exploit." It weakened Hitler's war against Russia "in ways that could not have been predicted in the spring of 1941."[14]

Between April and August, the British "acted decisively in the important areas—Iraq, Syria, and Iran—to protect and guarantee her all-important oil supplies for what turned out to be the rest of the war."[15] Oil from America had to be shipped across the Atlantic, with its pockets of U-boats, and paid for from Britain's shrinking currency reserves.

When Wavell's counteroffensive, code-named "Operation Battleaxe," failed in mid-June—as a result of enemy mines and antitank fire from German tanks—Churchill decided to replace him because, as he confided to Anthony Eden (who was now foreign secretary), he lacked the mental vigor and resolve to overcome obstacles essential for a successful war.

But despite their mutual dislike, they continued to carry on a civilized working relationship. For example, Churchill wrote to Wavell on March 1, 1941:

Hearty congratulations on the brilliant result of the campaign in Italian Somaliland. Will you convey to General Cunningham the thanks and appreciation of His Majesty's Government for the vigorous, daring, and highly successful operations which he has conducted in command of his ardent, well-trained, well-organized army. Will you ask him to convey the message to his troops. Publish as you find convenient.

Wavell replied the next day, "Your congratulations are very much appreciated. I have conveyed your message to General Cunningham." No doubt he read the inference between the lines as to what Churchill wanted from his generals and what he generally failed to find. It was that ingredient that made generals great. Alexander, Napoleon, Frederick the Great of Prussia, Marlborough, and the Duke of Wellington all possessed it. It was *audacity— always audacity.* It was a characteristic that Churchill possessed himself. And so, unfortunately, did Rommel.

Long afterward, Wavell was to remark ruefully of the episode that he had not budgeted for Rommel after his experiences with the Italians. He was sent to India on June 22 and may have welcomed leaving with relief after agreeing with Churchill that new blood was needed. His replacement was General Sir Claude Auchinleck, known affectionately as "The Auk," because of his prominent beaky features.

The Balance of Power

No less important than Churchill's choice of frontline generals in North Africa was the bond that he established with President Roosevelt at Placentia Bay in Newfoundland during August 9–12, 1941. Their discussions ranged wide in order to establish the scope and boundaries for the new partnership between the Anglo-American Allies for the following years of the war.[16] Although not yet active in the war, Roosevelt's administration had already provided Britain with considerable assistance, and this meeting would increase it. What was most important was the instant personal friendship and trust that materialized, with its appreciation of each other's abilities. They agreed that if they had to fight Germany and Japan, they should focus first on defeating Germany. It was one of eight items in a joint declaration that would be signed by twenty-four more nations. The declaration was almost like a Utopian manifesto that separated World War II from all other previous wars, which had been fought either for power, for material advantages, or for territory.

Both were unique individuals of enormous courage and integrity—although the latter quality has since been questioned by Roosevelt's critics. Nevertheless, it was fortuitous for the whole world that they were brought together at that time and agreed with each other on the most important goals and tactics. It must have been particularly heartwarming for Churchill with his admiration of the United States and the warm feelings he always held for his American mother.

The Auk

Generals can have their sharply honed skills blunted by battle stress. And it is a matter of opinion whether Churchill was wise to replace Wavell with General Auchinleck. He certainly felt that Wavell's thinking was not as clear as before but might still benefit other battle centers with different pressures and problems. In fact, between April and August the British "acted decisively in the important areas—Iraq, Syria, and Iran—to protect and guarantee her all-important oil supplies for what turned out to be the rest of the war."

But Auchinleck, too, recognized that the British forces were not strong enough to seize the initiative. Meanwhile, he was continually bombarded with telegrams from Churchill calling for the relief of Tobruk. He endured them as civilly as Wavell had, but—like Wavell—formed his own conclusions and refused to be deterred by them or diverted into making a false move. Churchill wanted airfields established to protect routes between Alexandria and Malta. Auchinleck was more concerned to protect the Nile Valley and obtain oil from the Persian Gulf. He insisted on securing his base before anything else. Regardless of what Churchill demanded, he was fortunate to have two such level-headed generals as Wavell and Auchinleck to restrain his famous impatience or channel it into the right direction.

General Auchinleck waited confidently for Rommel to attack. General Ritchie, who commanded the Eighth Army, and he had planned an elaborate defensive position from Gazala (held by a South African division) to Bir Hacheim (held by the First Free-French Brigade) on a series of fortified points called boxes.[17] They were defended by an enormous array of minefields, beyond which armored troops and the 30th Corps were kept in reserve.

Rommel began his drive in moonlight on May 26 to 27. His armor swept around Bir Hacheim in order to engage at great speed with the British armor and destroy it. But the British armored forces resisted his attack and stubbornly countered it according to plan. Rommel's tanks fought on for several days, which created supply issues and problems replacing ammunition—a typical result of advancing too quickly ahead of supplies. His Afrika Korps engineers were obliged to clear shortcuts back through the minefields held stubbornly by British troops. His audacious plan had failed. But he regrouped within the defenses of the minefield and prepared for another battle to capture Tobruk.

Rommel's first attack achieved little. His attempt to break through British defenses was easily halted. Heavy fighting continued for three days, with the Afrika Korps now supported by the Italian Mobile Corps. It swung back and forth over a wide area. Running short of supplies and water, the Afrika Korps was forced again to make gaps in the minefield. More and more tanks and other vehicles were disabled or knocked out. Meanwhile, RAF night bombers attacked enemy communications and airfields while Rommel's tanks and transport withdrew into a gap, where he was harried by British troops aided by bombers and fighter planes. Rommel's failure cost Axis lives and battle material.

And in the usual seesaw of fate in the desert war, Rommel made a desperate move to obtain supplies of water. The only way to achieve his aim was to destroy the only brigade in front of him. As Rommel described it later on, "Yard by yard the German-Italian units fought their way forward against the toughest British resistance imaginable. The British defense was conducted with considerable skill. As usual the British fought to the last round of ammunition."[18]

The battle for Tobruk continued until Rommel regained the initiative in the North African campaign.

---

* Military historian Ronald Lewis claimed that "to leave O'Connor looking over Neame's shoulder was to prevent a desert-worthy general from exercising effective command."[19] Lieutenant-General O'Connor was out of action until he managed to escape from the Germans in December 1943 and would fight again in Normandy.

15

THE KILLER INSTINCT

THE BATTLE FOR TOBRUK RAISED QUESTIONS about its strategic value. Churchill thought it was vital for defense against Egypt. Hitler wanted it at all costs. And Mussolini wanted it in order to rule Egypt. But General Auchinleck had decided by now that the cost of holding the port was too great in terms of lost lives and war material. Although it was a useful supply base, it would have to be evacuated if it could no longer be held. Meanwhile, he felt it must be held, and no part of the Eighth Army should "be allowed to be surrounded in Tobruk." The view of the war cabinet was that "Tobruk should remain, as in the previous year, a thorn in the enemy's side."

Churchill, hurrying off to Washington, telegraphed Auchinleck to make certain that they all understood the same policy in presuming there was no question of giving up Tobruk. Auchinleck replied that the war cabinet interpretation of what he planned to do was correct, and that General Ritchie was putting what he considered to be an adequate force to hold Tobruk, even if it became temporarily isolated. To avoid any danger of ambiguity, the Auk also sent a message to Ritchie, declaring that he realized its garrison might be isolated for short periods until a counteroffensive could be launched. They all seemed to be generally communicating on the same wavelength.

Either way, Rommel, with overreaching audacity, renewed his offensive after pausing for two days, by taking El Adem, Belhamed, and Acroma in several rapid attacks on the same day. The next day, he defeated the Fourth Armored Brigade at Sidi Rezegh, leaving them with only twenty tanks. Tobruk was now isolated, but still held by the Eleventh Indian Infantry Brigade, while the enemy bombarded the port with artillery and dive-bombers.

Half an hour after the softening-up process, the Germans launched an attack with two panzer divisions, an Italian armored division, and a motorized infantry division. Since the British armor outside Tobruk had already been put out of action, Rommel was free to use his full force to attack the town with a single blow.

A British counterattack with tanks failed. But fighting continued all that afternoon and evening. The British general in charge held out until 8 p.m., then requested instructions. He was advised to leave, since resistance was no longer effective. He informed General Ritchie of the shambles and was told to use his own judgment. The Germans accepted his surrender the next morning at 7:45 a.m., and thirty-three thousand British troops were taken prisoner. Nevertheless, 199 officers and men of the Coldstream Guards and 188 South African Union forces managed to escape in trucks and drove for the Egyptian border.

The German capture of Tobruk without an anticipated long siege changed the enemy's plans, since it enabled a considerable amount of supplies to fall into their hands. The day after Tobruk fell, Rommel announced that the British Eighth Army had been practically destroyed. He intended to destroy the small British force that remained on the border and open the way to Egypt for German and Italian troops. Mussolini then postponed any further attacks on Malta, which was being bombed night and day, and turned back to conquer Egypt and revel in the glory.

Remnants of the Eighth Army withdrew behind the frontier to delay enemy forces. It was an option that Auchinleck chose from all others, and stuck to, regardless of Churchill's offer of reinforcements. Meanwhile, RAF fighter squadrons covered the Eighth Army's retreat to Mersa Matruh.

Auchinleck took over direct command from Ritchie but decided it was impossible to make a final stand there. The Germans broke through the front of the Twenty-Ninth Indian Infantry Brigade that evening, where the minefield was incomplete. Streaming through the gap, they encircled the New Zealanders and attacked them from three sides. The fighting continued all day. Soon after midnight the Fourth New Zealand Brigade moved due east across the country with its battalions deployed and bayonets fixed, and charged the enemy in line, taking them completely by surprise and routing them in hand-to-hand combat under the light of the moon.

Then the New Zealanders, under General Freyberg, broke clear of the fighting in a disciplined manner under cover of RAF planes. They united with their division eighty miles away at Alamein, which was situated only forty miles west of Alexandria and thirty-five miles north of the impassable Qattara Depression.

In Washington, Churchill obtained 300 of the latest Sherman tanks, the finest in the American army, and one hundred 105-mm self-propelled guns, as well as 65 Liberator bombers, under the lend-lease program, which had been arranged as a business deal with the Americans. He was conscious of the need to reequip the Eighth Army. With their two Halifax bomber squadrons, they would now have 127 heavy bombers to continue the war for Egypt.

Auchinleck's counterattacks pushed Rommel hard for the first two weeks of July. But Rommel reacted by renewing attempts to break the British line. He considered withdrawing a week later, since he was short of men, tanks, and artillery, and the RAF never let up harassing him. Both sides fought themselves to a standstill by the end of the month. Auchinleck took several thousand prisoners. And Egypt was still safe from the Germans.

Nevertheless, Churchill's political opponents were sniping at him for the delays in the North African Campaign and his lack of success. They wanted more victories and laid blame as well as praise on him. But he felt confident with the "Ultra" decrypts that provided him with a detailed picture of the German lines of battle in Greece and North Africa. He continued to prod Wavell in his campaigns in Abyssinia, Iraq, and Syria, still believing he was defeatist. Churchill couldn't understand that some of his generals might be battle weary, since he himself was so buoyed up by battles.

The "Ultra" decrypts also revealed that Germany was building up forces to attack Russia and obtain more German territory. With no victory in sight in North Africa, it would ease some of the pressure off British forces and might provide Churchill with a way out of the present stalemate.

In the meantime, the flight of Hitler's deputy, Rudolph Hess, who parachuted into Scotland in May, was being ignored as a matter of principle, leaving the public with an impression that either Hitler had sent him to negotiate another peace deal as a smoke screen while German troops invaded another nation, or Hess was a mental case.

Rommel's Letters Home

As German forces closed in on Alamein on June 30, Rommel paused to wait for the Italians to join him. He was aware of three "boxes" of British troops laid out in a thirty-five-mile stretch between the coast and a steep descent into the Qattara Depression. Each box was connected at intervals by small mobile columns from each division. But he was unaware of a new fourth "box" where he was waiting north of the Depression, which consisted of an impenetrable salt marsh and soft sand. The largest "box" on the coast was occupied by the First South African Division. This newly made fourth one at Deir el Shern was occupied by the Eighteenth Indian Brigade.

Nor did he know that he had been outstripped by the retreating British. Meanwhile, the Afrika Korps were held up in the box until they could capture its defenders—long enough to prevent Rommel from making a quick breakout before he could press on. Even when he finally did so, British aircraft bombed his supply columns by moonlight.

July 1 would prove to be the most dangerous moment of the North African Campaign. This was the first Battle of Alamein and was considered to be the most crucial. Rommel continued his attack the next day but had less than forty usable tanks left, and his troops were exhausted. Auchinleck made an assessment of the situation and realized that Rommel's forces were too weak to attack.

By July 3, Rommel had only twenty-six tanks left for battle and was stopped by British armor. It was not long before he was halted. Another German division panicked from sheer exhaustion and was driven off by a New Zealand battalion.

Rommel wrote home saying, "Things are, unfortunately, not going as we should like."[1] When he wrote home the following day, he admitted their strength was exhausted—they were near to complete collapse. General Auchinleck had regained the initiative. The Auk ordered his forces to attack the Afrika Korps and give the enemy no rest. The Eighth Army was to destroy them in their present position.

Early the next morning, the Australians attacked the enemy near the coast and overran several Italian divisions. Rommel wrote to his wife, "Things are going downright badly for me at the moment, at any rate, in the military sense. The enemy is using his superiority, especially in infantry, to destroy the Italian formations one by one, and the German formations are much too weak to stand alone. It's enough to make one weep."[2]

The New Zealanders attacked at night on July 21. But German tanks came up and counterattacked in the dark, causing confusion. With daylight, the enemy battered the foremost New Zealand brigade. The Fifth Indian Division failed to reach its objective and also failed to clear a gap in the minefield for the Twenty-Third Armored Brigade. When two other tank regiments advanced to attack, they could obtain no information from the Indian Division whether the mines ahead of them had been cleared. Consequently, they drove into a trap, coming under heavy fire from German tanks and anti-tank guns, which sent them into a minefield where they were stranded. Only eleven tanks came out. A hundred and eighteen were lost (compared with the German loss of only three).

After four days for reorganizing and regrouping, the British made a final attempt to break through the German front. The Australians captured the ridge by moonlight and the Fiftieth Division made a good beginning. But the commander of the First Division held them all up because he was dissatisfied with the narrow gap in the minefield. By the time the leading tanks began to move through the minefield, there had been enough time for German tanks to rush in and pin them down. The British infantry were cut off and the Australians were driven off the ridge.

Auchinleck decided to suspend the attack, as many of his troops showed signs of exhaustion and disorientation, which caused a tendency to surrender if isolated. The battle was disappointing for the British. And by the beginning of August, Rommel's tank strength had increased to more than five times what it had been. He had been close to defeat by mid-July. And he was unable to afford any huge losses—like the seven thousand prisoners taken by the British.

The biggest British armored offensive, named "Operation Crusader," was launched on the night of November 17. Although Auchinleck's tanks were not in good shape, the Eighth Army had been enlarged into two corps. The attack surprised Rommel, but the tank battle was checked at Sidi-Rezegh. Rommel counterattacked, but Auchinleck's forces held. And the Afrika Korps was pushed west of Tobruk, The Eighth Army, commanded by General Ritchie, pushed Rommel all the way back to Cyrenaica and El Agheila by the end of the year.

It was at this point that Japanese aircraft attacked part of the U.S. fleet at Pearl Harbor. The incident drew off two Australian divisions from the North African campaign, which had to return home where they were now needed to defend Australia.

The Japanese Threat

The Japanese threat to Australia was seldom far from Churchill's thoughts. But other priorities took precedence according to immediate challenges and the limitations of troops and war material. Until Japan's preemptive strike on the U.S. fleet, Churchill was always against diverting forces from the Mediterranean Basin, where his target was to get Italy out of the war; the priority of the Royal Navy there was to protect the British Isles. Fragmenting Britain's sea power by sending battleships to the Pacific would cripple its effectiveness. But he promised to defend Australia in the event of a serious attack on it or Singapore.[3]

There had been plenty of discussion in the Admiralty from 1937 to 1939 about sending the fleet to Japan, which had turned from its traditional cautious attitude to the outside world to a belligerent one, incited by secret military societies of hotheads. But every argument had ended with an admission that to do so would leave the British Isles vulnerable to the German and Italian navies. The Royal Navy was simply not big enough to fight on two fronts so far apart. Churchill was against it. And the realization began to sink in that the Japanese fleet was more modern; Britain's new battleships were still under construction.[4] Fortunately, the U.S. fleet had been growing precipitously. It had even been viewed by some as a threat. But not by Churchill.

Prior to Japan's entry into the war, he considered that the Japanese were "a prudent people." But one of the remarkable characteristics of the Second World War was how Japanese soldiers—like the Germans—lost their individual human capacities and became mere robots manipulated and controlled by superior officers who wound them up like clockwork toys. Humanity had disappeared and individuality was subsumed into nationalism.

Nevertheless, it was Japanese prudence that caused them to destroy eight American battleships at anchor in Pearl Harbor before entering into an aggressive and total war in the Pacific.

To prevent Japanese landings in Malaya and Thailand, the Admiralty sent two British ships, in the open and without air cover, to deter Japanese aggression: the *Prince of Wales* and the *Repulse*. It was old-fashioned gunboat diplomacy, which had worked for Britain in past centuries. But instead of awing the Japanese, Japanese aircraft sank both ships, with a loss of 840 British lives. Churchill claimed it was his biggest shock in the war. It also shook the Royal Navy's complacency.[5] (What they had not taken into account was that Japan had been one of the first nations to emulate the English Industrial Revolution and arm itself with modern weaponry, and had already shown its prowess by beating Tsarist Russia in the Russo-Japanese War in 1904–05.)

The sinking of the two British ships by the Japanese was followed by two Canadian battalions surrendering at Hong Kong, the fall of Singapore to smaller Japanese forces than the British and imperial ones, and the beginning of the barbaric Japanese prisoner-of-war camps for those of the 139,000 Allied troops who had not been killed. Blame for the destruction of Force Z fell on Churchill. But the commander of the Eastern Fleet, Admiral Phillips, who sent the ships, had assumed that the mere sight of the British navy would awe the Japanese. So had Churchill. But the Japanese navy took pride in its own powerful fleet of state-of-the-art battleships, as well as its aircraft and its troops, led by Admiral Nagumo Chuichi.[6] Another shock was that the Japanese Zero fighter planes that destroyed the British ships were superior to Britain's Hurricanes or Spitfires.

The warships sent by the Admiralty were intended as a bluff. But it was poorly conceived and popularly attributed to Churchill. Nevertheless, every commander has to take risks, particularly the most brilliant ones, or nothing is achieved in war or peace. Historian Christopher M. Bell praised General Alan Brooke and Admirals Pound and Cunningham for often deflecting Churchill from possible errors of judgment by their sound advice.

Brooke's diary shows how he and Churchill felt at the time, when he wrote, "If the army cannot fight better than it is doing at present, we shall deserve to lose our Empire." Churchill felt despondent at the lack of heroism when the imperial forces outnumbered the Japanese invaders but simply gave up. Both were made aware of the complacent and arrogant army culture that had grown out of empire and left the British occupying troops in Asia only half-trained, poorly equipped, and lacking in proper leadership and morale.[7]

Churchill fell ill from exhaustion soon after returning from the United States and was confronted by one disaster after another. When two German battle cruisers escaped from the Royal Navy and the RAF in poor visibility, it was much publicized and created a mood of defeatism. Then, when British troops surrendered to the Japanese in Singapore after the disaster of the failed gunboat diplomacy, Churchill was attacked in Parliament, as well as by the press and the Australian government. And pro-Soviet demonstrations in Britain demanded a second front to relieve the Russians when Britain was not yet ready for it.

At the same time, the flow of useful tactical information from decoders at Bletchley Park came to a sudden stop when the German navy changed its Enigma cyphers by adding another cylinder. The result was heavier losses of convoys at sea from German U-boat wolf packs in the North Atlantic. In 1942, 1,769 Allied ships and 90 neutrals were sunk.[8] Churchill realized that the British could be starved to a point of collapse.

Neither the British public nor the news media conceived of the enormous impact of possible starvation in the British Isles. Starvation had already resulted in the deaths of millions in China and would face Russia, France, and Germany, even Malta and Bengal. But Churchill, with his tactical experience of naval blockades in the First World War, always managed to keep Britain well fed. So no one collapsed in the street from hunger in Britain during the war. No one reported in at work that they would not be returning before going home to die from malnutrition and exhaustion, as happened in Russia.[9] Nor did they ever have to step over starved bodies in the streets.

Meanwhile, the Japanese drove British, American, and Dutch forces out of China and Southeast Asia and were in a strong enough position to threaten India and Australia. Now Churchill was concerned about the Japanese army advancing through Burma to the Indian border, with a possibility of a seaborne attack on India and air raids on British shipping in the Indian Ocean.[10] He was soon confirmed in his view that Britain could not stretch its resources to the East. The War in the Pacific became America's war. And the Japanese would suffer heavy losses from American forces in the Battles of the Coral Sea and Midway in May and June of 1942.

Rommel's Afrika Korps

At the beginning of 1942, the Afrika Korps and the Eighth Army faced each other off at El Agheila—by which time the Axis had already lost 24,500 dead and wounded since the launch of the campaign, and 36,500 taken prisoner. The British had lost only half that number.

Rommel's forces attacked and captured Benghazi on January 21. He expressed great respect for Auchinleck, whom he thought cool and skillful and who would not allow himself to accept second-class solutions. General Auchinleck's problem was that they were often not carried out in the way he wanted. It was a failure in the British army culture and lax training.

Rommel was finally given the go-ahead by the OKW to take Egypt and seize the Suez Canal.[11] After his capture of Benghazi, the British mined the line for forty miles. They outnumbered Rommel's forces by this time. Nevertheless, his offensive against the Gazala Line on May 28 began three weeks of heavy fighting. Field Marshal Carver calculated he averaged only two and a half hours of sleep in every twenty-four hours at the time. Rommel now threatened the rear of the Eighth Army. And General Ritchie anxiously withdrew to Halfaya on the Egyptian border. Tobruk was besieged. And it fell to the Afrika Korps after a combined attack with aircraft.

The fall of Tobruk was viewed as the biggest blow to the British in the entire war. It was also another shock to Winston Churchill, who was embarrassed when handed a note of the news on a visit to Washington. Now he had to explain the reasons for the defeat to the House of Commons, as he had previously done about the humiliating defeats in Greece, Crete, and of Force Z in Singapore.

Auchinleck was in a perfect defensive position by this time. And the Afrika Korps was exhausted and overextended. But Rommel was bolstered by his victory and believed British morale would be at a low ebb, so he attacked the British on July 1. Battles went back and forth until both sides settled down to refresh, refit, and retrain for the summer, and Rommel laid a massive minefield to protect his forces.[12]

Auchinleck warned the high command in London that the counterattack could not be launched until September in order for him to train reinforcements in desert conditions. It brought Churchill to the front to assess the situation for himself. But Churchill and Brooke had already decided that General Auchinleck was not sufficiently offensive in his attitude, that neither he nor the gentlemanly Wavell possessed the killer instinct. They replaced him in early August with General Sir Harold Alexander who would be commander in chief, and with Lieutenant-General Bernard Montgomery who would now be in command of the Eighth Army.[13]

"General Sir Claude Auchinleck did not really deserve to be removed from his command in North Africa," wrote historian Andrew Roberts. He held the Afrika Korps from breaking through British defensive lines on the Ruweisat Ridge at the first battle of El Alamein in early July, when he took seven thousand prisoners, and made excellent plans for an autumn counterattack. Military historian Antony Beevor agreed.[14] Churchill offered Auchinleck command of Middle East forces instead. But he refused because it was a demotion. He was given command in India but never served in battle again.[15]

What Churchill wanted in a general were flair and zest for battle, which were part of his own nature after charging on horseback with saber drawn as a young man in the imperial cavalry at Omdurman. Instead, both Wavell and Auchinleck possessed a heavy sense of responsibility. And despite Britain having acquitted herself so well in the air in the Battle of Britain, it had been a defensive battle. Churchill knew that battles are won by being on the ground and on the offensive. And he needed a dramatic victory to please the electorate and the media and impress the Americans, whom he wanted as allies. He was the leader of a parliamentary democracy that could vote him out of office if it was dissatisfied with his performance.

Meanwhile, he was disenchanted by the atmosphere at military headquarters. "Ever since 1939, visitors to Egypt had been dismayed by the lassitude pervading the nexus of headquarters, camps, villas, hotels, and clubs that lay along the Nile. An air of self-indulgent imperialism, of a kind that confirmed the worst [class] prejudices of Aneurin Bevan, persisted even in the midst of a war of national survival."[16]

Churchill's first choice had been Field Marshal Sir Alan Brooke who, as chief of the Imperial General Staff, thought highly of Auchinleck and didn't want his job. Brooke claimed the shortage of good generals was due to the huge loss of young officers in the First World War.[17] Churchill's second choice was General Gott, who was killed the following day in an air crash. General Montgomery, who was Brooke's protégé, was brought out to fill a vacancy that no other British general seemed strong enough for. And Montgomery was the only general with the audacity to exploit the situation by refusing to attack the Germans until he was adequately equipped and his troops were properly trained to win the war in North Africa. By that time, Churchill had no other choice but to accept: it seemed there was no one else.

The Spartan General

General Montgomery's family came from the north of Ireland. He was as cool and hard and ruthless as the two generals who had preceded him. But whereas their appearance and demeanor conformed to military convention, Monty's did not. He was a short, wiry man who had learned to be pushy in order to ensure he was not overlooked. He was as eccentric in manner as Winston Churchill. Churchill established his brand image with his unconventional hat and huge cigar, his melodramatic voice and colorful phrases. Bernard Montgomery wore a cocky beret instead of the traditional officer's peaked cap, and he swaggered with self-assurance from having observed the mistakes that caused unnecessary bloodshed in the trenches on the 1914 Western Front.

He'd fought and been wounded twice at Cateau, Ypres, and the Somme in the First World War. He'd studied at the Royal Military Academy at Sandhurst with General Sir Alan Brooke, and he'd taught army officers at the Staff College in Camberley. He was as ambitious and argumentative as Churchill, but—unlike the prime minister—he was dour and ascetic and neither drank nor smoked. He had been nicknamed the "Spartan General." But, like Churchill, he was also a great communicator and show-off. Montgomery possessed an ability to inhabit the skin of his military opponent and view the campaign from the enemy's perspective so as to know what he thought and what he was most likely to do next. He was "disciplined, focused, adaptable, a meticulous planner, quick to dismiss the incompetent, respectful of the Germans' capacity for counterattack." But "Montgomery was irascible, opinionated, and egotistical." He "was also the greatest British field commander since the Duke of Wellington. . . . If Montgomery was vain, he had plenty to be vain about."[18]

The first thing he did was address his new troops and tell them what he planned to do and what he wanted *them* to do. Then he pinned a portrait of Rommel to the wall of his trailer to study his character and get inside his head. It was not long before the troops under his command had developed sufficient respect, admiration, and even a camaraderie that they were comfortable enough with him to refer to him almost affectionately as "Monty."

It was now four years since that moment during the Munich crisis and the Phony War in 1938 when Joseph Kennedy and others forecast that it would take that length of time to reach military and air parity with Germany. This was a turning point from just surviving, as Britain had so far managed to do, to having enough well-trained troops and war material to enable the Allies to get the war over and done with, in order to save millions of Allied lives.

That endeavor was assisted by the lack of coordination between the German services, where everyone was out for his own ends. There was jealousy and deadly rivalry. It arose largely from Hitler's own leadership style. Since the dictator had to have his own way, he avoided meeting with more than one general at a time, so he could browbeat and resist being outnumbered. The result was that each service knew next to nothing about the others. Göring controlled the air force almost on his own, and the German navy was a mystery to all. Although Prussia was not landlocked, it had always relied on its army. Access to the North Sea and the Baltic was only from its narrow northern border, and most of its historic battles had been on land because the Germans were primarily landsmen, not sailors, hence, their apprehension at the prospect of crossing the English Channel.

16

THE DESERT FOX

General Auchinleck had accepted Brigadier Dorman-Smith's original plan and Field Marshal Alexander had approved it. Montgomery also accepted the plan in principle and made no radical changes. His intention was to threaten any advance by the enemy by holding the area between the sea and the Ruweisat Ridge. The major issue depended on the effective defensive action arising out of the Auk's well-chosen position of the armor. The only area of the front where a quick penetration by the enemy could succeed was between the "box" held by New Zealanders on the Alam Nayil Ridge and the Qattara Depression.

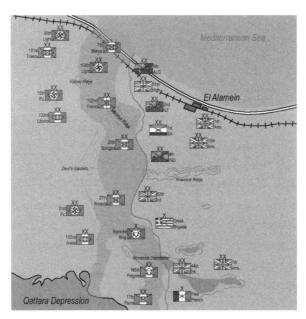

The second battle of El Alamein: October 25 to November 11, 1942, led by General Montgomery

Normal conditions in the North African desert were sweltering hot days and freezing cold nights, incessant mosquitoes, clouds of aggressive flies, and scorpions, amidst the sunbaked boredom of a typically featureless and altogether empty desert, intermittently broken by sandstorms that lasted for days.[1] Tanks were like ovens in the heat of the sun—another good reason to move off at night. Perhaps it was the typical desert boredom that triggered energetic action in the Allied troops and the Afrika Korps as some kind of relief. But it required enormous self-discipline. That was hardly the case with the administrators in their cushy jobs close to the hotels and cocktail bars of Cairo, whom fighting troops referred to as the "Gabardine Swine." Some were so isolated from the realities of the war by their daily bureaucratic paperwork that they had no idea of the dire straits they and the British Empire were in.

Rommel had received two fresh parachute brigades during the lull in fighting—a German one with 200 tanks in two panzer divisions and an Italian armored division with 240. He had also been sent more drafted men and supplies. He planned to attack at the end of August. The Italian tanks were old and obsolete models, but his panzers were of the most modern designs. By comparison, the British possessed 700 tanks, of which 160 were the best American Grants and had the advantage in strength of weapons.

The fortified British front was held by four infantry divisions, the Seventh Light Armored Division and the Tenth, with two armored brigades. In addition, the reequipped Twenty-Third was placed under Major-General Gatehouse's command after the battle commenced. And another division was brought up to Alam Halfa Ridge.

It was obvious that Rommel would head for the box near the Qattara Depression, so a surprise attack from him was impossible. He would have to rely on his typical timing and speed. In fact, Rommel planned to capture the mined belt under cover of night. He would drive the Afrika Korps thirty miles east before daylight, then turn toward the Eighth Army's supply area. By doing so, he expected to entice the British armor into a chase with opportunities to trap and destroy it. Meanwhile, the Italian Mobile Corps would provide protection until he had won the battle. He relied on the slower reactions of British command, which was not as impulsive as him; it always took them longer to arrive at decisions and put them into effect.[2]

In any event, the Afrika Korps couldn't start until close to 10:00 a.m. because the mined area was far deeper than he'd anticipated. The delay provided opportunities for bombing attacks by the RAF. The Korps commander was wounded very early on, and the Afrika Korps was commanded by his chief-of-staff, Lieutenant-General Bayerlein. They carried on by changing direction and heading for the dominance of Alam Halfa Ridge. It was where the British Twenty-Second Armored Brigade was positioned beside an area of soft sand that limited maneuvering.

The British Eighth Armored Brigade was positioned ten miles away from the Twenty-Second, since Montgomery knew he could rely on their individual strengths; each was as strong in armored vehicles as the entire Afrika Korps. Rommel attacked the Twenty-Second. But he was held up by continual air attacks from the RAF and delayed arrivals of fuel and ammunition. Then his panzer columns came under heavy storms of fire from British tanks and support artillery. His several advances and attempts at flank maneuvers were held in check until nightfall. Rommel's tank attack was aborted more by his fuel shortages than anything else.

The shortage of fuel prevented any large operations at sunrise on September 1. The Afrika Korps had already suffered considerable losses from the nighttime battering it had received from British bombers, as well as the artillery of General Horrocks's Thirteenth Corps, which continued throughout the day. Rommel now found himself in a "very awkward predicament."[3] At that point, Montgomery planned a counterattack to gain the initiative. It involved trapping the Germans with a cork in the neck of the bottle into which they would have to be pushed. He also organized a pursuit force.

The panzers now had only a day's fuel left, which meant they could move only sixty miles. They were bombed almost nonstop for another night, and Rommel decided to withdraw. The German forces thinned out in their westward retreat, and Montgomery refused to allow his army to follow them in case they were being lured into a trap. Monty also planned an attack for the night of September 3–4. Meanwhile, Rommel continued to withdraw. The Afrika Korps had gotten as far east as it ever would and had suffered three thousand casualties, which was nearly twice the number that the Eighth Army had received. Most importantly, Rommel's stocks of fuel were exhausted.

The British launched their bottling attack on the enemy's rear flank that night. But it became badly confused and was broken off.

The Afrika Korps continued to withdraw, then appeared to be making a stand on high ground on September 6. Montgomery decided to discontinue the battle. But British troops were encouraged by Rommel's retreat and felt the tide had turned. Montgomery had already imbued them with a spirit of confidence although the question remained as to whether the Eighth Army should have cut Rommel off. But Montgomery may have recognized that Rommel was already defeated when he was checked from dashing into Egypt at the first Battle of Alamein, which was the real turning point.

In the meantime, Churchill and the British government waited impatiently for Montgomery to launch an offensive and achieve a decisive victory. It took another seven weeks, since Montgomery was prepared to wait until he had completed all his preparations and could be more certain of success. He planned his starting date according to the phases of the moon, since it would commence with a nighttime attack. It required darkness to confuse enemy fire and moonlight to clear gaps in his minefields. Hence, the darkness of October 23 and the full moon of the twenty-fourth.

El Alamein

The Eighth Army's artillery opened up with a massive bombardment on October 23 at 9:40 p.m., coordinated with an attack from the air by Wellingtons and Halifax bombers. About six thousand artillery men fired about 882 guns with about a million shells during the battle.[4] Sometimes as many as a thousand guns flashed and roared simultaneously as they lit up the sky: "The barrage could be heard in Alexandria, some sixty miles away."[5] It carried on for five hours. Then it broke off at 3:00 a.m.—to be resumed at 7:00. Sappers went on ahead to clear paths through the minefield for the infantry. They were marked with white tape. The pipers played as the British infantry advanced along the line.

The two Dictators: Adolf Hitler admired the Italian leader, while Benito Mussolini took care to avoid having Hitler as an enemy.
(The United States Holocaust Memorial Museum.)

eld Marshal Hermann Göring, Chief
the German Air Force and a leading
member of the Nazi Party.
(The Imperial War Museum of the
United Kingdom Government.)

The Munich Crisis: 1940. Britain's Prime Minister Neville Chamberlain waves a piece of paper signed by Hitler, which he naively believed promised "Peace in our time." Lord Halifax can be identified by his bowler hat, leaning on his umbrella, standing back and to Chamberlain's right, to give him more room.

itish Prime Minister
msey MacDonald. "No
e knew what he was
ing to say or what he had
st said."
*he George Grantham Bain
lection at the US Library of
ngress.)*

*British Prime Minister Stanley Baldwin with wife and
daughter. Churchill avoided attending his funeral, saying
"It would have been better for our country if he had never
lived."*
(Bain Collection at the US Library of Congress.)

*e dapper British Foreign Secretary Anthony Eden
ith US Secretary of State Cordell Hull.*
nited States Government, World War II Database.)

*Chancellor of the Exchequer
and Hitler appeaser Sir Samuel
("Slippery Sam") Hoare—
wept like a guilty child in
Parliament when found out.*
(The United States Library
of Congress's Prints and
Photographs division.)

The young Winston Churchill with his fiancée Clementine Hozier. They married in 1908.
(http://worldroots.com)

Britain's Wartime Prime Minister Winston Churchill in 1944.
(Wikimedia Commons.)

Women's Air Force plotters in 1940 Battle of Britain.
(The Illustrated London News, "Responsible Work by the WAAFs: 'Plotting' Our Aircraft," November 28, 1942, p. 608.)

British General Bernard Montgomery in a Grant tank at El Alamein in 1942.
(The United States Government. www.archives.gov)

German General Erwin Rommel, nicknamed "The Desert Fox" by the British.

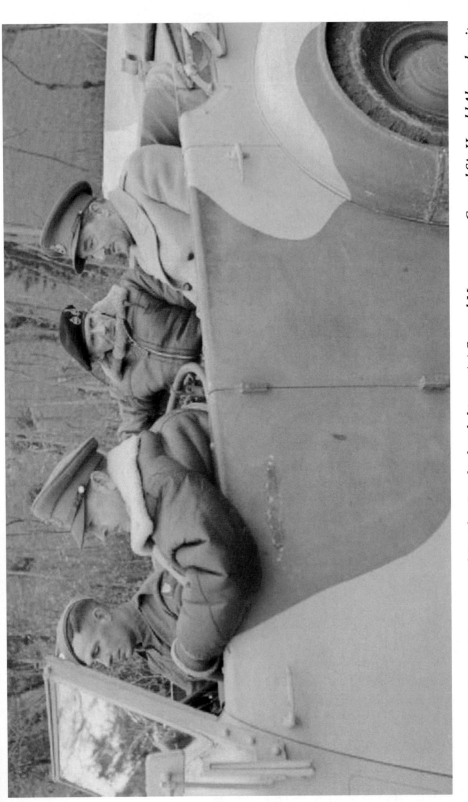

Churchill's closest military adviser, General Sir Alan Brooke, beside his protégé General Montgomery. General Sir Harold Alexander sits in front.

The Nazi war against unarmed women and children. Warsaw 1943 victims for the Nazi gas chambers.

(Polish Institute of National Remembrance.)

Free Polish Battle of Britain pilots in RAF 303 squadron. 1940.

Young Russian women snipers guarding Ukraine. Few survived the German onslaught.
(Wikipedia.)

British women code-breakers at Bletchley Park working a Mark 2 Colossus in 1943—th *first ever programmable electronic computers.*
(UK Government National Archives.)

A British Enigma machine used for breaking German military and naval codes.
(Sperling on Wikipedia.org)

Just before D-Day. The British Army Sixth Airborne Division being briefed in England for the Normandy landing. June 4–5, 1944.
(UK Imperial War Museums. United Kingdom Government.)

General Eisenhower encouraging US parachutists of the US 101 Airborne Division in Britain before they board their aircraft for the D-Day invasion of Normandy on June 5, 1944.
(US Army Photograph, US Library of Congress.)

German forces surrendering in Saint-Lambert-sur-Dive. 21 August 1944.
(Library and Archives Canada.)

Left to right, Generals Patton, Bradley, and Montgomery sharing a joke in Normandy, July 7, 1944, at Twenty-first Army HQ.
(United Kingdom Government.)

General Mark Clark being awarded a DS(by President Roosevelt in Ita in December 1943.
(US Library of Congress.)

General Douglas MacArthur returning to the Philippines.
(US National Archives and Records Administration. Photographer, US Army Signal Corps Gaetano Faillace.)

General George Marshall with US Secretary of War Henry Stimson.
(US Federal Government.)

The three greatest British field commanders who fought in the critical desert war against German and Italian troops: Field Marshal Sir Archibald Wavell (in the center), now Viceroy of India, with Field Marshal the Viscount Montgomery of Alamein (on left), and Field Marshal Sir Claude Auchinleck, now Commander-in-Chief of the Indian Army. June 17, 1946.
(Imperial War Museum, United Kingdom Government.)

French resistance leader and Commander of the Free French forces, General Charles de Gaulle, who would become President of France.
(Imperial War Museums, United Kingdom Government.)

Ruins of Coventry Cathedral two days after the German Luftwaffe bombed the city in an air raid on the night of November 14, 1940.
(Imperial War Museum, United Kingdom Government.)

Anne Frank at school at age eleven. She was victimized and hunted down by the Nazis in Hitler's war against women and children. (Wikipedia. Website Anne Frank Stichting, Amsterdam.)

Dead bodies at Stalingrad in 1943. (Wikimedia.)

British Prime Minister Winston Churchill on the Rhine in wartime, March 25, 1945, with Generals Alan Brooke and Montgomery and several US generals. (United Kingdom Government.)

Dead bodies of former Italian Dictator Benito Mussolini and his mistress hang upside down in public in Milan after being machine-gunned to death by anti fascist partisans. (Photograph by Renzo Pistone.)

The "Big Three" leaders. From left to right, Soviet Marshal Josef Stalin, US President Franklin D. Roosevelt, and British Prime Minister Winston Churchill, at the 1943 Teheran Conference.

(The US Army.)

Soviet Field Marshal Georgy Zhukov, one of the greatest generals of World War II. (Time Inc.; photograph by Gregory Weil.)

Prime Minister Winston Churchill with the new American President, Harry S. Truman, and Marshal Stalin, just before the "Big Three" Potsdam Conference. (Harry S. Truman Library, National Archives and Records Administration.)

Field Marshal Sir Bernard Montgomery decorates the Russian Generals after victory against the enemy. Deputy Supreme Commander in Chief the Red Army Marshal Zhukov, Marshal Rokossovsky, and General Sokolovsky at the Brandenburg Gate Berlin, July 12, 1945. (Imperial War Museum United Kingdom Government.)

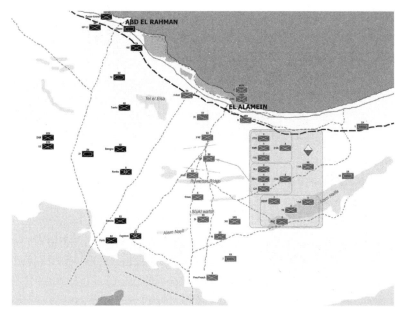

The second battle of El Alamein. Disposition of forces on October 3, 1942, between Allied Armies led by General Montgomery against General Rommel's Afrika Corps.

The creeping barrage subdued enemy fire. And the Eighth Armored Brigade made it to the Miteiriya Ridge. But they were the only ones, since the others were caught up by the congestion. And the depth and intensity of German minefields held up the action so that it was already daylight when the British tanks were still being delayed. They only reached the far side of the mines on the second morning, and the infantry suffered heavy losses while pushing through. The advance cost them two and a half thousand casualties from enemy mines and booby traps.

Nevertheless, the wedge driven into German defenses intimidated the German commander defending them, who panicked and sent in their vulnerable tanks only a few at a time during the day in futile attempts to halt the Allied expansion. Montgomery's army inflicted heavy losses on the defending panzers until, by evening, the Fifteenth Panzer Division had lost three-quarters of its tanks.

British superiority was greater than ever before. The Eighth Army's fighting strength was 230,000, whereas Rommel had only 27,000 Germans and less than 53,000 Italians. Montgomery also had 1,440 tanks, compared with Rommel's 260 German and 280 obsolete Italian ones. The odds in Britain's favor were six to one. And added to the British Grant tanks were now 500 of the latest Shermans. The British also enjoyed greater air superiority than ever before. Air Commander-in-Chief Sir Arthur Tedder had 96 operational squadrons to draw on with a total of 1,500 modern aircraft. The Germans and Italians possessed only 350.

New industrial designs and greater productivity proved crucial. And so did the ability of the Royal Navy's submarines to cut off supplies to the Afrika Korps. Nearly a third of supplies shipped to the German desert forces were sunk by the British in the Mediterranean. They included oil tankers—hence Rommel's fuel shortage. Before the British offensive even commenced, the panzers had only three issues of fuel in hand instead of the thirty they needed. The British had orchestrated a well-executed stranglehold on German power. It included holding up food supplies from the enemy, leading to a spread of dysentery and jaundice among German troops. Its victims included Rommel himself. He was laid up in Austria in August but recovered in time for the attack on Alam Halfa.

Rommel's convalescence was cut short by Hitler ordering him to return to Africa. He arrived at Alamein on the evening of October 25, when his defenses were already battered and half his tanks had been destroyed.

"Operation Lightfoot," as Montgomery named it, attacked a four-mile stretch near the coast. He'd decided to keep it simple because of shortcomings in training in the British army; otherwise, a bolder plan could have exploited the British superiority in arms. Nevertheless, he was known for his "unflinching determination." As mentioned, the German minefields held up the action. British tanks only reached the far side of the mines on the second morning, and suffered heavy infantry losses as a result. A subsidiary attack came up against similar problems, and was abandoned.

The British resumed their advance the next day, October 26, but were checked. Now the massive wedge was surrounded by a ring of German anti-tank guns. British losses multiplied, while Montgomery displayed supreme confidence, knowing his triumphant grin was infectious. Nevertheless, he realized his attack had failed.

Monty tended to claim, after the event, that everything had gone according to plan; in fact one of his strengths was his ability to change plans according to new conditions. Now he immediately gave his forward troops a rest and designed a new plan called "Operation Supercharge," which—combined with his grin—encouraged the troops.

This new offensive opened at night on October 28, with a thrust to the coast, but became delayed in German minefields. Rommel benefited from the delay because his resources were fast evaporating. He had only ninety tanks left by now, whereas the Eighth Army possessed over eight hundred on the spot. British superiority had risen to eleven to one in their favor.

But Montgomery brought Lightfoot to an end on October 29, upsetting Anthony Eden in London. Eden convinced Churchill that Montgomery had given up the fight halfway through. The prime minister berated Brooke, since Monty was his protégé: Had Britain not gotten a single general who could even win a single battle?

Brooke defended Monty to Churchill and was backed by Field Marshal Smuts of South Africa, who gave the benefit of the doubt to the man on the spot. But Brooke had begun to have his own uneasy doubts about Montgomery.

No Exit

Rommel wrote to his wife the next day, "I haven't much hope left. At night I lie with my eyes wide open unable to sleep, for the load that is on my shoulders. In the day I'm dead tired. What will happen if things go wrong here? That is the thought that torments me day and night. I can see no way out if that happens."[6]

Meanwhile, Montgomery saw that his coastal thrust had miscarried, and he reverted to his original line of attack by launching "Operation Supercharge" on November 1. But, although he was flexible, his forces were not. Nor was Montgomery as confident as he showed himself to be. Enemy resistance was greater than expected, and he felt he might have to break off his offensive.

His leading armor was confronted by an unexpected screen of antitank guns he'd thought were further away, and his position was too cramped to counterattack, losing a considerable number of tanks. What was left held on, and the brigades that followed managed to push through the gap. But they were checked beyond the Rahman track and lost about two hundred more tanks by nightfall.

Fortunately for Montgomery, "Rommel was at the end of his resources."[7] Montgomery had the advantage of being able to read Rommel's Enigma communications. He knew the Germans were short of men, ammunition, food, water, and—most disastrously—fuel, from reading Rommel's letters.[8] The Afrika Korps had barely thirty tanks left in action, whereas the British still had six hundred. It gave them increased superiority of twenty to one. The Italians had been badly beaten and were nowhere to be seen.[9]

With the possibility of being outflanked from the south, Rommel decided to fall back to Fuka in two stages and had begun his withdrawal when he received an order from Hitler to hold Alamein at all costs. It was a "stand or die" order. Rommel was bemused. "The Führer must be crazy," he incautiously remarked to a junior officer. Apparently he was to be sacrificed to another of Hitler's whims.

Afrika Korps commander von Thoma was captured in the confusion. It was an opportunity for the British to cut off and destroy Rommel's entire army. But Hitler's permission to withdraw arrived the next day, and the Germans moved off fast. The Afrika Korps left the field in fairly good order, although those with no transport surrendered or were captured: twenty thousand Italians, ten thousand Germans, and nine generals. The British—too cautious, hesitant, and slow—lost the opportunity to capture the rest. But that night, Montgomery invited the captured General von Thoma to dinner in his tent.

British troops followed the German retreat on the evening of November 5. The New Zealand Division headed for Fuka but was slowed down while taking Italian prisoners. They arrived at midday on the fifth, to be held up again, this time by a possible minefield. The Seventh Armored Division was held up at the same location before discovering it was a dummy, laid previously by the British. By the time that the three pursuit divisions closed in on Fuka, Rommel had slipped away.

The First Armored Division went in pursuit. But driving rain on the coast put a halt to it. And the British troops failed to cut off Rommel's getaway to Sidi Barrani on the seventh. "Only the rain saved them," wrote Montgomery afterward. "Four crack German divisions and eight Italian divisions had ceased to exist as effective fighting formations."[10] He organized a special pursuit force, but Rommel slipped away again and avoided several attempts to cut off his retreat.

Although Rommel had not been captured, his forces were broken and the Germans and Italians had been shaken off the map of North Africa before rolling it up. Churchill would end his history of the affair by remarking, "Before Alamein we never had a victory. After Alamein we never had a defeat."[11] It expressed the importance of the campaign to the Allies in World War II. Nevertheless, it was Churchillian rhetorical hyperbole, because there had been plenty of British victories before El Alamein: in the air in the Battle of Britain and on the ground in North Africa. But Churchill tended to brush aside defensive actions, because he knew that wars are won only by taking the offensive.

The Eighth Army had killed and captured thousands of Germans, and captured twenty thousand Italian prisoners with 450 tanks and a thousand guns. In return, they suffered 13,500 casualties. The Desert Fox would have to be fought another day. Meanwhile, he slipped away again on November 12 and reached Mersa Brega, where Hitler ordered him once again to "hold the line at all costs." In spite of that, Rommel was convinced the North African Campaign was over and the Germans had lost.

But there was a sequel. Hoping to describe the reality of the situation to Hitler—with whom he thought he was on unusually good terms—he flew to meet him in Rastenburg, East Prussia. His reception was chilly. "Hitler flew into a fury." The dictator repeated that there would "be no withdrawal from the Mersa el Brega line" and would not tolerate any further argument. Rommel was shocked that Hitler refused to listen to facts that did not coincide with the false delusions in which he had imprisoned himself and everyone else.[12]

17

THE ANGLO-AMERICAN ALLIANCE

WHILE THE BATTLE FOR EGYPT WAS being fought in the North African desert, Churchill heard that the Japanese navy had made a preemptive strike on the United States by bombing part of the American fleet at Pearl Harbor on December 7, 1941. He was jubilant that it brought the United States into the war on Britain's side. It meant that Britain would no longer have to fight alone in a total war against the three most powerful enemies. It was also the first intimation that the Allies would win the war, since the Second World War was fought between the mighty industrial potential of Germany, Britain, the United States, and Japan. For example, most of the untrained and inexperienced British army simply hung around to no purpose in Britain because they had insufficient arms and armor, vehicles and ammunition, to enable them to fight.

"Well then," de Gaulle remarked, when he heard about the Japanese attack, "this war is over. . . . The outcome is no longer in doubt. . . . Nothing can resist the power of American industry."[1]

When Churchill first visited Moscow in August 1942, he received from Stalin an account of a conversation between Russian Ambassador Molotov and Ribbentrop that took place in Berlin during a bombing raid by the RAF the previous November, which Stalin was convinced had been contrived by Churchill to target the two ambassadors.[2] Ribbentrop had led Molotov to a deep underground air-raid shelter and shut the door.

"Now we are here alone together," Ribbentrop said to Molotov, "Why should we not divide?"

"What will England say?" Molotov replied.

"England is finished," Ribbentrop remarked dismissively. "She is no more use as a power."

"If that is so," said Molotov, "why are we here in this shelter, and whose are those bombs which fall?"[3]

Different Attitudes

The difference between Britain's approach to war and the methods of the two police states was striking. German officers and men would either die fighting or at the end of a pistol from a Gestapo officer assigned to the unit. Disobedience was not tolerated. Since the secret police were everywhere, they inspired constant fear and anxiety. The Gestapo, who were selected from the SS, had been set up in 1933 to enforce Hitler's will on everyone. Commissars (or political officers) served the same purpose in Communist Russia and held the same rank as a unit commander. The result was that the Germans fought ruthlessly and with cold discipline or were shot by their own side. The Russians fought like wild beasts to protect their land, and commissars used their pistols to enforce Stalin's orders. Both dictators were guaranteed that their troops fought to the last bullet and the last man. But Britain was a democratic country that relied on cooperation instead of coercion.

Now that the United States was their ally, Churchill was eager to cooperate with President Roosevelt to choose the most vital priority to bring the war to a close as soon as possible. And he recognized that the Americans were untrained, inexperienced, and unproven in battle.

President Roosevelt listed all the alternatives to an Allied landing in Europe (originally planned for 1942), which the British government and President Roosevelt agreed they were not yet ready to launch. In Roosevelt's mind, the loss of the Middle East could result in the loss of Egypt and the Suez Canal, Syria, and the loss of oil wells in Mosul, the Persian Gulf, and the loss of Iranian oil.

The occupation of French North Africa was also on the agenda, and Churchill believed it had attracted the President. Originally code-named "Gymnast," it could effectively provide relief for the Russian front by drawing off a number of German divisions and air forces. But it was understood from the beginning that they could not rely on an invitation or guarantee from Vichy-France, and there would be resistance in some quarters to an Allied landing. The British government proposed that U.S. General Marshall command the campaign in 1942, which they code-named "Torch."

The significance of Operation Torch to the war effort was that British generals showed considerable caution about entering Europe again with a ground force after the previous catastrophe of Dunkirk until Germany had been weakened on the Russian front. And France's position was potentially explosive as the Vichy-French came more and more under German control. General George Marshall's 1942 plans for an early return to France were considered to be much too risky and potentially dangerous by General Brooke, who was now chairman of the British Chiefs of Staff, as well as chief of the Imperial General Staff. Brooke viewed Torch as a good opportunity for U.S. forces to obtain battle experience for more significant future operations against well-trained and more powerful German forces. And both American and British officers needed experience of amphibious operations for the future invasion of the continent of Europe. Brooke was an Irishman from the north, with characteristic "toughness, diligence, intolerance, Christian commitment, and a brusqueness that sometimes tipped over into ill-temper. His sharp brain was matched by extraordinary strength of purpose."[4]

Marshall and Brooke were the two driving forces behind a combined Allied strategy. Alternative ideas and options were aggressively debated from 1942 onward. Some discussions occasionally included stand-up arguments, since Churchill was no longer the sole warlord, but now part of an Allied team. Fortunately, Marshall and Brooke respected each other and were gentlemen.

President Roosevelt saw the necessity of a land operation against Germany, probably in 1942, whereas the British knew the Allies were not yet ready for it. On the other hand, some Americans strategists favored a Pacific Campaign.

Led Down the Garden Path

When Churchill visited him at his country house in Hyde Park, New York, the President was prompted by the fall of Tobruk to favor undertaking Operation

Torch against French colonies in North Africa in 1942. And George Marshall was given the responsibility of implementing it, although he had reservations. He pointed out that Torch would effectively place an attack on the French mainland on the back burner. He tended to view it as a distraction from the main objective and considered the British had led the Americans down the garden path.[5] Nevertheless, he was committed to undertake the operation for the President, since it was his duty.

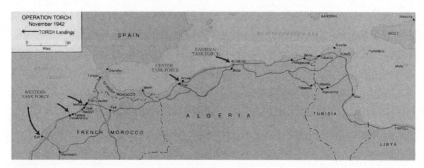

The Anglo-American Alliance 1942 landings on French North Africa. Code-named "Operation Torch."

At least three hundred warships and four hundred other vessels would carry more than 105,000 troops. Three-quarters would be American and the rest British—33,843 from the eastern seaboard of the United States and 72,000 from the south coast of Britain. U.S. General George Patton would be a driving force behind the military expedition. He was renowned for his bellicosity and his forthright remarks that spared no one. He was known as "Old Blood and Guts"—not always affectionately. He admitted to what he called "the white-hot joy of taking human life."[6] And he always sported a matching pair of pearl-handled revolvers. He believed he had been reincarnated several times, always as a warrior. When he admitted he did things by sixth sense, it turned out he meant that, regardless of clear military instructions; he acted on his own instincts as the mood took him at the front line.

Operation Torch was very well supplied with women's nylons as well as bazookas, 7,000 tons of coal as well as 3,000 vehicles, five pounds of rat poison as well as 1,000 Purple Heart medals for soldiers wounded in action,

750,000 bottles of mosquito repellant as well as one hundred thousand dollars in gold and 60 tons of maps.

Acting General Dwight Eisenhower would be in charge of the operation. General George Marshall was his mentor. "Ike," as he was affectionately called, possessed the right temperament for it—good-natured but firm with prima-donna generals. He was a well-organized administrator who won the respect of all the generals responsible to him. But he had never commanded soldiers in combat. The other generals included Montgomery, Omar Bradley, and Mark Clark. Vanity, ambition, and backbiting would be rife among them, with a frequent attitude of "them and us" between the Americans and the British, whom they called "Limeys."

There would be nine separate landings at three different French ports in Africa. And each encounter would be challenged by different levels of touchiness or resistance from Vichy-French forces. Consequently, it was agreed beforehand that British forces should sew a Stars and Stripes insignia on their sleeve, since "the French hate the English more than the Americans."

Marshall left for England after the Hyde Park meeting with Ambassador Harry Hopkins, and Roosevelt confirmed his view that a war with Germany should take precedence, since defeating Japan would not defeat Germany. On the other hand, it was obvious that defeating Germany meant the inevitable defeat of Japan, "probably without firing a shot or losing a life."[7] Meanwhile, Torch would be a useful test to see how well the British could work with untested and insufficiently trained American allies.

Admiral King's war was against the Japanese. He proceeded to reinforce the Pacific region of the war, which he planned to control through the U.S. Navy and the Marines. Up to three hundred thousand troops would be under General Douglas MacArthur's command. He was the prima donna of the Pacific War and had skillfully managed to create—at least for the media and in the minds of the public—an image of a man of destiny, posing authoritatively for the news cameras as professionally as a film actor, with his corncob pipe clenched between his teeth, while he gazed meditatively into the far distance. General MacArthur was an extreme right-wing Republican and disliked President Roosevelt intensely. Eisenhower regretted that MacArthur had been evacuated from the Philippines, and King hated him.[8] Admiral Nimitz, on the other hand, was an accomplished professional who just got on with the job of war.

The agreed division of responsibilities left Britain with the China, Burma, and India campaigns. The Americans would control all operations in the Pacific and South China Sea, defending Australia and New Zealand. MacArthur set up his headquarters in Brisbane. To his credit, he replaced the Australian plan to defend the continent in the interior with his own strategy to defend it in the Solomon Islands. He insisted that the Japanese must be prevented from setting foot in Australia. His island-hopping strategy was masterly in leaving large numbers of Japanese troops stranded as he swept by to the Philippines.

Fighting in the island jungles was as brutal as in Soviet Russia. But instead of fighting in subzero temperatures, the ever-present dangers came from tropical humidity with dengue fever, malaria, and typhus, as well as dysentery. And there was tropical cover that Japanese snipers used to advantage. "Clothes fell to pieces, skin became infected from insect bites, and both sides were half starved."[9] A thousand Papuans acted as bearers for the Australian forces.

Operation Torch

Torch was a credit to Churchill's leadership, since he had persuaded reluctant U.S. military chiefs and the President of the United States to agree to it against their wishes. They would have far preferred to sacrifice a force of untrained, outnumbered, and ill-equipped British troops to an unwinnable invasion of France, which the British military knew would be a monumental disaster. Only when the United States finally fought German forces did they admit grudgingly that Churchill was right and they had been wrong.

U.S. General Mark Clark made a secret visit to Algiers in a diplomatic prelude to the landings. And Robert Murphy, who was the chief American diplomat in North Africa, had been preparing the way by discreetly sounding out French officers, particularly General Mast who commanded the troops in Algiers. The question was who would be the most suitable French leader. General de Gaulle was ruled out because of his association with Churchill against Dakar, Syria, and Madagascar, and its embarrassment to French officers who were now loyal to the pro-German Vichy government. The rec-ommended choice was General Giraud, who had escaped from the Germans in the fall of France. As Giraud remarked, "We don't want the Americans to free us; we want their help to free ourselves, which is not quite the same." Giraud and de Gaulle detested each other.

De Gaulle had powerful emotions and a short fuse, stemming from his admiration for Napoleonic France and the emperor's defeat by the British, as well as the shame of subsequent French defeats by Germany. He was arrogant and autocratic. To an officer who wished to join him, he shouted, "I detest the English and the Americans. Get out!"[10] Evidently the fact that he needed help was humiliating and beneath his dignity. His well-meaning helpers were intolerable to him, while the Allies thought him ungrateful and found him impossible to work with.

When all preliminary steps had been taken, U.S. General Patton and the American armada approached the coast of Morocco on November 6, after a smooth crossing. But heavy seas and high surf from a storm made landings impossible until the eighth. They made a main landing at Fedala, north of Casablanca, and at two other locations. Some mishaps from inexperience caused further delays. Confusion and hesitancy were expected from the French as loyalty and expediency conflicted. Meanwhile, defensive fire from coastal batteries was slow in coming, and American gunners subdued it when it did. American inexperience also caused confusion at the beachhead, since their boats and troops were overloaded.

A new French battleship, the *Jean Bart*—still incomplete and confined to its berth—opened fire on Admiral Giffen's U.S. covering group. The group comprised the battleship *Massachusetts*, two heavy cruisers, and four destroy-ers. They returned fire, silencing the French battery and the battleship. But the engagement had distracted the U.S. landing force from the escape of French craft. Those vessels included a light cruiser, seven destroyers, and eight submarines that slipped away toward Fedula. Fortunately, Admiral Hewitt ordered their interception, and the covering group cut off their retreat.

The French survived by using smoke screens and submarines, and losing only one destroyer. But another was sunk in a second engagement. Only one of the eight French ships returned undamaged. Two others sank in the harbor and some others were badly damaged there by bombing. Then the French batteries and *Jean Bart's* guns opened fire again on the American troops.

Political developments in Algiers changed after that situation, since the French navy had been subdued in a battle on the very first day, which "had an old-style flavor."[11] The advance in Algiers took place without opposition on day two. Less progress was made on day three. But the French authorities of Admiral Darlan ordered a cease-fire on the tenth, pending an armistice.

Landings at Oran came up against greater opposition. The plan to capture the port depended on a double envelopment after landing. And cooperation between the American military force and the British naval force proved effective. A light armored column drove inland from the beachhead at Arzeu, and a smaller one from another landing point, to capture the airfield south of Oran. Their objective was to close it down before reinforcements could be landed from elsewhere. The landings were on time and the surprise arrival encountered no opposition. Disembarkation and unloading were slowed down by overloading troops, but the unloading of medium tanks carried in transports went smoothly after the Arzeu harbor was captured.

On the other hand, a rash attempt to take Oran harbor by direct assault suffered a serious reversal. It involved two small British cutters carrying four hundred American troops. The timing was bad, late enough for French units to be warned and prepared by the other landings. And a large American flag failed to prevent French fire that crippled both vessels, killing half the troops and crews. The rest of the Americans were taken prisoner by the French.

French Resistance

The landing party advanced from the beachhead and reached Tafaraoui airfield soon after 11:00 a.m. But the advance was halted before La Sénia airfield, as well as another column. Their converging infantry met stiffened resistance at the approach to Oran, where the whole plan of operations was dislocated by a French counterattack. U.S. General Fredenhall diverted forces from other missions, while La Sénia airfield was captured in the afternoon. But most of the French aircraft had already left, and the airfield was now unusable as a consequence of heavy French shellfire.

On the third morning, they launched a concentric attack toward the city of Oran. Their infantry attacks met with checks again from east and west, but their armored advance parties managed to drive into the city without opposition, and the French commanders agreed to surrender.

Landings at Algiers went smoother and quicker as a consequence of cooperation from the French commander in chief, General Mast. Otherwise, attempts to force an early entry into the harbor were resisted. Two British destroyers carrying an American infantry battalion and flying American flags immediately encountered heavy fire. One was hit badly and withdrew, while the other succeeded in disembarking her troops after the fourth attempt. But she was forced to cast off and withdraw under French shellfire, even though it was aimed only at stopping the landing party, rather than destroying it.

At daybreak on the seventh, the USS *Thomas Stone* was temporarily disabled 150 miles short of Algiers by a torpedo from a U-boat. Otherwise the seaborne approach met no more trouble at sea or from the air. Landings at Algiers were made by the Americans and some British Commandoes. The main British landings were on the beaches of Castiglione, where French troops had been instructed to offer no resistance. They reached the Maison Blanche airfield—where there was only token resistance—soon after 6:00 a.m. The British force took only eight hours to reach Blida airfield at about 9:00 a.m. Their advance on Algiers, however, was threatened when they encountered three French tanks at a strongpoint. The coastal battery also refused to surrender. It had to be bombed twice by warships and dive-bombers before yielding.

Troops landing west of Algiers were met with a friendly reception, with General Mast coming out to meet them. But he was relieved of his command by the Vichy-French, and they encountered resistance afterward. Nevertheless the collaborators of the Allies in Algiers aided the landings by welcoming and guiding the American troops. Opposition was generally paralyzed by the time of the landings. And the radio station was taken in readiness for a broadcast by General Giraud. But movement was too slow for what was needed.

When the Americans failed to appear by 7:00 a.m., the limitations of the collaborators' influence on their countrymen became manifest. Moreover, when they broadcast an appeal in the name of Giraud, who had also failed to arrive as expected, this fell so flat as to show that the Allies had overestimated the influence of his name. They soon began to lose control of the situation, and were brushed aside or put under arrest.[12]

Meanwhile, Murphy sent an urgent message to wake up Admiral Darlan. The admiral agreed to send a message to Marshal Pétain, reporting the situation. He asked for authorization to deal with it on the marshal's behalf, but then found himself almost under guard because the villa was surrounded by an armed band of anti-Vichy French. They were driven away by *gardes mobiles,* who arrested Murphy.

"Then Darlan and [General] Juin, eyeing one another like suspicious cats, went off to the headquarters in Algiers. From here Juin took steps to regain control, releasing General Koeltz and other officers who had been arrested by Mast and his associates, while putting the latter under arrest in their turn. Darlan, however, sent a further telegram to Marshal Pétain, just before 8:00 a.m., in which he emphasized that "the situation is getting worse and the defenses will soon be overwhelmed"—a palpable hint that it would be wise to bow to force majeure. Pétain's reply gave the authorization requested."[13]

Only a few hours later, Hitler put pressure on French Prime Minister Pierre Laval to accept his offer of German air support, and the Axis powers prepared to send forces to Tunisia. It triggered a race for Tunis—where "Rommel was shepherded warily toward the Tunisian frontier by Montgomery's forces."[14]

THE RACE FOR TUNIS

HITLER HELPED TO RESOLVE THE SITUATION and clarify all doubts in a search for an answer of how to free the French from an ambiguous situation and restore their self-respect. The Vichy-French government had taken possession of the unoccupied part of France in the Midi and the Massif Central. It had so far managed to stall Hitler's demands for armed support against Britain, but was under heavy armed pressure. Laval had already survived several encounters with Hitler and Mussolini. Now Hitler demanded air bases in French Tunisia. Laval continued to hedge by shifting the responsibility onto Marshal Pétain. But Hitler's patience had been pushed to its limit, and he ordered his mechanized forces and six Italian divisions to invade the rest of France at midnight.

German aircraft started to arrive near Tunis soon afterward on the afternoon of the ninth. The airlift was multiplied from the eleventh on. French troops in the vicinity were disarmed, and tanks, transport vehicles, guns, and stores were brought to Bizerta by sea.

The Allied cause was helped by the shock to French commanders in the south and in the French colonies. General Clark talked to Admiral Darlan and urged him to order the French fleet at Toulon to sail to a North African port and to order the Governor of Tunisia to resist the Germans. Clark was so frustrated at their postponements and delays that he threatened to place all the French leaders under arrest and lock them up on a ship in the harbor unless they came to a favorable decision in twenty-four hours.[1] He had to threaten them again because of Darlin's and General Juin's evasions and changes of mind.

Dealing with the pro-Nazi Darlan was abhorrent to all the Allied leaders. But Churchill came up with a solution to their moral doubts with a remark in a private letter to Roosevelt. The President liked it so much that he made it public. It was alleged to be an old proverb of the Orthodox Church: "My children, it is permitted to you in time of great danger to walk with the devil until you have crossed the bridge."[2]

Darlan finally agreed to cooperate with the Allies. But he was assassinated on Christmas Eve by a twenty-year-old Royalist in de Gaulle's circle.[3] Even so, had they not pressed Darlan to cooperate, the Allies would have had a tougher time, with greater losses of Allied lives, since there were 120,000 French troops in French Morocco, French Algiers, and French Tunisia.

The race to Tunisia began with seaborne landings. Two convoys sailed from Algiers transporting the British Thirty-Sixth Brigade and the Seventy-Eighth Division, with their stores. They arrived at Bagie on the morning of the eleventh, but landed on the beaches to avoid a possibly hostile reception from the French and lost valuable time. In any event, the local reception turned out to be friendly.

But it took two more days to bring in protective fighters, resulting in some of the ships being destroyed in air raids. Other Allied troops advanced overland from Algiers, followed by armored columns with Crusader III tanks and the two-pounder armed Valentines that were better armed.

The Afrika Korps was drawn across the Tunisian border in early February and made a stand at the Mareth Line in its first major attempt to stop Montgomery since El Alamein.[4] Even as the soldiers dug in to prepare for the encounter, Rommel flew west for a counterattack in a sequence of five battles for the Kasserine Pass, where he was up against Major-General Fredenhall's Second Corps. The actions showed why Marshall's original idea for an early attack on northwest France was unpractical.[5]

On the sixteenth, General Nehring, who formerly commanded the Afrika Korps until he was wounded, arrived to command the Axis forces, which by now consisted of an understrength parachute regiment in two of the battalions at Tunis. On the seventeenth, General Anderson ordered the Seventy-Eighth American Division to attack Tunis and destroy the enemy forces. The Germans rapidly thrust west, and the French troops fell back.

Despite the gung-ho attitude of the irrepressible two-star General Patton and several other U.S. generals, Rommel's attitude toward them was unambiguous when he stated, "The Americans had no practical battle experience, and it was for us to instill them with a deep inferiority complex from the start."[6]

Rommel's thrust was launched early on February 19, when he swung the Afrika Korps around to advance through the Kasserine Pass, which was held by U.S. Colonel Stark. Stark stopped him and had his own troops reinforced. Rommel attacked again the next day. But now he was resisted by a stubborn British armored squadron with infantry and a field battery under Lieutenant-Colonel A. C. Gore, sent to support the defense of the pass. Gore's forces were overcome when a panzer battalion was brought up and all his eleven tanks were knocked out. "The enemy was amazed at the quantity and quality of the American equipment captured more or less intact."[7]

Americans and British forces reached the pass after three days and organized Italian POW burial parties to bury all the corpses they found there.[8] After the defeat of General Eisenhower's superior force of U.S. troops at the Kasserine Pass, Alexander remarked on the inexperience of the Americans: "final victory . . is not . . . just around the corner." Fredenhall was replaced by Patton. The unnecessary loss of life was not unnoticed by the British public—envious of the higher standard of living of the GIs—who criticized the Americans for throwing their weight around to little effect. They were weary of war after three years of it.

It was in that weary and ungenerous mood that many hoped Germany and Russia would destroy each other, while Americans were happy with the thought of the British Empire collapsing at the end of the war, and Britons relished any news of American defeats. The same war weariness was felt by Britain's industrial workers, who initiated unofficial strikes.

Nevertheless, Rommel seemed depressed, according to Field Marshal Albert Kesselring, who was the commander in chief in the south and had overall responsibility for the Mediterranean Basin. He visited Kasserine to confer with Rommel and found him in a depressed mood. He wrote afterward that "Rommel was physically worn out and psychologically fatigued." He noted that "he had undoubtedly turned into a tired old man."[9]

The defeat of over four thousand Allied troops who became prisoners of war in Italy, and were marched from the Colosseum and through Rome by Mussolini, ended any mood of overconfidence by U.S. generals—although the Kesserine Pass was recaptured by the Allies a few days later. Meanwhile, Rommel complained that he was not getting the supplies he needed. Patton attacked his rear, while the British Eighth Army attacked the Mareth Line on March 20.

The effect of Patton on one side and Montgomery on the other side of Rommel led to competition between the two generals, both possessed by pride that led to enmity, since both of them were inordinately vain. Wrote Patton in his diary, "When I think of the greatness of my job and realize that I am what I am, I am amazed, but on reflection, who is as good as I am? I know of no one."[10] Each was wary of the other, sensing a rival who might overshadow him. Montgomery no doubt recognized an impetuous maverick when he saw one, and Patton was jealously afraid of being outshone by the brilliant front-line commander. They were reluctant partners and jealous rivals.

Meanwhile, Hitler continued to make the same mistakes as before and followed them by issuing "stand or die" orders that were of no advantage to anyone but the Allied forces.[11]

The Offensive

The battle was followed by German dive-bombing. Skirmishes continued for some time with each side outwitting the other, until U.S. Lieutenant-General Anderson's planned offensive to capture Tunis began on the twenty-fifth. German strength had been tripled during Anderson's lengthy pause to consolidate his thoughts and his troops, so that he was unsure whether he now possessed sufficient strength to gain his objective. General Eisenhower hurriedly reinforced him with more American units. But only part of the reinforcements arrived in time. Anderson was rated "not much good" by Brooke.

The three-pronged Allied offensive started late and advanced cautiously as far as only twelve miles in the first two days while a small parachute battalion of German engineers fell back before it. The offensive carefully pushed on twice as far, until the Americans ran into an ambush on the twenty-eighth that German parachutists had prepared for them. They were forced to abandon the larger attack against strengthening defenses on the thirtieth. That, in turn, resulted in the failure of an amphibious assault by an Anglo-American commando unit, which was forced to withdraw.

The center prong of the offensive was formed by the British Blade Force, strengthened by an American light tank battalion. They were stopped by ten German panzer tanks and two infantry companies. They managed to knock out eight of the tanks with 37-mm antitank guns. But both sides became confused by the "fog of war." The Allies were more cautious than the bolder German troops led by General Nehring—except for Major Rudolph Barlow, who had been sent on a mission at the edge of the Djedeida airfield and, seizing an opportunity that presented itself, had swept in with seventeen tanks and destroyed twenty newly arrived enemy aircraft. So Nehring became more cautious and hastily pulled back.

The battles continued to ebb and flow as victory that had been in one army's grasp was snatched away by the other.

General Eisenhower remarked later of the constant complaints of no air cover and astonishing exaggerations about the conditions and damage from U.S. soldiers not used to war, with such remarks as, "Our troops will surely have to retreat; humans cannot exist in these conditions."[12] Many were former farm boys who had enlisted because they were out of work, not well enough trained for the job, untried and untested in battle conditions.

On the other side, Field Marshal Kesserling reproached Nehring for being too cautious and defensive in the face of much larger forces. He told Nehring to regain lost ground. So a counterthrust was made by three panzer companies on December 1. The Tenth Panzer Division had just arrived with a fresh panzer battalion. The result was that the Allied spearhead force barely escaped the Germans and had to abandon their equipment and transport. And the Germans took more than a thousand British prisoners and more than fifty tanks.

Recent German reinforcements included five of the new fifty-six-ton Tiger tanks, which were monsters, known as a secret weapon and being tested in combat.

The Allied commanders renewed their offensive also with increased strength. But now Nehring was inspired to increase his gains by an outflanking maneuver south of the Medjerda River and recapture Medjez el Bab. First they attacked an observation post on December 6, overrunning the defenders. The newly arrived commander of the British Fifth Corps ordered the withdrawal of his troops to a position near Hill 290 and obtained Anderson's agreement to a longer withdrawal to the west of Medjez el Bab. But Eisenhower turned down the proposal.

Writing to a friend on the seventh, Eisenhower remarked, "I think the best way to describe our operations to date is that they have violated every recognized principle of war, are in conflict with all operational and logistic methods laid down in textbooks, and will be condemned in their entirety by all Leavenworth and War College cases for the next twenty-five years."[13]

On December 10, the Germans resumed their flank thrust with about thirty medium and two Tiger tanks. They were checked two miles before Medjez el Bab by a well-situated French battery. Then they became bogged down attempting to outflank the guns by moving off the road. But the problem was only temporary. Then they were obliged to withdraw when threatened by a detachment of American Combat Command B. And then Combat Command became confused while withdrawing from an exposed position after dark. They reversed on a false rumor of a threat and turned off on a muddy track near the river, where the remaining tanks and other vehicles were bogged down in mud. They were left with only forty-four tanks fit for action, having lost three-quarters of their strength. This catastrophe reduced the prospects of the Allied push to Tunis.

Colonel-General Jurgen von Arnim replaced Nehring on the ninth, taking supreme command of the Axis forces—now known as the Fifth Panzer Army. With the arrival of more reinforcements, they expanded their cover of Tunis and Bizerta into a bridgehead. Allied Intelligence estimated that the Axis forces possessed approximately twenty-five thousand fighting troops and ten thousand administrative personnel, with eighty tanks—which was actually more than they had. It compared with the Allied strength of about forty thousand troops—twenty thousand British, twelve thousand Americans, and seven thousand French. The odds in Allied favor were more than two to one. But numbers weren't everything: there was the matter of American inexperience and French loyalty.

Anderson decided to use the full moon to start an offensive on the twenty-fourth with a nighttime assault. The Americans mounted preliminary attacks on Longstop Hill and Hill 466. But both developed into seesaw battles because of bad weather and confusion, and the main assault was postponed.

Eisenhower and Anderson abandoned the proposed offensive because of the setbacks and torrential rain that began to turn the ground into a bog. It was clear that the Allies had lost the race.[14]

But ironically, the Allied failure in Tunisia turned out to their advantage, since it encouraged Hitler and Mussolini to pour in huge reinforcements and build up a defense of 250,000 men, while the sea at their backs was dominated by the Allied fleets. It meant the Axis troops would be trapped if defeated. They were overwhelmed in May. Their defeat allowed the British a jubilant run on Sicily in July, which Churchill described as the soft underbelly of Europe.

THE RUSSIAN CAMPAIGN

FÜHRER DIRECTIVE NO. 21 WAS SENT to the most important people in the Reich. It began: "The mass of the Russian army in Western Russia is to be destroyed in daring operations, by driving forward deep armored wedges, and the retreat of units capable of combat into the vastness of Russian territory is to be prevented."[1]

The Wehrmacht launched a surprise attack on Soviet Russia before dawn on Sunday, June 22, 1941. They destroyed about 1,200 aircraft on the ground in the morning. The chief of Russia's Bomber Command had little choice but to commit suicide the next day. The Germans followed up by destroying 90 percent of the Red Army's new Mechanized Corps in the first week of fighting. General Zhukov phoned Marshal Stalin to inform him of the German invasion, and Stalin went into shock. When a Politburo delegation arrived to visit him, Stalin at first suspected they intended to arrest him.[2] As soon as he recovered from his initial shock, he had five million people conscripted into the armed forces, including eight hundred thousand women. But he walked around in his apartment in a daze for a week.

It took six months for two hundred new divisions to be readied for battle. By the time Marshal Stalin became supreme commander, Russia had lost 4,800 tanks, 9,480 guns, and 1,777 planes.[3] German bombs began to fall on Moscow on July 21. When civilians panicked, Lavrenti Beria, who commanded the Security Police (NKVD), placed roadblocks on all main exits from the city and shot anyone who tried to escape.

Given that the Soviet Union appeared to be defeated by late August of 1941, with about half its territory, half its population, and half its industrial and agricultural production in German hands, Russia's recovery under Stalin was extraordinary.[4] Only four months later, the Russians had killed

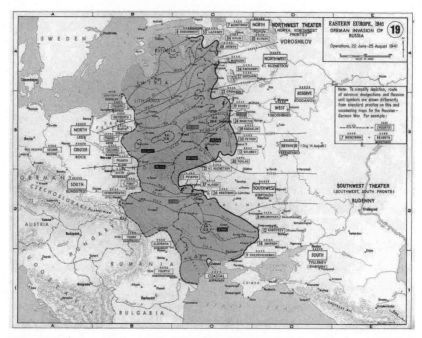

The 1941 German invasion of Soviet Russia, code-named "Operation Barbarossa."

more than 200,000 Wehrmacht troops, wounded 726,000, and captured 400,000, leaving another 113,000 incapacitated by frostbite.[5] Nevertheless, Soviet Russia would need help.

At first, British and American generals were dubious about whether the Russians could survive the German onslaught, until Soviet Russia turned the enemy back from Moscow in December 1941. The Allied attack in Dieppe on August 19, 1942, was intended to help them by diverting German forces away from Russia. But it turned out to be a disaster, particularly for the Canadians, three-quarters of whom were killed in the first six hours. Lord Mountbatten was blamed for faulty intelligence and planning.

Churchill's first conference in the Kremlin lasted nearly four hours. Present were Marshal Stalin, Foreign Minister Molotov, Marshal Voroshilov, Averell Harriman, and the British ambassador to Moscow. The agenda began immediately with the Second Front. Churchill had met Molotov before in London; since then the subject had been discussed exhaustively between the British and American governments. Stalin already knew from Molotov that the Allies were preparing for an invasion of Europe in 1943, and he wanted it earlier. Stalin's view was that wars could not be run without risks, and that troops must be blooded in battle to have any idea of their real value.

When they moved on to the bombing of Germany, Stalin "emphasized the importance of striking at the morale of the German population."[6] He had immediately grasped the strategic importance of Operation Torch. It would hit Rommel in the back. It would overawe Spain. It would produce fighting between Germans and French in France. And further, it would expose Italy to the whole brunt of the war. Churchill reminded him that it would also shorten the sea route through the Mediterranean to Sicily and the toe of Italy, and then north, up through to the rest of Europe to Germany.

He and Marshal Stalin established a friendly and respectful meeting from the beginning as they sized each other up. But they argued vigorously for two hours at their next meeting, when Stalin made a number of disagreeable remarks about the way the British army fought the Germans, as a preamble to pushing again for a Second Front in 1942. He explained that the Russian people were suffering in dreadful conditions to save their land from the Germans and survive. He had nothing but praise for the RAF in the Battle of Britain. Churchill's frank and determined attitude won him over, and each knew instinctively that the other could not be bullied into changing their plans. Nevertheless, Stalin repeated his arguments for an earlier Second Front in an aide-mémoire he handed to Churchill before he left.[7]

"[Soviet Ambassador] Maisky repeated Russian demands for an immediate Second Front, pointing out that if Russia were defeated, the British chance of winning the war might well be gone forever."[8] The same claim could be made if Britain had been defeated, or the United States. Each now depended on the others. It was a case of "one for all and all for one."

Aid to Russia

Churchill visited Moscow again at the end of the year, resolving to aid Russia as much as was in Britain's and America's power. Millions of Russian soldiers and airmen were holding back the German onslaught with great courage in dreadful frontline conditions the West couldn't even imagine. But Stalin was as confident that he would win as Churchill was confident in a British victory. Churchill recommended to President Roosevelt that they should give the Russians direct military help by placing a strong Anglo-American air force in the Caspian Sea. Roosevelt agreed.

Disagreement with Russia came on October 15 when Molotov demanded that Hitler's deputy, Rudolf Hess, be tried as a war criminal. Hess was now in British hands after flying on his own to Scotland and dropping in a field by parachute, where he'd been captured. Stalin feared that Hitler might have sent him to negotiate a separate peace between Britain and Germany so he would be free to concentrate his forces on defeating Russia.* Churchill chose to dismiss the request as understandable in the circumstances and emphasized to Foreign Secretary Eden that the only thing that would have any positive effect was fighting and winning.[9] He continued to admire the commanding and purposeful character of Marshal Stalin, whom he respected because Stalin was determined not to allow another inch of Russian territory to fall into German hands.

President Roosevelt was just as single-minded in his resolve: "I feel sure the Russians are going to hold this winter, and that we should proceed vigorously with our plans both to supply them and set up an air force to fight with them. I want us to be able to say to Mr. Stalin that we have carried out our obligations one hundred percent."[10]

It is almost impossible to determine exactly when Winston Churchill became the twentieth-century man of destiny and the greatest hero in the entire history of the English-speaking peoples.

---

* Although Hess was thought to be Hitler's closest confidant and therefore most probably sent to Britain by him to negotiate peace, it turned out to be untrue. Hess had always opposed war with England, but he had been sidelined by Nazi rivals and decided to negotiate peace on his own. He parachuted into Scotland without first having made contact with anyone who had the authority to negotiate peace terms. There was evidence of an unhinged mind when he believed he had once met the Duke of Hamilton, whom he thought had significant power in England. Hess was easily captured, since he broke his ankle on arrival. When interviewed by Lord Beaverbrook, the Lord Chancellor, and others, he began to realize that no one was prepared to listen to any peace terms. Mental illness remained with him until he committed suicide in Spandau Prison in Berlin in 1987 at the age of ninety-two.[11]

His judgments and actions affected everybody's lives. As soon as he was mature enough to think and understand and feel clearly, he seemed to have been aware of taking part in great historical events. That awareness of his possible position in history began in childhood, where some of the influences that would make an impact on the world met and shaped him into a patriotic hero in one of the most cynical and ruthless centuries of our age.[12] And yet, they were England's years of glory as much as Elizabethan England had been when it shaped the English character. His knowledge of history gave him a sense of perspective, proportion, and purpose. It was this that enabled him to build a personal friendship with Stalin and Roosevelt and persuade them to follow the wartime strategies he preferred.

The Arctic Convoys

British and American ships began carrying aid to Russia on a large scale at the end of September 1941. British convoys sailed to Murmansk in North Russia, since ice blocked Archangel in winter. The German navy and air force hurriedly increased their strength in Norway and attacked the Arctic convoys in the spring of 1942. The British eastbound convoy PQ 17 sailed to Russia at the end of June, carrying aircraft, tanks, and other vehicles.

The British Admiralty ordered the vessels to scatter, to make them more difficult targets for attack, believing it was about to be overwhelmed by German warships on July 4. Instead, they were attacked by enemy aircraft and U-boats. Out of the 36 vessels, only 13 survived the attacks. Only 87 aircraft were delivered (with 210 lost); 164 tanks were delivered (but 430 were lost); 896 vehicles were delivered (but 3,350 were lost). Only two-thirds of the other cargo reached port.

Later British convoys of merchant ships were given far greater escorts, so that German aircraft and U-boats suffered greatly. Forty Arctic convoys sailed from 1941 on. Of 811 ships, 720 now reached their destination; 58 were sunk and 33 turned back. They delivered 5,000 tanks and 7,000 aircraft. They lost 18 warships and 98 merchant ships. The Germans lost the *Scharnhorst* battle cruiser, 3 destroyers, and 38 U-boats in attempts to stop the convoys arriving in Russia.

The strength of the German U-boat fleet had risen to almost 250 by the end of 1941. Hitler decided to send them to penetrate the coastal route between Newfoundland and New York, with instant success, since the Americans were not yet ready to protect their shipping. U-boats sank thirty-one ships off the United States and Canadian coasts. Many U-boats with some of the best commanders were already hunting for defenseless shipping in the Mediterranean. Others were in Norwegian and Arctic seas. Now they spread to Florida and preyed on oil tankers in the Caribbean Sea as the scale of shipping losses grew. Losses to U-boats in February rose to seventy-one ships, all but two sunk in American waters.

To ensure shortening the turnaround time of convoy ships when in ports and under repair, Churchill formed a Battle of the Atlantic Committee and chaired it himself.[13] "'The U-boat at sea must be hunted,' he declared, 'the U-boat in the building yard or in dock must be bombed. The Fokke Wulf, and other bombers . . . must be attacked in the air and in their nests.'" There was a net improvement of thirteen days in turnaround time as a result. And he urged as a high priority antiaircraft guns for merchant ships. When he explained the convoy problem to Roosevelt, the President informed him that the United States would extend its patrol area and report any Axis raiders operating west of that line.[14]

But the British had not overcome the losses from U-boats, and Churchill was shocked that German industries were now replacing and even exceeding them. Then British losses fell sharply in July 1941, attributed to greater protection from more destroyer escorts supplied by the United States and production from British and Canadian shipyards. Even so, Britain's bombers had to be diverted from destroying German industries to attacking German warships until Bomber Command was allowed to use its whole weight on German industrial cities. Churchill worried about the full use of long-range bombers for that purpose.[15] Then came a study, known as the Butt Report, which suggested that only about 5 percent of bombers actually dropped their bomb loads within five miles of their targets. It severely changed Churchill's confidence in the value of the bombing raids. There seemed to be no certain method to win wars. By autumn 1941, he realized that it was essential to get ground troops onto European soil to defeat the German forces.

THE BATTLE FOR STALINGRAD

THE POINT AT WHICH STALINGRAD BEGAN to feature in Hitler's plans was when Leningrad and Moscow refused to be defeated by German troops, and were even launching counteroffensives against the Wehrmacht in December 1941. Hitler's response on May 8, 1942, included forces from Italy, Rumania, Hungary, and Slovakia, although they were not as reliable or effective as German troops. The German dictator made a desperate attempt to capture Stalingrad and the Caucasus at the same time. "If we do not capture the oil supplies of the Caucasus by the autumn," Hitler said, "then I shall have to face the fact that we cannot win this war."

The German spearhead had already surged 350 miles by July 28, and now the panzers had only 40 more miles to go to breach the Volga. Stalingrad was under siege by the last week in August, and another German army had reached the oil fields in Chechnya.

Most German soldiers were overwhelmed by the immensity of the Russian plains. The endless space was simply too large to take in. They were stupefied by rivers wide enough for artillery to barely be able to fire across the expanse, and the endless rolling steppes that seemed to lead nowhere. Burning heat turned to subzero windchill and blizzards swept across the bare, open spaces. They were demoralized by the vast distance they had traveled from home. German infantrymen marched for thousands of miles day after day until they felt lost in another world. They had won their battles so far, but as they drove deeper and deeper into an enormous unknown terrain, they wondered if they would ever return home.[1]

Young German conscripts in the German army suffered in unexpectedly appalling conditions. "Wearing clothes looted from peasants, its frost-bitten soldiers, with unkempt beards, noses peeling and cheeks burned by the cold, were unrecognizable from those who had advanced eastward the previous summer, singing marching songs."[2] Historian Antony Beevor described their typical practice of sawing off the frozen legs of corpses and thawing them over a fire to get the boots off for themselves. Their immediate enemy was subzero temperatures in which frostbite could turn to gangrene and result in amputation. Overworked army surgeons in field hospitals "simply threw the sawn-off hands and legs outside" onto growing piles of body parts in the snow.

Winter clothing had not arrived. Expecting to peel off the customary padded jackets from dead Russian peasants, they found the corpses froze quickly and too solidly for that. Dysentery was commonplace and presented the problem of continually lowering their trousers in icy winter temperatures—particularly when it was not unusual to come across troops from either side frozen to death while in the act of fighting each other. "Some of them were leaning against each other, others hugging each other. Some propping themselves with a rifle, others holding a sub-machine gun. Many of them had their legs chopped off."[3]

Despite the hardships of the Russian campaign, the hardiness and discipline of German troops was extraordinary, and they were well organized, frequently taking winning initiatives in battle against Russian troops.

Incendiaries

Lieutenant-General Paulus, who commanded the Sixth Army, had thrust his troops down the north side of a corridor between the River Don and the Donetz. On August 23, 1942, women and children dug antitank trenches and piled up berms to defend oil tanks and prevent German troops from crossing the River Volga, while the German Sixth Army reached the bend of the River Don and proceeded to cross it in boats, then build pontoon bridges across the water. Paulus believed he could take Stalingrad in twenty-four days.

Only three months earlier, Paulus had been a newcomer to the Russian front and been shocked by the force of the Soviet army. But this time he was supported by intense bombardment from the air, where General Wolfram von Richthofen meticulously carpet bombed the city of Stalingrad for two days with twelve hundred aircraft. Using incendiary bombs right from the start, Stalingrad, with a population close to a million, soon became a fire-balled inferno of roaring flames. Young women fired the antiaircraft guns until all of them were killed by the bombs or incinerated by the flames from the incendiaries. It was the noise of the antiaircraft batteries that first warned Russian civilians of the air attack that would kill forty thousand of the population. Those young women, not long out of high school, were the front line of Stalingrad's defenses.

Meanwhile, the famine in encircled Leningrad had killed close to a million that winter. But the Russian defense forces had survived the German stranglehold.

Stalingrad was under siege by the last week in August, while other German forces had reached the oil fields in Chechnya. On September 2, Hitler gave orders that "the entire male population should be eliminated" on entering Stalingrad. He was fixated on this city, apparently because it was named after Stalin, and the men he relished planning to destroy were a symbol of his intention to crush Marshal Stalin. It was like a personal vendetta. In the absence of real gains, symbols became more and more important for him.

From the moment of occupation, German military police began searching house to house for communists and Jews. Raping Russian women began. Almost simultaneously, the NKVD destroyed any defeatist attitudes by executing thirteen thousand Russians for cowardice or desertion. Civilians were trapped and crushed between the murderous embraces of two brutal and irresistible forces.

Meanwhile, Britain had been forced to stop sending military supplies to Russia by convoy after twenty-nine Allied ships had been sunk by German aircraft and U-boats, out of a convoy of thirty-four. Churchill felt he should visit Stalin and explain the problem. It was one of Churchill's worst periods, starting with the loss of Tobruk. This would be his first visit to Moscow, together with Averell Harriman. He told Stalin about the RAF bombing raid on Cologne first, before telling him about the delays in the Second Front. Stalin merely sneered that "someone who was unwilling to take risks could never win a war." But after a visit to Stalin's home, the marshal's mood changed under the influence of alcohol, and Churchill thought he had made a friend.

Street Fighting

The Battle for Stalingrad became a major struggle for possession of the city. When Khrushchev asked Major-General Vasily Chuikov what he intended to do, Chuikov replied that they would defend the city or die in the attempt. It would require persistence and cunning to wear the Germans down. Knowing the Germans disliked close combat, he resorted to vicious street fighting from house to house and block to block in urban streets, with advances and retreats fought stubbornly and relentlessly from shattered warehouses to steelworks and bombed factories, "night raids by fighting patrols of men armed with sub-machine guns, grenades, knives and even sharpened spades. They attacked through cellars and sewers."[4] Fighting took place day and night, "from floor to floor in ruined building blocks." The Germans described it as a war of rats, with efficient Russian snipers who seemed to be concealed everywhere, in bombed-out buildings and cellars and on rooftops. German officers were a prime target.

All the advantages of blitzkrieg and tank warfare were lost in the closeness of city and suburban streets and industrial zones. Snipers were more effective here than armored tanks with cannons. And bayonets and knives and hammers were more deadly in close combat than guns. Russian soldiers learned to embrace their enemies in order to be close enough to slide in the blade of a knife. German soldiers who were accustomed to firing shells from a distance were unused to the harsh conditions and the shortages of supplies, where they were closer to death than to life, with Russian soldiers fighting desperately to win in any way they could.

The urban street fighting lasted from the end of August 1942 to the beginning of February 1943. The street battles among the factories in the industrial areas of Stalingrad alone lasted for six months. The Wehrmacht occupied 90 percent of the city at one point. But General Vasily Chuikov's Soviet Sixty-Second Army was indefatigable despite 75 percent casualties. He had to be as stubborn and ruthless as Zhukov.

But Stalingrad was not intended to be the German army's primary goal—that was to cut the flow of oil from Astrakhan up the Volga to northern Russia and to give cover for the German southern advance.

The Germans took 625,000 Russian prisoners and seven thousand tanks, six thousand artillery pieces, and more than four hundred aircraft, in July and

August. Despite thousands of German casualties, the relative ease and speed of the campaign tempted Hitler to pursue two different strategies simultaneously—to occupy Baku for its oil and take Stalingrad instead of moving on.

When Rostov fell to the enemy for the second time, it became a rallying cry with Stalin's Order No. 227—"Not a step back!" Stalin's Order meant that no one was permitted to retreat without official orders to do so. And anyone who surrendered would be treated as a "traitor to the Motherland." He would be shot and his family would be liable to imprisonment.[5] "Panic-mongers and cowards must be destroyed on the spot. The retreat mentality must be decisively eliminated."

"The people are losing faith in the Red Army," Stalin claimed. It meant, "Iron discipline, harsh punishment, and no retreat without authorization."[6] It also combined an appeal to patriotism.

Once again, when Marshal Stalin and Winston Churchill met, Stalin requested the British to open a Second Front to draw off German troops from Russia. But Britain did not have enough landing craft available to cross the English Channel, and the Allies were not yet ready for a "Great Invasion" of the continent of Europe. Stalin was still dissatisfied. To urge on the Allies, he confided that he did not believe Hitler had enough divisions to fight two campaigns simultaneously.

That was the background when Stalin recalled Field Marshal Georgy Zhukov from the Western Front and appointed him Deputy Supreme Commander to fight the battle for Stalingrad "unwaveringly, ruthlessly, and with unshakable conviction."[7] Zhukov was one of the greatest field generals of World War II. And yet, only three years previously, he had kept a bag packed ready for prison during Stalin's purge of the Red Army, when thirty thousand high-ranking Soviet officers had been arrested for interrogation or torture by the NKVD. Fortunately for Stalin and Russia, the paranoid hysteria of the "Great Terror" had passed Zhukov by.[8]

The Turning Point

The turning point of the war on the Eastern Front came in the spring of 1943 as an aggressive Russian tidal force swept the German army away from Stalingrad.

The Germans withdrew to Rosin, while the rest formed a strong and firm bridge-head. Russian troops pressed them back to the line where the Germans had launched their offensive the previous summer. The German troops suffered huge losses as the Russians regained all the territory they had lost in the year past.

> The advance of a Russian army is something that Westerners can't imagine," wrote historian Liddell Hart. "Behind the tank spearheads rolls on a vast horde, largely mounted on horses. The soldier carries a sack on his back, with dry crusts of bread and raw vegetables collected on the march from the fields and villages. The horses eat the straw from the house roofs—they get very little else. The Russians are accustomed to carry on for as long as three weeks in this primitive way, when advancing.[9]

Marshal Zhukov was in command of the Russian armies west of Kiev. His forces penetrated thirty miles a day. General Manilovsky overcame the Germans' untenable position and began a scissors movement, capturing a port at the mouth of the Dnieper river bend and cornering part of the German forces. General Konev's armored forces struck in the direction of the Dniester.

The German onslaught on Russia, code-named "Operation Barbarossa," had been quick and ferocious when Hitler invaded on June 22, 1941, the day prior to the anniversary of Napoleon's fatal mistake of invasion in 1812. Now Hitler's delusion of annexing Russia was shown to have been just as suicidal. Then, the emperor of France had been forced to retreat before the end of the year by Field Marshal Kutuzov's Tsarist forces, whereas Hitler was not driven out for three long years of bitter and destructive fighting. For the Russians— just like the British—"did not see they were beaten."[10]

Now, the sweeping advance of the Russian counteroffensive to the west was unstoppable. The might of the onslaught fell on the German Army Group Center commanded by General Busch. He knew that, although the Russian offensive last winter had failed to break down the German defense forces, it had been a narrow margin between success and failure. They had fought like wild beasts. He and his officers were anxious about their chances of resisting the Russians again. The German army wanted to withdraw to the historic line of the Beresina River, ninety miles to the rear. But Hitler was against it, so there was no question of arguing—he preferred to have German troops die rather than retreat or give in. And the Germans were afraid of what would happen to them if the Russians took them prisoner, as many were. Being a prisoner of war of either side meant a slow death from starvation or freezing to death, which was more painful but quicker.

Stalingrad

Fortunately, despite their huge losses, the Russians still had immense reserves, so that when Stalingrad did not fall as Hitler wished, he grew threatening and dismissed General Halder as chief of staff after he had unsuccessfully attempted to persuade Hitler to abandon the city. Hitler seemed to recognize that his gamble on defeating Soviet Russia had failed. He replaced him with a younger man motivated by a new promotion. But he, too, wavered soon after seeing the reality of the immense barren wastes of the broad Russian front and the peasant brutality of the troops that matched their own German ruthlessness. Now Hitler's rage turned to Rommel's retreat in North Africa.

Nevertheless, the outside world still expected to see a Soviet collapse in Russia and a German advance in North Africa. Only with hindsight do we see the vast difference between perception and facts.

Russian troops made small exploratory attacks to test the German resistance of their thin front lines. But Hitler was determined to hold Stalingrad for the prestige it would give him.

Meanwhile, the Germans were running short of supplies, tanks, and air support. And while Hitler was encouraged by the perilousness of the Russian position, his generals and frontline troops were demoralized by the awful fighting conditions, in which it was too cold to wash. Sentries who fell asleep never woke up.[11] And soldiers were too exhausted to lift a comrade onto a stretcher, leaving him to freeze to death on the ground. Men were desperate to escape. In the meantime, the Russians waited patiently and watched the German exhaustion reach a tipping point—just as the great Field Marshal Mikhail Kutuzov had done with Napoleon's Grand Armée in 1812.

Then the brilliant quartet of Russian generals chose the right moment to strike. Zhukov, Vasilevsky, Voronov, and Konev soon turned the tide against the enemy. They encircled the German Sixth Army and a corps of the Fourth Panzer Army. In only a few days, German troops who had flooded without hindrance into Russia began to recede like an outgoing tide.[12]

By the time that Stalin's chief of staff, Vasilevsky, was targeting Berlin in his mind, the Russians had received streams of new American vehicles to motorize their infantry brigades and move faster than on foot, and the monstrous new King Tiger tanks were equipped with 222-mm guns instead of the old 88-mm. The tanks were also more heavily armored than before. The Russian numerical superiority against the enemy was now five to one. Soviet forces prepared for the "Great Envelopment" of General Paulus's Sixth Army.

The Russian offensive began on January 12, 1945. Ten armies of seventy-two divisions were deployed with the support of two air armies. And, fortunately for the Allies, Hitler had focused his troops on the Oder, at the expense of leaving the Rhine exposed to British and American attacks.

Fog hanging over the battlefield kept the air force on the ground but cloaked General Konev's advance as the Russian armed forces thrust forward on a broad front. Zhukov launched his offensive as his right wing wheeled toward Warsaw and his left wing to Radom on the fourteenth and sixteenth. Rokossovsky's forces also struck on the fourteenth. Warsaw fell on the seventeenth. Konev captured Cracow on the nineteenth. They had advanced a hundred miles on a four-hundred-mile front, so that Konev's forces struck German soil on January 20, as each of the four leading generals outdid the others in a competitive victory over the demoralized German armies.

Chaos and confusion were everywhere, with the roads strewn haphazardly with the usual battered and broken vehicles and abandoned chattels that invariably got left behind on the fringes of battlefields.[13]

On January 23, Hitler told General Paulus he was forbidden to surrender. A week later he promoted him to field marshal to ensure he wouldn't, since no German field marshal had ever surrendered his forces in the field. Paulus was captured a week later and his army collapsed. Hitler was disgusted that he didn't shoot himself rather than be taken prisoner. Some nine thousand other Germans and their Russian volunteers were taken prisoner by the Russians.

They were the only survivors of Hitler's gamble on taking Russia. Out of the more than a quarter of a million who had invaded, many died in captivity; just as many Russians died in German POW camps. Only about 11 percent ever returned to Germany. As for the Russian volunteers who had helped the Germans or fought for them, most appeared to have been clubbed to death by the NKVD after they surrendered, to save the cost of using valuable bullets.

The Russian Offensive

Space was the Russians' friend; it enabled them to maneuver and baffle the Germans. And, as a result of America's supplies, large numbers of motorized infantry followed close behind their tanks. The enormous Russian pincer maneuver resembled the one the Germans had undertaken three years earlier. And only some of the German trapped forces succeeded in slipping out before it closed on the others.

German troops made a modest stand near Minsk before continuing their retreat. The Russian advance was likened to a semicircle of spear points, each thrusting toward its own separate target—Dvinsk, Vilna, Grodno, Bialystok, and Brest-Litovsk. Russian mobile forces bypassed Vilna on each side as a center spear pierced it on the ninth. It fell on the thirteenth. Then another spear point entered Grodno.

The Red Army swept all German troops out of White Russia and even overran half of northeastern Poland by mid-July. Its western wing flew right into Lithuania and close to East Prussia. The Russian offensive south of the Pripet Marshes drove like two horns of a bull toward Lublin and the Vistula, and converged with Marshal Rokossovsky's drive north to Brest-Litovsk. Its left horn thrust through the German front near Luck and Lwow, which fell to Marshall Konev's forces on July 27. The Russian offensive was so vast that it stretched from the Carpathian foothills to northern Poland, Latvia, and East Prussia. And yet, even that offensive was subsidiary to the deep thrust in the center.

On August 1, German troops retreated over the bridge crossing the Vistula in Warsaw, and Polish resistance leaders gave the signal for an uprising.

Nearly three years later, and with a loss of over thirty million German and Russian lives, the entire German invasion could be seen as a pointless and disastrous waste, and Hitler as, most probably, the biggest imbecile in history. The number of deaths in the Russian Campaign was almost half of the entire number on every battlefront in the entire war; it was estimated at about seventy million, with savage butchery, the like of which the world had never known before.

It seemed as if Hitler had been playing at tin soldiers with his generals, who didn't have the courage to oppose him. He was indifferent to their fate and considered the young German troops to be merely his own toys to be disposed of as he wished.

In spite of his years as a frontline courier in World War I and his formidable library of books on military affairs, which he carefully studied, including the famous Schlieffen Plan, "Hitler learnt nothing from the past," wrote historian Andrew Roberts.[14] Had he done so, he would never have sought war on two fronts simultaneously. And yet, when General Halder informed him that transport would be ready, he chose June 22 for the attack code-named Barbarossa. An earlier date would have given problems of wet spring weather. He claimed later that an earlier start would have given him victory before winter arrived. But "it was too wet to invade very much earlier" with heavy trucks and tanks getting bogged down in the mud and abandoned in rural back lanes.[15]

General Heinz Guderian claimed afterward that, after the briefing on Barbarossa, he was convinced that disaster loomed. But according to him, everyone else was optimistic and "impervious to criticism or objections."[16] Nevertheless, General Blumentritt wrote in a letter long after the event, in 1965, that the war was lost when Hitler attacked Russia in 1941, without having peace in the West.[17] But the general never said so at the time. No one criticized the plan. And Hitler believed that the whole Russian edifice would collapse from an attack.[18]

One of Hitler's purposes was to ensure that Britain had no allies and would sue for peace after Russia's defeat. "With Russia smashed, Britain's last hope would be shattered. Germany would be the master of Europe and the Balkans." As for the Russian Slavs, he told his generals, they would last only six weeks.[19]

Chief of Staff General Halder kept warning against Hitler's overconfidence. He pointed out that new Russian divisions seemed to appear from out of nowhere. He noted in his war diary how Hitler "explodes in a fit of insane rage and hurls gravest reproaches against the General Staff when faced with reality. . . . This chronic tendency to underrate enemy capabilities is gradually assuming grotesque proportions and develops into a positive danger."[20]

Historians continue to speculate when the turning point of the war was reached. For the British, it was between the first and second desert battles at El Alamein, when Britain's wartime industries finally caught up with Germany's. For the Russians and Germans it was when the full force of the defense and retaliation in Leningrad and Stalingrad swung in the Allies' favor. Stalin learned of Field Marshal Manstein's intended assault with his Eleventh Army and launched a preemptive attack known as the "Great Envelopment." Hitler had thought the Russians were finished and planned to crush them finally with overwhelming force. Instead, the Russians encircled them and struck them from Leningrad and the Volkhov Front, crushing the German invaders toward the end of August.

Manstein's desperate attempt to break through the Russian cordon and relieve the garrison from the southwest in December failed.[21] And when a Russian offensive threatened his flank, the general was forced to retreat back behind Rostov-on-Don. The German chances of resisting the tide diminished when General Manstein was dismissed for remarking that Hitler's strategy made no sense. When the Red Army surrounded about 290,000 German troops in an area about sixty by forty kilometers, Hitler kept the bad news secret, but rumors soon filtered out. And when Paulus requested seven hundred tons of daily supplies to be flown in by the Luftwaffe, Göring promised him only half that amount. Looking for someone else to blame for the imminent defeat, Hitler chose the Rumanians, whom nobody liked. They were refused rations. Meanwhile, the German forces sought cover and dug in to the frozen ground, since most of the wooded areas had been destroyed or taken for firewood.

Starving civilians greeted the Red Army. But the trapped German forces had been told they would be relieved, and they believed the Russian campaign would soon be over. However, bad weather prevented supplies arriving.

"Operation Ring" began with the usual bombardment by heavy artillery. The Russians sent in tanks. The Rumanian troops deserted. The Red Army advance was ruthless. The German troops were now short of ammunition.

Some fought on, others, beset by battle fatigue, shell shock, and frostbite, were too demoralized, and they surrendered. On January 22, Hitler ordered the Sixth Army to fight to the end. Four days later, several German officers shot themselves rather than be taken prisoner by the Russians. Ninety-one thousand German troops were captured but could not be fed, and there was no medical help. Despite that, German propaganda told of a valiant "Last Stand." By now, over half a million German troops had been killed.

Finally, Marshal Paulus and his staff were captured by the Russians on February 2, and Marshal Voronov reported that all resistance had ceased. The BBC announced the German defeat. The German war, which had begun with the speed of a blitzkrieg, had long since been slowed down until the German forces lost their initiative. Their troops were exhausted and their supply lines could no longer be sustained.

Communications between Warlords

On the same day, Prime Minister Winston Churchill wrote to Marshal Stalin in reply to Stalin's telegram to President Roosevelt, in which he had asked about the slowing down of the Allied operations in North Africa. The British Eighth Army, Churchill wrote, had since taken Tripoli. They hoped to enter Tunisia in force shortly and drive the enemy from the Mareth and Gabes positions. Churchill described the clearing and restoring of the harbor at Tripoli, which was being undertaken speedily. He explained the limited condition of the present line of communications to Benghazi and partly also to Cairo, 1,500 miles away. The First Army was reinforced by strong American forces and was bringing its supplies forward before attacking the enemy together with the Eighth Army as soon as was possible. Wet weather was a serious factor, and so were communications. However, he hoped that the enemy would be completely destroyed or driven from the African shore by the end of April—perhaps even sooner. [22]

THE WAY AHEAD

CHURCHILL COULD ALREADY SEE CRACKS IN the "grand alliance" by 1943. Until then, he had impatiently dismissed any discussions about the postwar world as distractions from the task of defeating Hitler and the Nazis. And, although he'd quieted the Socialists in his Coalition government from talking about their postwar political ambitions, they had not stopped planning privately. Stalin, too, was already planning the shape of a postwar Communist Europe. And President Roosevelt's postwar international order—with his hostility to imperialism and militarism—was revealed by his attitude to the Royalist de Gaulle with his own delusions of grandeur.[1] Roosevelt wanted to see the old French Empire dismantled of its colonies in postwar France by a pro-American government.[2] He also posed a threat to a postwar British Empire, whereas neither Churchill nor Eden could imagine anything other than what it had previously been. But because of Churchill's own sentimental desire for friendship and even affection from the Americans, Eden complained that Churchill's indifference to postwar planning would simply result in "America makes a policy and we follow." Nevertheless, Churchill still insisted on victory rather than ideology.

It came at a time when there was still some doubt about who had committed the murders of ten thousand Polish officers discovered buried in the Katyn Forest. Germany, which had been guilty of murdering millions, now sanctimoniously blamed the Russians for the bodies found in the Katyn Forest. The Russians looked guilty when attempting to ignore the accusations. It was hardly a basis for good faith.

The 1943 Casablanca Conference placed a further strain on the triumvirate, with President Roosevelt almost turning his back on Churchill to demonstrate that the two English-speaking leaders were not ganging up on Stalin—so that Churchill began to feel they were both ganging up on *him*. He did not like the idea of Roosevelt and Stalin settling the fate of the world.[3] Nevertheless, there was more appreciation of British victories at El Alamein, when the United States Army had barely dipped its toes in the battles of the Second World War. The British were still the more experienced partners in the Anglo-American alliance. They continued to regard the U.S. military as beginners, which Admiral King, with his dislike of English arrogance, resented. Churchill felt satisfied that British forces had now reached a level of success from which there would be no backsliding, even if he were killed in an accident on one of his side trips to the Balkans or elsewhere. After three years of his leadership, the threat to Britain's survival no longer existed. From now on the power struggle depended on numbers of trained troops, and war materials coming off assembly lines. (Nineteen forty-four would be the peak year when modern U.S. production and assembly-line methods flooded the arms industry with a broad range of military equipment, ammunition, weapons, ships and aircraft, tanks and trucks, and other transport to support the Allied forces. Even so, it was dwarfed by the flow of products now emanating from Soviet factories for Russian troops.)

It was agreed to invade Sicily in June (although it was eventually delayed until July). Churchill—a great face-saver in conflicts with the Allies—also agreed on an invasion of Europe, providing that enough landing craft were available. But he privately considered it unlikely to happen. The American President was as genial as usual and joked with Stalin at Churchill's expense. His close associates knew that beneath his debonair attitude was a hard-nosed political schemer. He was "selfish and superficial," according to General Dill, who interceded between him and the British as an honest broker. It was his needling side that he showed more and more as the United States became more deeply involved in the alliance. Even his mask of geniality disappeared. "He always enjoyed other people's discomfort," wrote American diplomat Averell Harriman. Roosevelt even attempted to arrange a secret meeting alone with Stalin, hosted by the U.S. ambassador in Moscow who was devoted to the Soviet Union.[4] And he was now sufficiently self-confident to tell the news media that the Allies would demand the unconditional surrender of the Germans.⁵ It annoyed Churchill, who saw it would make German troops more determined.

Allied Tensions

The Americans put more and more pressure on dominating the British on the agendas: it was now a case of "he who pays the piper calls the tune." And very different fundamental approaches between the American and British Allies caused considerable tensions, since Britain's limited resources had always forced it to be adept at subtle innovations and peripheral approaches, such as enticing an enemy to fight at times or places where it was at a disadvantage. U.S. generals viewed it as wasting resources on secondary objectives. They preferred a more direct approach. It raised the question of two different fundamental strategies. One had been used successfully in Europe and elsewhere ever since Alexander the Great. It was to strike with maximum force at the weakest point in an enemy's defense. It was what military strategist Carl von Clausewitz called the "strategic objective" or *Schwerpunkt.*⁶ That was what Churchill favored.⁷ The other strategy, which the U.S. generals preferred, was to use maximum force at the most powerful point that would achieve total collapse.

American military negotiators continually failed to understand their unique position, in that only the United States could afford to choose its objectives first, with a firm assumption that resources would always be found to fulfill them. Britain was far poorer in resources and had to wrestle to find them before deciding if it dared to commit its troops. The Americans regarded that as vacillation. But there had never been enough suitably armed and well-trained British troops or landing craft. The result was that U.S. top brass often maligned the British. Eisenhower, who attempted to discourage. Anglophobia, thought the British military were hesitant—but he had never commanded forces in battle against professional German troops.

America's military leaders were made aware that the British were still traumatized by the bloodbath on the Western Front in the First World War. And it was certainly true that British generals did not have the stomach to lead their forces into untenable positions in which they might get bogged down in ghastly conditions, like the trench warfare of 1914–1918, until wiped out by bigger, better-armed, or better-trained enemy troops—whereas American generals seemed more apt to calculate and consider impersonal statistics instead of people. But General Marshall thought most British generals were weak and afraid to fight. On the other hand, Brooke and Montgomery viewed Marshall and Eisenhower as incompetent generals fit only for administrative functions.

Regardless of differing personal opinions, the rivalry spurred both sides on, because they possessed far more qualities in common than the mere irritating habits that divided them. Major conferences of the military advisers to the "Big Three" must often have sounded like the disputes of 1776 all over again, when "the British regarded the Americans as ingrates, and they were. The Americans regarded the British as overbearing and presumptuous meddlers, and they were."[8] There was duplicity on both sides—just as there had been with the convenient and subtle affair of the American Declaration of Independence, which the people in both countries had wanted, since they depended on each other for everything encapsulated in the motto of the United States of America. "*E Pluribus Unum*" is emblazoned on its official seal depicting an eagle readying itself for flight with outstretched wings. It is generally translated literally from the Latin as "one out of many." But it can also mean, more colloquially, "one for all and all for one," as the popular novelist Alexander Dumas phrased the motto of his three fictional heroes in his bestselling classic *The Three Musketeers* in the following century. What the friendly musketeers meant was, "united we stand, divided we fall," which was a call to arms used by the United States in the Second World War, and one that Churchill evidently cherished when he originally proposed the grand alliance of Britain and the United States and Soviet Russia.

But Eisenhower, too, failed to understand that British forces were still too limited in number to use a strategy of total force, so they had to be more subtle instead. And their very different mind-sets often brought discussions to impatient and angry confrontations. "As one general remarked, 'The American Army does not solve its problems, it overwhelms them.'"[9] And by 1942 both Britain and the United States felt able to consider combining forces in a heavy and direct assault on Europe that was aimed at 1943, when the strategic objective was to break through the Atlantic Wall. Even then it had to be held back for another year because of preparations and the buildup of overwhelming force.

Tensions caused by those disagreements were made even more severe by the contempt felt by the military for ineffectual Cabinet Ministers and distrust of the military by the politicians. History rarely records such rage between allies that frequently came close to blows and had to be overcome by aides.[10] For example, furious and determined arguments ensued over a proposed naval operation named "Culverin," which involved the recapture of Singapore and Borneo. Churchill became so distracted from the major war objectives by his insistence on an imperial campaign to chase the Japanese out of former British colonies in the Indian Ocean that there seemed to be no stopping him from running riot. But by October 1944, an outline of a compromise strategy for the British fleet in the Pacific had been thrashed out. Despite Churchill's opposition against fighting in the endless swamps of Burma, General Slim's Fourteenth Army was obliged to invade Burma in the north.

Meanwhile, the creative destruction caused by improved armaments in war obliged Sir Archibald Sinclair and Lord Cherwell to recognize that air superiority was making battleships obsolete—an argument that Churchill must have realized was true but found hard to swallow at first. He finally accepted as fact that ships would play only a minor role in future wars, and he watched the navy being run down afterward with equanimity. The use of aircraft carriers would also come to an end later on, since they were simply floating targets for attacking aircraft.[11]

Operation Husky

Churchill traveled to Washington for a third conference there in May. What he hoped to discuss was the extension of the Mediterranean Strategy. At their first session on May 12, he described the collapse of Italy as the "great prize" they would be awarded after invading Sicily. He claimed that Italy's surrender would be the beginning of Hitler's doom. Then would come an invasion of the Balkans. But General Marshall wanted to close down the Mediterranean war and no one but Churchill was interested in the always disagreeable and undependable Balkans. When Churchill persisted with his rhetoric, Roosevelt told him to "shut up."[12] That was the point when they all began to realize that the President of the United States was very tired, perhaps even a very sick man.

Churchill was heard to express his views on the postwar world order at the British embassy: it was to restore the nineteenth-century world of great-power politics.[13] Eden began to draft a long paper in which he described his own vision for the future. Its objective was to avoid the mistakes of the two decades between the end of the last war and the beginning of this one, 1919–1939.

In the meantime, the British had outlined their own plan for the next campaign, which was code-named "Operation Husky." It would be a converging sea approach and invasion of Sicily, to be headed by Eisenhower as supreme commander, with General Alexander as his British deputy. The two army field commanders chosen were Montgomery and Patton. It was approved by the Combined Chiefs of Staff on May 13, a week after the German and Italian collapse at Tunis.

As far as the Americans were concerned, Husky was a Mediterranean mission, whereas to Churchill it was the simplest way to enter Europe by using Sicily as a stepping-stone to land in the south of Italy and advance northward toward Germany. But the American military's skepticism of Churchill's melodramatic rhetoric and his proposed tactics—at this stage of the war—arose from a suspicion that he was using it to lay the groundwork in the Mediterranean to strengthen the British Empire's postwar interests.

The Americans did not share his interest in history or his impulsiveness in wanting to put his ideas into practice. There was a cultural difference. Despite his pro-American sentiments, Churchill was a European with all it meant in terms of culture. He lived in Europe and had traveled over Europe, while they were North Americans who viewed Europe skeptically as a place from which early American settlers had fled because of its ancient religious superstitions and hatreds, its intolerance of new ideas, its oppressive governments with their secret police, and the suppressions of liberty. They were not wrong. But Britain was part of Europe, which Churchill understood. They did not. As American military men, all they wanted was to get most economically and efficiently from A to B, and then swiftly back home again.

The Teheran Conference

Churchill was sixty-nine when he crossed the Atlantic on the *Queen Mary* for the "Big Three" conference in Teheran on November 30, 1943. He heard, on the way, that Mussolini had been dismissed and replaced by Marshal Badoglio, who was having secret talks with the Allies about the possibility of an armistice. Churchill's imagination soared at the possibilities of a neutral Italy or an Italy breaking its alliance with Germany and even changing sides. But the Americans were determined to clip the wings of his imagination and use their greater size and power to get him to toe their line.

He prepared his notes, listing artificial harbors as one of the key elements required for the invasion of the South of France, now code-named "Overlord." He could see it as the most spectacular amphibious operation of the war, and somewhat scary. These conferences of the "Big Three" leaders would decide which was to be their priority and if the Italian landing was even necessary.

Roosevelt was noticeably worn and ill but was staunchly in favor of Overlord. So, of course, was Stalin, who spoke in his usual quiet but decisive voice. His self-assurance at the summit meetings came largely from knowing a great many secrets about his allies beforehand from Communist agents placed in British Intelligence and also close to the American President. There was, for example, what historian Sir Max Hastings called "the Washington and Berkeley five hundred" who passed information to Soviet Intelligence.[14]

Brooke wrote in his diary that the reason for Stalin's support of the President was that he thought the Germans would push the British and American forces back into the sea. It would distract the Germans from the Russian front and also weaken the Anglo-American Allies, so that he would be free to control Europe afterward. Stalin got what he wanted. And so did Roosevelt.

As soon as Churchill realized Britain was finally safe, he lost his focus and thought up a multitude of schemes to prop up the old imperial order by restoring overthrown monarchs in the Balkans and Greece and retrieving lost colonies of the British Empire (which would end up throwing off the colonial yoke to gain independence instead). Author and journalist H. G. Wells wrote that he seemed to have completely lost his head and must go. Fortunately, the Americans ignored him. Even his rhetoric had declined into shapeless meandering. His power to shape events was gone. Nevertheless, noted Brooke, "He has probably done more for this country than any other human being has ever done."

The one fear on Stalin's mind was that the Germans might dispose of Hitler and make peace terms with the Anglo-American Allies, while the Allies feared that Stalin would make peace with Hitler—since he'd mentioned at the conference that the Germans had put out peace feelers to him.

After the Teheran Conference, Churchill remarked that he realized for the first time what a small nation we are.[15] And yet, he said, he was the only one who knew the right way home.

Regardless of his suspicions of the American military wanting to take over, he trusted in his personal relationship with Roosevelt and hoped for an Anglo-American Alliance after the war. But Mrs. Roosevelt had remarked at dinner on August 14 at their country home in Hyde Park that the Soviets would feel threatened if they thought they were opposed by an Anglo-American combination. And it became clearer at subsequent conferences that Britain was not only the smallest of the Big Three, but that what Churchill thought of as his personal friendship with the U.S. President was of little use if Roosevelt was determined to forge a special relationship with Stalin.

Whereas the British tended to view the Americans as insular and naive former colonials who were often crude, the Americans considered Britain conservative, old-fashioned, and imperialistic. As it would turn out, it was Churchill who was naive to imagine that he even had a friendship with the President or that the relationship would be valued after the war was over. Roosevelt was more subtle than they thought, and the American military more pragmatic. And the Americans did not want to get bogged down in a Mediterranean war.

Most importantly, Overlord was confirmed as the major operation for 1944, largely because Stalin was eager for it. Stalin and Roosevelt were also keen that Germany be dismembered and her power destroyed so that it was no longer a threat. Churchill was against it, no doubt remembering what the Treaty of Versailles had done to Germany: perhaps the major ingredient that caused the Second World War.

It was about this time that Churchill became gradually aware of the irony of his situation. He had denounced Chamberlain in 1938 for appeasing Hitler by being ready to give him other nations' territory in exchange for hollow promises of a bit of peace. And yet he now found himself constantly appeasing Stalin over the Poles, whom Britain had gone to war to protect in the first place. Stalin still refused to recognize the free Polish government, which had escaped to England when Hitler's troops invaded Poland. The aggressiveness of the London Poles toward Stalin didn't help.

What he wanted was a Polish government that was friendly with Russia, not the London Poles. And Churchill was obliged to conciliate the Russians because they were allies.

He reflected on how, only six years ago, he had denounced appeasement as unworthy of a great nation like England. And yet, in January and February 1944 he put pressure on the Poles to accept border changes in Russia's favor. Wasn't that what Chamberlain had unforgivably done to Czechoslovakia when *he* had been prime minister? And, of course, just as it had not been enough for Hitler then, it was not enough for Stalin now. When his early morning waking thoughts were not about how to appease Stalin, they were how to conciliate President Roosevelt. So much for glory!

But the war was not over yet.

GATEWAY TO EUROPE

THE ALLIED CONQUEST OF SICILY CAME about as a compromise between the American and British Combined Chiefs of Staff at the 1943 Casablanca Conference. They finally decided they were not yet ready for the much bigger alternative Operation Overlord. But the Sicily operation could be an effective means to divert some of the German pressure from the Russian front—although that could have been more to placate Marshal Stalin's desire for a Second Front in Europe. In Churchill's own mind it was a gateway through which to chase the Axis armies all the way back home.

It did not turn out to be the walkover that Churchill anticipated, although it may look like one in retrospect, or when glancing at a map. Instead it was "a hazardous leap, hedged with uncertainties."[1]

It was also a prime example of the part that personal foibles and follies play in the erroneous judgments and actions of emotional and irrational dictators with total power. Egotism, pride, and vanity, as well as delusions of grandeur, persuaded them that they must "save face" in Africa. And their armies paid the price for their pumped-up view of their own self-importance while they sacrificed other people's lives.

Added to Hitler's personal delusions of world conquest was the successful deception that British Intelligence played on his character weaknesses by convincing him that Sicily was not the Allies' real objective. It resulted in the further folly of both dictators pouring so many troops into Africa that they were left with too few to defend Europe. Part of that temptation arose from their own immediate success in the Allied shambles of the opening advances of Eisenhower's first landings to occupy Tunis. It encouraged them to believe that they could occupy Tunisia indefinitely if they poured in more reinforcements. Rommel had personally argued with Hitler for more troops in Europe instead, but without success.

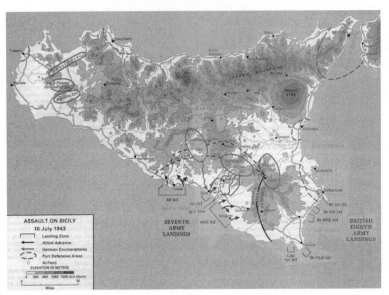

1943 Allied landings in Sicily. Code-named "Operation Husky."

The capture by the Allies of the eight Axis divisions in Tunisia included most of Rommel's veterans and the pick of the Italian army. It left Italy almost bereft of defenses. They would otherwise have provided a very strong barrier across the Italian gateways into Europe, and the Allies' chances of success would have been small.[2] Churchill was jubilant that the whole of North Africa had been cleared of enemy troops, with a quarter of a million taken prisoners of war.[3]

In Mussolini's case, General Roatta, who had previously commanded Sicily, convinced Il Duce that larger German reinforcements were essential there in order to protect Italy. The Italian garrison in Sicily possessed only four field divisions and six coastal defense divisions with poor equipment and low morale. Germany's Fifth Panzer Division was on its way to Sicily, but it had only one tank unit. And a rebuilt "Herman Göring" panzer division was sent toward the end of June. They were commanded by the Italian General Guzzoni and broken up into five separate groups around the 150-mile parameter of the island.

In fact, Hitler's forces were overextended because of the broad German conquests over huge tracts of territory. Hitler had become convinced that the

Allies' target was not Sicily but Sardinia, because of faked documents found on the corpse of a "British officer" that washed ashore on a Spanish beach—another successful British deception.

Even so, the Italians still possessed six effective, modern battleships that might be used against or even prevent the Allied landings.

The Assault of Sicily

The initial assault of Sicily included three thousand ships and landing craft, carrying 160,000 men, 14,000 vehicles, 600 tanks, and 1,800 guns. The convoy was assembled and escorted across the seas and concentrated on the battle area at the right time.[4] It included eight British divisions and six American. The Naval Force was 80 percent British; the air force 55 percent American. It was under the supreme command of General Eisenhower, with General Alexander in command of the Fifteenth Army Group, Air Chief Marshal Tedder of the Allied air force, and Admiral Cunningham of the Allied naval forces. General Montgomery was in charge of the British assault with his Eighth Army. And General Patton commanded the United States Seventh Army.

General Alexander's plan recommended a week of preliminary bombardment to neutralize the enemy's navy and air forces. The British Eighth Army would then assault Cape Murro and Pozzallo to capture Syracuse and the airfield. It would then thrust north. General Patton's army would land between Cape Scaramia and Licata to capture the port and a group of airfields. A powerful force of British and American parachute troops would drop or be landed by gliders beyond the beachheads and seize key points, then aid the landings.

Only four convoy ships and two LSTs were lost to U-boat attacks. The Allies' air superiority was great, with 4,000 operational aircraft against about 1,500 Axis aircraft. But when the convoys began arriving at their assembly areas on July 9, a sudden storm arose with a high wind in the afternoon. The landings were threatened by the pitch of the sea, and it affected the gliders and parachute landings. Airborne troops became scattered. And 47 gliders, out of the 134, fell into the sea.

But the storm provided one advantage; it distracted the Italian defenders and gave them a false sense of security in believing there would hardly be an attack that night. In any case, most of them were demoralized and tired of the war. And most were Sicilians, who were aware that the harder they fought the more their homes would be destroyed.

The Allies landed on July 10 and quickly overran the beach defenses with little resistance and few shots fired. Mass surrenders took place. Responsibility for defense fell on two German divisions that were reinforced by another two. But one dangerous attack was launched by the Herman Göring Division with its new fifty-six-ton Tiger tanks against the Allies, before they were successfully established. Then German tanks arrived next morning from the plains and overran the American positions. But effective naval gunfire broke up their attack. And another German column of tanks was stopped in the same way.

The Fifteenth Panzer Division arrived at the American front the next day, after the Herman Göring Division had moved off to advance on the British position, which had so far met with little opposition. Allied troops had been sheltered from the start by their own air and sea domination.

In the first three days, Montgomery's force cleared the entire southeastern part of the island. Then he ordered a break through into the plain of Catania and a major attack on July 13, while a parachute brigade captured the bridge over the River Simeto. Although only half the parachutists managed to land in the right place, it was sufficient to secure it intact. But they were prevented from a swift clearance of the island by German attacks. Meanwhile the American Seventh Army advanced east and north to occupy Palermo on July 22.

A new push was planned to start on August 1 with two fresh infantry divisions—the American Ninth and the British Seventy-Eighth. The character of Sicily and its terrain had been described as a triangle of mountainous country. It favored the defenders, and the Allied armies became increasingly cramped, preventing them from deploying their full superiority in size. Nevertheless, the vigorous competition between Montgomery's and Patton's troops resulted in swift victories until they converged on Messina. They captured 5,500 German troops, and 13,500 wounded were evacuated to Italy, with only a few thousand killed. British losses were 2,721 killed, 2,183 missing, and 7,939 wounded. The Americans lost 2,811 troops killed, 686 missing, and 6,471 wounded. Altogether, the assault on Sicily caused the downfall of the Italian Dictator Benito Mussolini and the surrender of Italy.

23

THE SOFT UNDERBELLY

—————

On June 18, General Alexander reported to Churchill that he could destroy the German forces in Italy, if his own forces were not weakened. After that, there would be nothing to prevent him from marching on Vienna.[1] Churchill was eager to back Alexander's operation, since he had already begun anxiously anticipating the dangers of a postwar Communist Europe.

He'd also had other presentiments while waking in the morning hours and considering his options for the day. Even as early as 1944, Churchill was aware of change, as a consequence of fighting against the Germans, dealing with the Italians, supporting the Russians, and working with the Americans—all of whom had different values from his own. On the one hand, he was a romantic with dreams of saving mankind, and they were not. But the old imperialist order with its honor and patriotism was turning out to be a hollow concept. "What is honor?" Shakespeare has his cynical Falstaff ask himself, as if seeking the truth; he is dismayed to find that all he can come up with is "a word."

Contemplating his hollow explanation, he is driven to ask another question: "Who hath it?" And he is compelled to answer ruefully, "He that died on Wednesday."

Churchill as a war leader had carried the heavy burden of millions of such deaths by now—many of them from unintended consequences.

Nevertheless, he had absorbed honor as a child and been formed by it as a youth. He was still driven by it in abundance. So was Anthony Eden. Both refused to allow their resolve to be weakened by Falstaff's type of cynicism, which they thought dishonest. Eden's Minister of State had written to him in the latter part of 1943, saying, "It is possible that the part we have played in this war will appear to historians as the last brilliant flare-up which illuminates the darkness of the decline of British power and influence."[2] Britain's foreign policy toward France and Russia was already subordinated to American interests. But Churchill refused to be distracted by defeatist thoughts, since he still had a war to win, and winning required focus.

With all the profound thinking of Eden and Churchill about Britain's future in the postwar world, diplomat Sir Harold Nicolson read the writing on the wall more clearly than either of them when he wrote, "The upper classes feel that all this sacrifice and suffering will only mean that the proletariat will deprive them of all their comforts and influence, and then proceed to render this country and Empire a third-class state." There was also concern among upper middle classes that democracy would result in falling standards and ethical values to that of the lowest common denominator. Already, by the close of the war, there was a schism between people who distrusted all forms of authority, including politicians and institutions, and those who feared the results of socialism.[3]

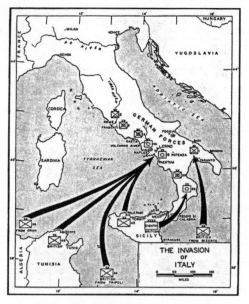

The Allied Italian Campaign.

Italy Surrenders

Meanwhile, the announcement of the Italian surrender was broadcast on the air as the Allied armada neared the Salerno beaches for the landing that evening, with the troops keyed up for battle. According to Churchill, the change in the situation had an unfortunate psychological effect—they thought their task in Italy would be a walkover. The officers immediately tried to correct that assumption by reminding them there was bound to be strong resistance from the Germans. And, in fact, the Germans acted immediately.

According to military historian Liddell Hart, there were only six weak German divisions left in the south of Italy and two divisions near Rome to cope with the double burden of meeting the Allied invasion and, at the same time, holding down their former Italian allies who were turning on them.[4]

Against Rommel's recommendations, Hitler decided to pour troops down to the south of Italy. It left his forces weaker on the Russian front and also distracted him from preparing to defend against the anticipated Allied landings in Normandy. Instead, he wanted to hold as much of Italy as he could and for as long as possible. Hanging on to useless territory had been more typical of the First World War, and it was one of Hitler's worst failings.

Rommel had arrived in Greece on July 25, when he received a telephone call telling him that Mussolini had been deposed and he must return to Hitler's headquarters in East Prussia. The next day he was given his orders "to assemble troops in the Alps and prepare a possible entry into Italy." By the beginning of September, he was in command of eight German divisions in the north of Italy, while Field Marshal Kesselring commanded the German forces in the south.

Kesselring was known as "Smiling Albert." He was a Bavarian bourgeois, and was therefore looked down on socially by Prussians aristocrats under his command. Nevertheless, they obeyed him.[5] They did so because he was vicious. Although not entirely responsible for the massacre of 335 Romans who were taken to the Ardeatine Caves, south of Rome, and shot in the back of the head in groups of five as a reprisal by the Germans against Italian partisans who killed thirty-two SS men, it had been undertaken with his full and prior knowledge.[6]

At more or less the same time, a hardened German airborne division, the Second Parachute Division, was flown close to Rome under the command of General Student, with instructions from Hitler "to disarm the Italian forces around Rome." The Italians withdrew and left Rome to the Germans. With no Italian resistance, the Germans were able to send reinforcements to Kesselring's Tenth Army down south.

The Salerno Landing

Meanwhile, the Allied assault convoys entered the Gulf of Salerno for the landings, escorted by a strong British fleet. Perhaps due to a storm, there was little initial resistance other than a minor air attack. The assault landing on Salerno was covered by an overwhelming artillery barrage from the shore of Sicily by 600 guns and the fire of 120 naval guns. The assault force consisted of the Sixth American Corps and the British Tenth Corps. The attack was opened by General Montgomery's Eighth Army on September 3 when he crossed the narrow Straits of Messina from Sicily and landed on the toe of Italy. The Anglo-American Fifth Army under General Mark Clark disembarked in the Gulf of Salerno at midnight on September 8. And General Dempsey's Thirteenth Corps landed on the beaches near Reggio.

As Kesselring said later, if the Allies had landed by air on Rome instead, his forces would have been cut off and forced to evacuate the entire south of Italy. Instead, the Allied landings came exactly where they were expected. German artillery surrounded the beachheads and the Allied landings were attacked by at least six German divisions.

Three battalions of the U.S. Eighty-Second Airborne parachutists were dropped almost at the water's edge. The German positions were bombarded by strategic bombers from the Northwest African Air Force. And Allied naval guns gave close supporting fire. Above all, the Fifth Army stubbornly and resolutely held the beachheads.[7]

Regardless of the heavy German defensive activity, Montgomery had been ordered to secure a bridgehead on the toe of Italy. He was also to assist Mark Clark's Fifth Army. But no attempt was made to coordinate their operations. And the plan for the Eighth Army landed them on a most unsuitable part of the coast, described as a narrow and mountainous area, ideally suited for ambush by bandits or obstruction by German troops.[8] Fortunately, there were only two German infantry battalions near the toe, and they were situated over ten miles away from the beaches.

Three thousand Italians were picked up as prisoners by the Fifth British and First Canadian divisions, and they cheerfully offered to help unload the British landing craft. The landings were otherwise quiet, giving a sense of false security. But German troops reacted speedily to the slow Eighth Army toiling through mountainous terrain; nearly three German divisions arrived from the north. A regiment of German parachutists arrived from the east. The new German radio-controlled and glider bombs caused losses to British ships. But huge Allied air force bombings were focused on hampering approaching enemy reinforcements and scattering their concentrations.[9]

On September 11, the Italian Battle Fleet was in the hands of the British navy, and over a hundred merchant ships had been scuttled to avoid capture by the Germans. All Italian captains responsible were shot by the Germans. As Italian Fascist forces collapsed the following day, Mussolini was rescued by Hitler.

While the battle raged in Salerno, General Alexander decided to use audacious tactics at Taranto, a port that could serve a whole army. Six thousand hand picked men embarked on British warships and, on the same day as the Salerno landings, the Royal Navy steamed into Taranto Harbor and boldly deposited the troops onshore without any opposition. The only hazard was one cruiser that struck a mine and sank.

Alexander took the initiative to establish his presence at the front, to ensure that he could observe what was happening and to avoid the huge losses of millions of soldiers in the previous war, when generals remained at headquarters without any idea of the awful conditions they were sending their troops into at the battlefront. It was good for morale. And he continually reported what was happening to Churchill. Churchill was in mid-ocean on the way home from Washington, and eagerly imagined that, once the battle for Salerno was won, "Naples and the Foggia airfields were spread out before us."[10] A few days after returning to London, he was back at his simultaneous multiple observations and his multitasking. As he emphasized, war is never a matter of one thing at a time.

The Anzio Beachhead

Meanwhile, the Allied troops in the south of Italy were "badly stretched both tactically and administratively," according to Eisenhower. The Americans concentrated on opening the harbor at Naples so that, within two weeks, five thousand tons of supplies a day could be brought in. And the two airfields were made usable for six RAF squadrons. The Anglo-American Fifth Army entered the city of Naples (its initial objective) on October 1. It had taken them three weeks, with seven thousand British and five thousand American casualties. It was the price of choosing an obvious landing point and sacrificing surprise.[11]

Conditions in Naples were chaotic. Law and order had broken down, with corrupt local authorities and Mafia criminals. Bread and water were hard to find, and there were continual food riots. Trading prostitution for food was commonplace. The Allies had to organize military hospitals for venereal disease, typhus, and other illnesses.[12]

They took another week to reach the Volturno River, as a consequence of "muddy roads and soggy ground," where three German divisions had withdrawn to make a stand against them.

They launched a nighttime attack on the German position on October 2. But the river crossing was stopped by German counterattacks, according to Kesselring's orders to stay on the river line until the sixteenth, before withdrawing fifteen miles north—near the mouth of the Garigliano River—through a cluster of hills, since the field marshal hoped to make a stand at the Cassino defile.

The islands of Sardinia and Corsica had fallen to the Allies. And General Alexander continued to send optimistic reports to Churchill while the prime minister sent enthusiastic congratulations to all the generals. Montgomery, despite still getting his supplies and administration together in the south, could already see himself with the Eighth Army in Rome. The Italian fleet was secured, and the Italian army and air force were no longer enemies of the Anglo-American forces. German troops had been neutralized after fierce fighting. And the Allied forces had now eased themselves out of the boot of Italy to advance north.

But regardless of Benito Mussolini's fall from power, he was now engaged with reviving a Fascist government with the help of Hitler. Italy, headed by King Victor Emmanuel, and its new Badoglio government, had now become a common cause for most Italians who opposed the Fascist regime. There were also intrigues against the monarchy and Badoglio. Churchill, as usual, was single-minded in his determination not to get involved in foreign politics, but to focus solely on fighting the war.

Inching their way up the spine of Italy to their next objective, the Allied troops had advanced only seventy miles beyond Salerno and were still eighty miles from Rome, as a consequence of General Montgomery's careful and orthodox textbook consolidation of each advance to establish a firm base and make sure of supplies before moving on. But the mountainous terrain was difficult and the rainy weather was bad as the Allies fought their way north, coping with booby traps and muddy mined roads, sullen and rebellious villagers and towns, and dealing with rearguard actions. They crossed rivers where bridges had been destroyed and suffered from all kinds of illnesses, from trench foot to pneumonia and dysentery. There were an estimated forty thousand battle casualties on the way, with fifty thousand noncombat casualties and about twenty thousand desertions. The rain would turn into sleet and even blizzards when autumn turned into winter.[13] And "no sooner had one river or mountain been crossed than another barred the route."[14]

The biggest criticism of the Allies' sluggishness was that they failed to exploit amphibious power. And by now, Churchill's optimism had given way to frustration and anger that none of the landing craft in the Mediterranean had been put to use for three months.[15] He said the same of the Adriatic side. He described Anzio as "a story of high opportunities and shattered hopes."[16]

The only suitable landing beaches beyond the German flank were at the small holiday resort of Anzio, where the amphibious attacks by the Allies took Kesselring by surprise—he had expected a landing more dangerous to him, north of Rome. The Allies were almost unopposed as a result: by the British, north of the town, and the Americans just south of it. But the German reaction "was rapid and resolute," as reinforcements arrived from the north and the south. Hitler was determined to stand fast and firmly, to scare off any more Allied landings in Italy. Elements of eight German divisions were brought up and assembled around the Anzio beachhead in the first eight days.[17]

Since Eisenhower and Group Commander Harold Alexander knew from the Ultra cypher of Hitler's decision (of October 4) to support Kesselring's plans to fight south of Rome—and since Churchill was convinced Rome was the key to Italy—they devised a plan for the Fifth and Eighth Armies to take Rome together.[18]

Field Marshal Kesselring now had fifteen divisions in his Tenth Army and another eight in the Fourteenth Army in the north to hold the Gustav line, as it was called. So the obvious response by the Allies was to make an amphibious landing behind that line. Assault craft were provided for landings in January on the Anzio beaches, south of Rome. But the battle didn't work out for the Allied forces, who had expected to meet confused and exhausted troops. Instead, the enemy fought with tenacity, while the Fifth U.S. Army's offensive was "disjointed in delivery." The British Tenth Army started well with a successful nighttime crossing of the Garigliano River on January 17–18. But Kesselring sent a large proportion of his reserve divisions to the front. And an attack on the American Second Corps resulted in the almost complete destruction of the two leading U.S. regiments.

"The life expectancy of a forward observation officer was a mere six weeks." And they would have seen the full horrors of the war at Anzio: the wounded with filthy, sodden uniforms—mostly British but some Americans—buried in mud and blood, with ghastly pale faces, some carried in already dying, with shattered limbs and protuberances of intestines and brains through huge holes in their bodies.[19]

Despite fighting, often at close quarters, the Anzio operation did not meet its objectives. All that General Clark wanted was to be the first in Rome, and never mind the others. He was as keen on inflating himself for publicity as Patton. If he found the British already there, he said he would fire on them. No one was entirely sure whether he was serious or not.*

The Gustav Line

Although the beachhead was secured by day two, the first real push inland only began more than a week after landing on January 30 and was soon stopped by existing German troops. The U.S. Second Corps overcame the Gustav Line by attacking Cassino from the north, with the American Thirty-Fourth Division leading the assault. It took a whole week of heavy fighting to secure a bridgehead. But Lieutenant-General von Senger brought in more reserves to make his defensive position even stronger, so that the American forces were "heavily depleted and badly exhausted," and had to be withdrawn.

Lieutenant-General Freyberg's newly formed New Zealand Corps was brought in. Both the Second New Zealand and the Fourth Indian Division were veterans of the North African Campaign, and considered to be the best fighting division there. But his converging assault on Cassino changed nothing against the well-situated and stubborn defenses of the Germans. Major-General Tucker's more indirect tactics and wider maneuver through the mountains was another possibility, but he fell ill. And his division was tasked to assault Monte Cassino itself, with its ancient and imposing monastery at the summit. It had to be neutralized by heavy air bombardments. Now the German troops, who had not previously occupied it, moved into the rubble and established a firmer defense.

Repeated attacks that night by the Indian Division made no difference. They managed to capture Point 593 on the next night but were pressed back by counterattacking German parachute troops.

General von Mackensen was ready to launch a counterattack by mid-February, now that he had ten divisions surrounding the five Allied divisions and was reinforced by strong air support from the Luftwaffe. He would also use the new "Goliath" tanks, which—despite their name—were miniature remote-controlled tanks packed with explosives. The German attack on the Allied bridgehead commenced on February 16. But it happened that the numbers and mixture of German forces blocking the narrow road provided a crowded target for Allied artillery, aircraft, and naval bombardments.

The "Goliaths" didn't live up to their names. Nevertheless, the sheer weight of armies and arms pushed back the Allied forces. And a renewed assault by the German Eighteenth, together with the Twenty-Sixth Panzer Division, pressed them back toward the beaches. Nevertheless, the British and American troops fought desperately and effectively to check the German thrust, and "the assaulting troops wilted under the strain."[20] Another effort by the Panzergrenadier divisions was brought to a halt. Hitler ordered a fresh offensive that opened on February 28. But it was stopped without much difficulty by the American Third Division. After which von Mackensen was compelled by his losses to stop the offensive and withdraw to rest.

There were other attacks on Monte Cassino and heavy bombardments from the air and the ground in mid-March. But the elite First Parachute Division continued to hold the summit and not only survived, but checked further assaults by Allied infantry. They were largely protected by the rubble from the bombardments. Allied losses were becoming too heavy to continue the offensive, and the third battle for Monte Cassino was broken off on the twenty-third, for the planned breakout from the Anzio bridgehead.

The Germans troops doggedly held on for several more days, despite the Canadian Corps being thrown in to exploit the situation on the fifth. The German paratroops finally withdrew two days later. The Poles entered the long defended ruins of the monastery the following morning, after having lost nearly four thousand men in the effort.[21]

The assault on the Cassino front cost the Allies three months for an advantage of only about ten miles and huge losses of life.[22] Then, when the opportunity arrived to follow and destroy the withdrawing German forces, Lieutenant-General Mark Clark refused to obey his superior officer's orders.

Alexander hoped that by ordering this breakout attack for the twenty-third, there would be a strong and rapid thrust to Valmontone, to cut Route 6—the main inland road—and therefore cut off most of the German Tenth Army, which had been holding the Gustav Line. If that were achieved, Rome would fall like a ripe apple. But the prospect was marred by Mark Clark's differing views, and his eagerness that the troops of his Fifth Army should be the first to enter Rome. Kesselring's one remaining mobile division, the Herman Göring, was rushing to the scene to stop this thrust, and was being badly harassed by Allied air attacks. But at that stage, Mark Clark swung his drive directly toward Rome, with four divisions, while only one was allowed to continue toward Valmontone—and that was held up three miles short of Route 6 by the larger part of the three German divisions.

Alexander appealed to Churchill but did not succeed in changing Mark Clark's direction.[23] Clark openly ignored his orders from General Sir Harold Alexander, apparently in order to keep his forces intact for a triumphal arrival in Rome, rather than attempt to destroy the German forces on the Gustav Line.

---

* General Mark Clark set up his own public relations outfit with a staff of fifty to ensure everyone knew about his war efforts and the U.S. Army's, with the proviso that each press release "was to mention Clark three times on the front page and at least once on all other pages."[24]

Despite Patton's outstanding military skills, he was not an attractive man and seemed mentally unbalanced at times, so much so that "by the end of his career, the U.S. Army had placed a psychiatrist on his staff to keep an eye on him, and were monitoring his phone calls."[25] Top field generals are usually allowed some prima donna temperament, as a consequence of personality characteristics required in battlefront conditions. But jealousy over Montgomery's outstanding military ability led Patton and Bradley to gang up on him and, on one occasion, they both declared to Eisenhower that they could not serve under him. They even leaked damaging information about Montgomery to the press.[26]

24

HITLER'S SECRET WEAPONS

After Benito Mussolini escaped from antifascist Italian partisans with Hitler's help in September 1943, the puppet dictator was sheltered in a safe house in Munich with his daughter and her husband, Count Ciano, who had fled from Rome at the Italian surrender. The couple were now under house arrest on Hitler's orders. Hitler expected Mussolini to punish them for opposing Fascism. As far as he was concerned, they were traitors. All the other traitors who had been caught had been tried and executed in Mafia-type operations.

To put the war into perspective (which is a difficult task even now), Winston Churchill received a last letter from Count Ciano, who had been Italy's Minister for Foreign Affairs. He was still Mussolini's son-in-law. The letter was written when the Italian dictator turned on him and ordered his execution.

What he wrote was, in effect, that he was about to be executed for a crime. The crime was witnessing and, no doubt, revealing his disgust for the ruthless and cynical preparation of the war by Hitler and the Germans. He was, he claimed, the only foreigner to witness firsthand the preparations by the revolting Fascist gangsters who prepared to wage a bloody war on the world. "Now," he wrote, "according to the way of ruthless bandits, they have turned on me to destroy me as a dangerous witness. But," he added, "they are unaware that I wrote down everything in my diary some time ago, and have placed it and various documents in a safe place, as proof of the crimes committed by those people whom the 'tragic and vile puppet Mussolini' associated himself as a result of his vanity and disregard of civilized values." He went on to state that he was never Mussolini's accomplice in crimes against

Italy and humanity, or of fighting as an ally of the Germans. He insisted that the opposite was the truth.

Viewed in that perspective, it is easier to see the Nazis more as a criminal Mafia-type operation rather than having even the smallest semblance to a genuine political party.

Ciano received the death sentence, and Mussolini refused to revoke it, despite his daughter's entreaties. Early in 1944, Ciano was tied to a chair and executed by being shot in the back. [1]

Meanwhile, the battle for Italy had been hard and long, with soaking wet autumn weather turning into the sleet and blizzards of winter, and dysentery taking its toll. It was said that the Allies should have landed closer to Rome, instead of footslogging all the way up the spine of Italy to reach it. But, as it turned out, it was heavily guarded by German troops at that time and the Allies would have been slaughtered on the Albion Plains.

In June 1944, U.S. Lieutenant-General Mark Clark arrived in Rome after disobeying orders from his superior officer General Sir Harold Alexander to follow and destroy retreating German forces or tackle those holding the Gustav Line after the final battle at Monte Cassino. No doubt he expected applause for liberating the capital city. But Rome had already been declared an "Open City" by Kesselring, to prevent its destruction. So there was little or no German resistance by that time. Clark's Fifth and Eighth Armies included British, Canadian, U.S., French, and Polish troops, who took possession of a fairly docile Rome. Instead of being a critical episode, as all of them had thought, it was just another incident in the war.

On April 26, four months after Ciano was murdered, armed Italian Communist partisans captured Mussolini and his mistress with fifteen other leading Fascists in a German convoy. Forty-eight hours later, the dictator was tried and executed with Claretta Petacci by being shot with a sub-machine gun. After being thrown onto a heap of bodies in a square in Milan for the Italian public to see, they were hung up on meat hooks, upside down, to show they were infamous criminals, and also to prevent the hysterical and violent mobs from tearing them to pieces with their hands. The days of Fascism in Italy were over. But it took German forces in Italy another year before they surrendered.

Long-Range Weapons

German scientists had already begun to develop rockets and pilotless aircraft, or drones, several years before the war. Their top-secret experimental area was situated in Peenemünde on the Baltic coast. Nevertheless, British Intelligence reports mentioned what seemed to be going on there as early as 1939, by their references to "long-range weapons of various kinds." Then scraps of information and rumors began mentioning Hitler's Secret Weapons. The British Chiefs of Staff reviewed the Intelligence reports in the spring of 1943, and General Ismay made Churchill aware of the latest ones. Ismay suggested that Churchill might appoint Duncan Sandys to initiate more accurate information from suitable scientists, who might analyze the photographs of what looked like a special launching site, and provide whatever proposals might be made as to how to defend against it. He also warned the Minister of Home Security of the possibility of such an attack.

Duncan Sandys was now undersecretary at the Ministry of Supply. He had previously served in Norway with an antiaircraft unit and been disabled in a car accident while in command of Britain's first rocket regiment. He was also Winston Churchill's son-in-law.

His first report, which was circulated to the war cabinet, described the results of the most recent aerial photographs of the site at Peenemünde. He confirmed that the Germans had been attempting to develop a heavy rocket "capable of bombarding an area from a very long range," and that it might be far advanced. It was likely that the work had been undertaken side by side with the development of jet-propelled aircraft and rocket torpedoes.[2] In the meantime, Sandys sent the RAF a list of possible bombing targets of the most likely manufacturers who could be producing any of those weapons.

As Churchill explained in his memoirs, they examined all possible methods of tracing their trajectory and locating the firing point, then implementing Civil Defense and Security measures.[3]

Further reconnaissance photographs provided evidence of advances in manufacturing long-range rockets at Peenemünde, and of frequent experimental firings. It was noticed that the light antiaircraft defenses at the site were being reinforced. And it was estimated from the size of the rockets on the ground that their range could be about 90 to 130 miles. That indicated the Germans could already possess rocket projectiles that could be aimed at northern France, or even be targeted on London. And evidently both the rocket missiles and pilotless aircraft were being produced on a large scale. Churchill also carefully noted that no decisive progress had been made toward an atom bomb by the Germans.[4]

The Defense Committee decided that the experimental station should be attacked by the heaviest possible bombardment from RAF Bomber Command.

Hitler visited Peenemünde at the beginning of June in 1943. It was thought that his personal interest in Germany's so-called "Secret Weapons" was a sign of desperation—perhaps even his last hope. If so, they were doubly dangerous, since they could be launched as a last-ditch suicidal Armageddon to destroy civilization.

As for the possibility of a German atom bomb, doubts were based on scientific problems that had to be overcome with heavy water. Nevertheless, Hitler informed his military leaders at a meeting on June 10 that Germany had only to hold out, that London would be leveled to the ground by the end of 1943 and Britain forced to capitulate.[5] The appointed date for the destruction of London was October 20. And it was rumored that Hitler ordered thirty thousand rockets to be aimed at England's capital city.

The rockets were now described as V2s. It was estimated that manufacturing that number of rockets would be the equivalent of making 180,000 fighter planes, so it was considered to be an absurd claim. Nevertheless, the German Minister of Munitions, Dr. Speer, had given first priority to producing both weapons in that period of time. Five hundred skilled German workers were transferred from making antiaircraft weapons and artillery guns to Hitler's secret weapons. New British Intelligence revealed that the Germans also planned to launch pilotless aircraft (V1s) on London, and use very long-range guns.

Britain's Home Office immediately made plans for the wholesale evacuation of schoolchildren and pregnant mothers from London, at a rate of ten thousand a day, when the time came. Thirty thousand steel Morrison "table shelters," for inside homes, were transported to London. They had already been effectively used during the London "Blitz." Beneath their bolted steel tabletop was a cage for families to shelter in during bombing attacks. They often prevented deaths and injuries from being crushed by heavy falling masonry, or struck by shards of glass from shattered windows.

Britain's Defense Committee had the task of deciding not only to evacuate children and expectant mothers from London, but whether to evacuate the entire capital city.

Suicide Mission

On August 17, Air Marshal "Bomber" Harris, the Chief of RAF Bomber Command, sent fifty-seven heavy bombers to bomb Peenemünde by moonlight. Bomber crews were ordered to bomb from a lower height than usual in order to make direct hits on targets and cause as much destruction of the installations as possible. He emphasized that if they failed on the first night, the bombing raid would have to be repeated on the following night, and on any successive nights, if necessary. They were in the nature of suicide missions, since the bombers had no fighter escorts to protect them, and they were up against German fighter squadrons, antiaircraft batteries, and searchlights that crisscrossed to form a cone of light that trapped one targeted bomber at a time to destroy it. And, obviously, the Germans would increase their defenses and reinforce their armaments after the first bombing attack.

Selected skilled pilots and crews flew ahead of squadrons as "pathfinders" to mark the route and illuminate the targets for the others with flares or bombs. A master bomber circled intended targets and instructed other bomber crews by radiophone. They were the first to be isolated in the glare of searchlights, to be chosen for destruction by enemy antiaircraft guns and fighter planes.

In order to gain some time for surprise, a feint attack was made over Berlin as a deception by RAF Mosquitoes.

Despite cloud formations over Peenemünde, the RAF successfully achieved concentrated bombing on their prime targets. The parent factory was hit. And most of the pilots got away safely, Churchill reported, but German fighters caught them when they returned.[6] Forty RAF bombers were shot down in the raid.

Fearing further attacks, the Germans now concentrated manufacturing in underground factories and assembly plants in the Hartz Mountains, delaying the perfecting and production of the projectiles. They moved their experimental sites beyond RAF bombing range in Poland, where Polish underground agents kept watch on developments. They informed British Intelligence of trials of new weapons in January 1944. This led to more realistic assessments of their range and line of fire.

When one trial rocket fell beside the river without exploding, a Polish agent managed to roll it into the water and watched while the Germans finally gave up searching for it. The agent dismantled it that night. And a Polish engineer named Kocjan was picked up by an RAF Dakota at night on July 25 and flown to England with the essential parts of the projectile for examination. Kocjan decided to return to Warsaw, where he was arrested by the Gestapo and executed.

The bombing of Peenemünde, and subsequent raids on launching sites in France, postponed the German assaults on London by about nine months. That delay resulted in the French sites being overrun by General Montgomery's ground forces. It also resulted in the Germans having to use improvised sites in Holland, which were twice the distance from London and less accurate as a consequence. And the ensuing chaos of war caused on the continent of Europe after the Allied D-Day landings interfered with the transportation of rockets and projectiles from factories to launching sites.

Eisenhower would remark that "it seemed likely that if the German had succeeded in perfecting and using these new weapons six months earlier than he did, our invasion of Europe would have proved exceedingly difficult, perhaps impossible."[7]

As it was, Britain had to make plans against being assaulted by flying bombs. They included establishing three defense zones: a balloon barrage on London's outskirts, a gun belt beyond that ring, and an area for RAF fighters to operate beyond that. Supplies of electronic predictors and radio proximity fuses were hastened from the United States to enable antiaircraft gunners to shoot down any flying bombs they could target. And the RAF and U.S. air forces continued to bomb effectively a hundred or so rocket sites in northern France. This resulted in the Germans using less elaborate and better

Andrew Roberts: "Proponents of air doctrine in the bomber wings of the German, British, and American air forces in the 1920s and 1930s all believed that it was possible to win wars through bombing alone, with navies relegated to a blockading role and armies primarily used for mopping up and occupation."[8] Only actual experience in the Second World War would demonstrate that those tactics were wrong.

Meanwhile, the German Luftwaffe had bombed Warsaw in 1939, Rotterdam and Coventry in 1940, and Belgrade in 1941. There would be a tendency later on to sympathize with enemy civilians as victims. They were, of course, victims of war like everyone else. But the real victims who were being pressured with great intensity were the young RAF bomber crews—almost straight out of school—who had to undertake dangerous bombing missions over German territory, mostly at night, and who often never returned back home. It was a horrendous and terrifying voyage into the unknown, with the battering of antiaircraft shells and machine-gun fire from attacking fighter planes aimed purposefully at them as they hung perilously in the skies above their targets, while clearly spotlit for destruction by enemy searchlights.

RAF Pathfinders in their Sterling Bombers were the most vulnerable of all, because they drew off most of the enemy fire on themselves, as their navigators, observers, and bombardiers checked the sites against their map positions and became more and more exposed by every German spotlight in the zone. Not only were they set up in the cones of searchlights for enemy antiaircraft fire to strike them more accurately, but also for enemy fighters that buzzed around them and machine-gunned their own rear gunners, leaving them helpless. Nor did they or their comrades who followed them have protection from RAF fighter escorts, because there weren't enough Hurricanes for defense purposes. RAF bomber crews were dispatched on their missions in aircraft that were little more than flying coffins. RAF bomber crews even nicknamed the Wellington bomber the "Flying Coffin," because that is what it looked like.

Bomber Command attempted, whenever possible, to select particular German armament factories for bombing, which were at least 30 percent of their targets. The policy shifted to "destroying huge, heavily populated industrial areas," in order to dislocate production of war material—like ball bearings and synthetic oil—and demoralize the German working population. It was shown that, after bombing raids, workers failed to turn up at a bombed factory, because they were either looking after their families or couldn't reach their workplace because of the devastation caused by the bombings. Some left the most vulnerable cities for the safety of the countryside, where food was more likely to be available. There was no doubt that bombings interfered with and weakened the enemy war effort. "In the BMW factory in Munich, for example, some 20 percent of the workforce were absent in the summer of 1944, and in the same year absenteeism rose to 2.5 percent in the Ford plant in Cologne in the Ruhr."[9]

Air Chief Marshal Sir "Bomber" Harris was dedicated to a policy he inherited in 1942, believing it would shorten the war and save Allied lives. It would also divert and soften up German troops, rendering them less dangerous to Allied troops fighting them on the ground.

"Bomber" Harris was targeted for abuse because he was "particularly difficult to control" and "a cad." "Kill the Boche, terrify the Boche," he would say. But perhaps his biggest failing was not looking after his bomber crews by providing them with fighter escorts for protection.[10] On VE day he would write to apologize by letter to his sole superior, Lord Portal, air force marshal of the RAF, saying he was "borne down by the frightful inhumanities of war."[11] The public protested when his statue was unveiled on Whitehall.

"Bomber" Harris could be as flamboyantly persistent with his claims as Churchill in his attempts to destroy the enemy. He insisted that a bombing offensive on Germany could knock it out of the war "in a matter of months." His disdain for the defensive use of aircraft like Coastal Command appealed to Churchill as did his attitude of not wasting existing resources but using them to maximum effect. He advised on taking U.S. Liberators from Coastal Command for the use of raids on industrial cities by Bomber Command, whereas his superior officer, Lord Portal, considered that Lancasters were more suitable for strategic bombing.

At one time or another, most commanders were looking for a possible "killer blow" that would finish off either Italy or Germany. At the end, it would be left to President Truman to use the atom bomb on the Japanese for that purpose.

Meanwhile, losses suffered by RAF Bomber Command were far too great, even grotesque—150 aircraft in one month alone in 1942. At least 55,573

RAF bomber crew members lost their lives in the war, of whom 47,268 were killed in action on bombing operations, and 8,305 during training—representing a quarter of all the British military dead. The number of bomber aircraft that failed to return was 6,440—about double than lost by the U.S. Air Force, and 44.4 percent of RAF Bomber Command were killed.[12]

As a result of RAF bombings of the Ruhr and Hamburg, monthly growth in German armament production dropped to zero in May 1943 to February 1944.[13] Axis bombing raids on Britain also dropped between 1941 and 1945, roughly in proportion to the increase in RAF bombings of German cities.[14]

Aircrews

Most people have a reasonably accurate idea of what young daredevil fighter pilots were like in both World Wars. Plenty of books were written by and about them, and a number of fictional films were screened in cinemas with heroic story lines that appealed to millions of adventurous teenagers ever since the iconic Hollywood movie of *The Dawn Patrol* appeared in cinemas in 1930 (remade in 1938). But pilots of heavy bombers in World War II are rarely, if ever, profiled—perhaps because of the anger over "Bomber" Harris.

The main differences were that fighter pilots had to be able to think fast and accurately, and they required the killer instinct that Churchill attempted to imprint on his generals. They were tested for fast instincts and accuracy beforehand in cockpit simulators, and they failed if they didn't show enough measurable aptitude. Having no crew, they could be single-minded in their determination to hunt and kill the enemy. Bomber pilots, on the other hand, were required to possess a sense of responsibility for their aircrews and their aircraft. They were not necessarily slower, but more deliberate thinkers, because anything could happen suddenly and unexpectedly from enemy fighters in the air and antiaircraft fire from the ground, as well as unforeseen technical problems with their aircraft. Emergencies required instant reactions.

While RAF successes in the Battle of Britain had been defensive in protecting the British Isles, Air Chief Marshal Portal recommended using overwhelming force to break German morale with an offensive force of four thousand aircraft—despite the Butt report that claimed few bombs ever hit their targets. And Churchill, who was convinced of Germany's industrial vulnerability, agreed to expand the strength of RAF Bomber Command. The relative ineffectiveness of the Luftwaffe's bombing raids on Britain was ignored. That was when the RAF launched its bombing raid first on Mannheim on December 16, 1940, in retaliation for the German raid on Coventry a month earlier.

In July 1941, the bombing of German cities was ardently supported by Lord Trenchard, in view of the findings of the Butt Report, since cities were much easier targets that could hardly be missed, and evidence of bomb damage could be shown on aerial photographs. Bomber Harris was delighted, and he was determined to retaliate for the German bombing of London. But, unfortunately, Bomber Command's losses had been horrific—almost five thousand men and 2,331 aircraft in two years.

The lives of bomber crews possessed none of the glamorous attributes of Spitfire and Hurricane fighter pilots, who were known as the "Brylcreem Boys," from the popular brand of glossy hair cream used by men at the time. But there was a great deal of anxiety and tension involved in both cases as they waited to be called to the next briefing. Even so, they were volunteers who genuinely believed they were saving Allied lives and their families from the madness of war by getting it over more quickly. So they were as adventurous as fighter pilots, and much the same age, typically from about nineteen to twenty-four. However, many (around eight thousand) never experienced combat because they were killed in training crashes.

Crew briefings focused the mind. And there was considerable comradeship in which young men, straight out of school, bonded with their aircrews and other airmen. The RAF quickly became their new family after leaving home for the first time, while their real family receded more and more to the backs of their minds, since survival in combat had to be at the forefront. Pressures were considerable, from being targeted by antiaircraft flak over their targets to the loss of their crews from attacking enemy fighter planes. Seeing comrades spin out of control in the air when under attack or descend in flames was a daily occurrence. From the obligatory tour of operations consisting of a minimum of thirty bombing raids, "less than one RAF aircrew in five survived a thirty mission tour."[15]

The ordeal of aircrews being attacked by fighter pilots or antiaircraft fire left its mark on their minds. Despite what was known about shell shock in the First World War, few RAF psychiatrists understood it during the Second World War. It was only long afterward that posttraumatic stress disorder began to be understood as the shell shock that Freud diagnosed but that wouldn't go away, as he'd assumed it would. When aircrews were invalided out because of physical or mental incapacities from shattered nerves, their medical report invariably stated "NYDN" for "not yet diagnosed neurosis." RAF air personnel diagnosed with psychological stress numbered 2,989.[16] (Hence the success of the satirical novel named *Catch-22* for good reason. It was an attempt to laugh at the madness of war, the madness of flyers, and the madness of commanders who sent them on suicide missions. But helpless laughter when people are frantically attempting to survive relentless onslaughts is impossible in war. The novel had to be written with due cynicism by an American and published in 1961, long after it was all over and the Allies had won.)[17]

The first RAF bombing raid consisting of a thousand aircraft was undertaken over Cologne on May 30, 1942. The result of the furnaces created by incendiaries sent the U.S. Army Air Force to Britain to join in the bombing raids over Europe—the RAF at night, the USAAF by day. Each was as inaccurate at the other. And neither was escorted by fighter planes.[18]

Bad weather and heavy cloud formations caused a number of midair collisions and crashes on landing. "Many had the 'shakes,' and some suffered from fainting spells, temporary blindness or even catatonia." Symptoms were often delayed.[19] Some symptoms of PTSD (as it is now known) involve flashbacks or replications of the original incident that caused the trauma, numbed emotions resulting in an inability to feel happiness or enjoy normal relationships, an inability to sleep, exaggerated responses and impulsive outbursts of rage and aggression, poor memory and difficulty in concentrating, feelings of anxiety and apprehension, unpredictable behavior, and sudden emotional and lifestyle changes.

There are memorials all over the world to such young heroes. All that is left of them now are their names inscribed in row after row, as if lining up to be briefed for another raid. It is to such brave young men that all the following generations owe their lives.

25

D-DAY

Hitler's growing anger at the Allies was revealed by his increasing air offensives in England, for which he recklessly withdrew aircraft and aircrews from more important battle zones. The strength of the Luftwaffe in the Mediterranean in July 1943 had been 975. It dropped in October to 430, and then again to only 370 by January 1, 1944.[1] His reprisals against the British grew into a "Little Blitz" in the spring. It seemed he was satisfied that twenty good divisions were enough troops on the ground in Italy, without needing the Luftwaffe there as well.

The Allied Second Front, code-named Overlord, was not quite ready yet, but definitely planned to be launched in 1944. The D-Day objective was to use overwhelming force to subdue enemy forces as quickly as possible and save Allied lives. They knew that if the Normandy landings failed to be launched, it was likely that President Roosevelt would turn away from his Germany-First policy and send U.S. troops to the Pacific as a priority instead.[2] Meanwhile, right up until the last moment, there was plenty of speculation about where the proposed landings would be.

Meanwhile, in the five months before D-Day, Britain finally caught up with its promised targets to Russia by delivering over a million tons of supplies and weaponry on 191 ships.[3]

As the organization for the "Great Invasion" moved toward its final phase, the stalemate over Italy caused the Mediterranean front almost to vanish from everyone's mind with the imminent approach of Operation Overlord, now scheduled for June 6. Even with the present thirty Allied divisions, the British Chiefs of Staff feared heavy losses and a possible catastrophe. The Allied experiences of amphibious landings so far had been near disasters, like Salerno,

Anzio, Dakar, and Dieppe. And no doubt, the ghosts of Gallipoli still haunted Winston Churchill from the First World War. They had all been learning experiences for the Great Invasion. This time the planners would make sure of total air and sea supremacy, and restrain counterattacks by using advance bombing and airborne assaults on German fortresses. Twenty-five Allied divisions were planned by the end of June, and another fourteen to follow.

Meanwhile, about 176,000 troops had to be brought from their normal points all over Britain to the southern counties, stretching from Ipswich to Cornwall and the Bristol Channel, and distributed into camps from where they were marshaled to the coast. Then they had to be divided up into embarkation boatloads. They were protected from the air and by nearly seven thousand guns and rockets, and over a thousand barrage balloons. Southern England became a vast military camp, protected by the Home Guard, who manned antiaircraft guns and some coastal defenses.

Hitler knew the Allies had to attack in the West and that the decisive battles would be fought soon to decide the outcome of the war. Consequently, a great deal of work had been done on German fortifications in Normandy called the "Atlantic Wall." It was estimated that the Germans used two million slave laborers during the previous two years and eighteen million tons of concrete for deep bunkers and intimidating forts. They had laid minefields on beaches and in the sea. Tall wooden poles were sunk in fields to prevent gliders from landing. Rommel was put in command of Army Group B in January 1944.

"Watch Normandy," Hitler warned.

Meanwhile, Churchill knew that success in war is based on deception, and always would be. He had read the classics and would have known the story of the famous deception of the so-called wooden horse as Homer told it in the legendary Trojan Wars, General Sun Tzu's record of military deceptions in China, and the historical ones in Prussia by Frederick the Great, who took a personal interest in it. So did Winston Churchill. The objective was to mislead the enemy forces to their disadvantage in a continual effort to confuse and defeat them. So far, he had managed to ensure that most German troops were deployed somewhere other than where the Allies planned to attack. Most Allied reconnaissance flights had been sent over the Pas de Calais. And a false U.S. Army Group had been invented and placed across the Channel from

Calais, with a prominent public relations visit from King George. Dummy tanks were stationed outside the pretend headquarters with imitation landing craft and even stoves that smoked to show it was inhabited.[4]

False wireless traffic was sent and dummy landing craft and tanks placed in the Thames estuary. The best-known deception was hiring an actor who played the role of Montgomery in Gibraltar to lull any suspicions by German Intelligence that the invasion mighty be about to take place. Whereas the German army took for granted that an established port would be used to bring in supplies, Churchill had put great faith in the construction of a prefabricated, artificial Mulberry Harbour—built by two thousand men— which would be towed across the Channel from Devon and then sunk off two of the invasion beaches in Normandy.

From the Allies' point of view, the main value of the Italian Campaign lay in distracting Hitler from Overlord by keeping German troops tied up and busy fighting well away from the main battles that would end the war, which were the Second Front in the west and the Russian front in the east.

Field Marshal Kesselring decided to advance and make a stand against the Allied forces in Italy, while unaware that the major campaign was about to take place imminently in Normandy instead.

It had taken an endless number of Allied conferences over several years with heads of state and military leaders to reach an agreement on Operation Overlord. The landings took a great deal of planning, organizing, and training. The synthetic harbors, code-named "Mullberries," had needed to be designed and manufactured in the previous year, then towed over and "brought into action within a few days of the first landing."[5] Accurate timing of every activity and event was essential.

American troops had been landing in England for some time and gradually been absorbed inland, mostly along the south coast, facing targets not so very far away across the Channel.

"The theory and practice of amphibious operations," wrote Churchill, "had long been established by the Combined Operations Staff under Admiral Mountbatten, who had been succeeded by General Laycock." Now it had to be taught to everyone concerned with the proposed landings, as thorough training in modern warfare for the troops. Those exercises had already been going on inland of the south coast of England, and also as part of American military training in exercises with live ammunition, to be followed in rural areas of Sussex by Allied divisions that trained together. Lessons also from hard experience in failed attempts like Dieppe and the Dunkirk retreat were applied and rehearsed by the three armed services. They were concluded in early May.

Churchill expected all the activity to be observed from a distance by the Germans and had no objections since much of what could be seen was a ruse contrived to deceive the enemy. Special efforts were made so that they could be contemplated and passed on by pro-Nazi watchers in the Pas de Calais, where Churchill wanted the Germans to believe the landings were aimed.[6]

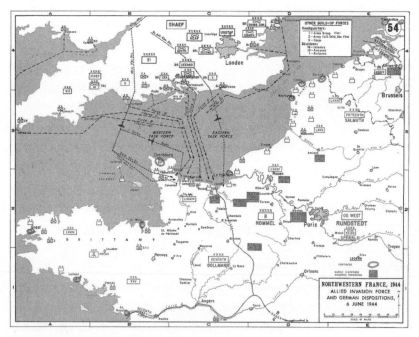

The Allied invasion of Normandy on 6 June 1944, code-named "Operation Overlord."

The Great Invasion

Churchill was awed by the prospect of the proposed Normandy landings and suffered from several changes of mind beforehand, even as he prepared for them and was involved in scheduling the dates. Like Eisenhower, he could imagine thousands of Allied bodies floating facedown in the Channel. But the Americans insisted on it to overwhelm and destroy the last German resistance. Fortunately, despite a post-colonial resentment toward Britain, which was reciprocated, the Anglo-American military accord worked—although the British Admiral Cunningham found it difficult to work with the icy and Anglophobic Admiral King. And, as military historian Max Hastings observed, "Eisenhower who privately liked the British a good deal less than his geniality caused them to suppose, deserved much of the credit." In particular, it should be added, for his extreme forbearance in the face of Montgomery's posturing.

Not everyone was able to pull a curtain across the acrimony between the two allies as Churchill managed to do during the entire war, with his calculated deceits and little white lies, vacillations, and innuendoes. The Alliance was far too important for Britain to be destroyed by pettiness and vainglorious competition under the stresses of war. Churchill's brotherly sentiments were genuine, whereas Roosevelt was motivated more by national and self-interest, since 1945 was the year for a Presidential election.

The final briefing for D-Day was given at St. Paul's School in Hammersmith, London, on May 15. It was Montgomery's old school, which he had commandeered when its classes were evacuated to the estate of the Marquis of Downshire in Easthampstead, Berkshire. Churchill finally admitted he was exhausted and passed work to others, then traveled to the south coast to make a tour of the embarkation ports beforehand. Bevin and Eden visited him on the train and discussed Britain's future after Churchill retired.

D-Day arrived on June 6, 1944. The leading assault craft were ready to hit the beaches in the largest invasion in human history. Landings were to be made on Normandy's beaches by five assault groups, code-named "Utah," "Omaha," "Gold," "Juno," and "Sword." The armada of seven thousand ships and landing craft carried close to 133,000 troops and were planned to increase to two million men. They included divisions from Britain, Canada, and the United States. The Allied troops would disembark and land on a coast "that the enemy had occupied for four years, with ample time to fortify it, cover it with obstacles and sow it with mines. For the defense, the Germans had fifty-eight divisions in the West, and ten of these were panzer divisions that might swiftly deliver an armored counterstroke."[7]

Despite the ultimately overwhelming size of the Allied forces, the enemy had nearly double that strength at the outset. Brooke, President Roosevelt, and Churchill all had pessimistic feelings of disaster, with the Channel a sea of floating Allied corpses.[8]

In the first edition of *Mein Kampf*, Hitler had written that the Germans have to be gulled in order to be led.[9] But he was unaware that he was being gulled and led to his own destruction by Winston Churchill throughout the entire war. The deceptions played on him to conceal the places and date of the D-Day landings were only a part of it. There was also a real and an imaginary network of British agents who supplied false information to the Abwehr, and also by German agents who had been turned by MI5. The information was completely trusted by the Germans.[10] The result was that half a million German troops remained stationary near the Pas de Calais up to June 26, guarding against an invasion that would never happen there.[11]

Meanwhile, the surge of Allied troops was held up by the sea crossing and the landing craft, in a kind of bottleneck, since only six divisions could be disembarked in the first seaborne lift, with three airborne divisions. It would take a whole week before they could land double that number. So there was considerable last-minute anxiety about breaking through the Atlantic Wall. A complicated assault operation of this size had never been attempted before, and its success depended on overcoming the hurdles of the enormous odds against it succeeding—hence the previous reluctance of the German generals to mount such an attack against Britain.

Now the invasion force approached the enemy coast by moonlight. The intention was to allow a short period of daylight to position the small craft and give accuracy and order to their deployment under cover of the bombardment. But if they took too long, the enemy would quickly recover from the surprise and fire on the Allied troops, who would be sitting ducks when landing. French Resistance forces were told to be ready for the invasion by a BBC broadcast on June 1 with the first line of a poem by Verlaine. Rommel was unavailable to give orders because he was celebrating his wife's birthday at home. As he would write later on:

Even the movement of the most minor formations on the battle-front—artillery going into position, tanks forming up . . . is instantly attacked from the air with devastating effect. During the day fighting troops and headquarters alike are freed to seek cover in wooded and close country in order to escape the constant pounding of the air. Up to 640 [naval] guns have been used. The effect is so immense that no operation of any kind is possible in the area commanded by this rapid-fire artillery, either by infantry or tanks.[12]

Lieutenant-General Speidel encapsulated what Rommel said, after it was all over—that the enormous air superiority of the Allies was so great that if they were not hurled from the mainland within forty-eight hours of arrival, then the invasion had succeeded.[13]

Up until lunchtime, German HQ was unsure whether it was a real invasion or merely a deception. Valuable time was lost while two panzer divisions were sent a hundred miles to the beaches, since Rommel wanted the Allies stopped before they were ashore. Runstedt thought they would have to be driven back since they couldn't be stopped from landing. According to Rommel, "The first twenty-four hours will be decisive."[14]

Forty minutes after a massive naval bombardment on the beach fortifications and villages at 5:50 a.m., the main American landings began at Utah and Omaha beaches. British and Canadian troops arrived an hour later on the other three beaches.

The Anglo-American Campaign

The matter of tides was crucial, since underwater obstacles would obstruct the landing crafts if they arrived at high tide. And if they arrived at low tide, the army would be exposed for longer to enemy fire while crossing the beaches. The right conditions for a landing were available for only three days in each lunar month. Eisenhower's target date had been either June 5, 6, or 7. He chose June 5. But if the weather turned out to be unsuitable, D-Day would have had to be postponed for at least two weeks, possibly even a month if they waited for the moon.

Bombardment from the air and offshore naval guns beforehand was essential to cover the first landing. And it had to be all along the French coast to maintain surprise as to where each landing would actually take place. To soften up the defenses beforehand, British heavy bombers attacked the ten heaviest German batteries that might prevent the landings. Then, about half an hour after first light, enemy defenses were assaulted by heavy and medium U.S. bombers and guns, as well as rockets from naval assault craft.

A great deal of thought was also given to deceiving the enemy, who expected an invasion at some place and at some time. The Allies had to conceal the place and time for as long as possible.

The major deception was to pretend that the invasion was coming from across the Straits of Dover. And the most obvious way to mislead the enemy was to simulate a concentration of troops in Kent and Sussex, to collect fleets of dummy ships in the Cinque Ports, and to rehearse landing exercises on the nearby beaches. And there was an increase in wireless activity.[15] All such deceptions were used, and many more.

Another distraction for the enemy was the announcement that General Alexander had led the Allied armies in the liberation of Rome the previous night. But instead of being the key to Italy, it turned out to be just another sideshow in a long journey up the leg of the continent.

The D-Day Landings

Twenty-three thousand men managed to get ashore at "Utah" beach, with only 210 killed or wounded, as a consequence of a current that swept landing craft two thousand yards from the designated area. German troops surrendered "in large numbers" when the airborne division blocked off most exits from the beaches.

Two-thirds of the American forces were planned to land on "Omaha" beach. Theirs was a very different situation. They lost ten times the numbers of troops as were destroyed at "Utah."[16]

The cliffs and bluffs at Omaha were in some places more than 150 feet above the sea wall at the end of the dunes; the inward curvature of the coast at that stretch helped German fields of fire to overlap; underwater sandbars and ridges snagged landing-craft; the powerful and well-placed fortifications (which can still be seen today) were not silenced by naval shellings; the anti-personnel mines, barbed wire and huge steel anti-tank 'hedgehogs' proved murderous obstacles; accurate German artillery fire, and above all a regiment of the 716th Infantry Division and units of the crack German 352nd Infantry Division, caused havoc. . . . These battalions provided 'by far the greatest concentration of German fire on the entire invasion front.'[17]

Although the ground seems to have been badly chosen for an invasion, "Omaha beach was the only feasible landing area between Utah and the British and Canadian beaches."[18]

American troops were landed on six thousand yards of Omaha beach, which soon became "a scene of confusion and destruction." Their ages averaged at twenty and a half years (younger than the British twenty-four or the Canadian twenty-nine). "They had to leap out of their landing-craft into a hail of machine-gun and mortar fire loaded down with sixty-eight pounds of equipment, including gas masks, grenades, TNT blocks, two ammunition bandoliers, rations, water bottle, and related kit. Many simply drowned when the water they jumped into proved deeper than expected."[19]

Many American troops had not seen combat before, and most were not in fighting shape when they landed after three hours and had been seasick in rough seas. "I never saw water that bad," one sergeant said. It prevented the Americans from having the necessary firepower to storm the beaches and escape from enemy gunfire. (There was less turbulent weather for the British troops.) The result was a chaos of "burning tanks, jeeps, abandoned vehicles, a terrific crossfire."[20] General Bradley observed it through his binoculars from one of the landing crafts. He could see they were pinned down on the beaches for seven hours. But at 1:30 p.m. they finally advanced up the heights beyond the beaches. Thirty-four thousand got ashore. But two thousand Americans were left dead on Omaha beach alone.

Fortunately, for the troops landing on "Gold," "Juno," and "Sword" beaches, there were no high cliffs to climb and more time for Allied naval bombardment to soften up the German defenses.[21] Despite the expected slaughter, the D-Day landings turned out to be the greatest triumph of cooperation and coordination in military history.

Two and a half hours later, Hitler—who still thought it was only a diversionary tactic—let General Rundstedt send two panzer divisions into battle. But it was too little, too late, and the air supremacy of the Allies slowed them down. Meanwhile, twenty-four German divisions still waited for what Hitler thought would be the real attack at the Pas de Calais. One result was that, although RAF Air Chief Marshal Tedder had forecast that Allied airborne troops would lose eighty percent of their men, the actual loss was only 15 percent.[22]

German troops showed a capacity for counterattack but were prevented by the overwhelming forces of the RAF and U.S. Air Force. The previous Allied bombing attacks on Luftwaffe factories were shown to have reduced the production of German fighter planes.

When fifteen-year-old Anne Frank heard of the landings, she was still hiding from the Nazis who planned to murder her. She wrote excitedly in her diary, "The invasion has begun!" It gave her hope of escape. But she would not live long enough to benefit from it. She was betrayed, arrested on August 4, and taken from her secret hideout to die in Bergen-Belsen death camp before it could be liberated by the Allies.

The Allies expanded their first landing into an eighty-mile-wide bridgehead. The Germans never did manage to launch a dangerous attack before the Allies broke out in exactly the way and place that Montgomery had planned. The German positions in France simply collapsed. But "the Allies were in great danger at the outset, and had a very narrow shave." The margin between success and failure had been incredibly narrow.[23]

Field Marshal Rommel's coastal defenses were overcome by 9:00 a.m. And Montgomery's advance inland with his troops to Caen began that afternoon.

A Visit to the Battlefields

Meanwhile, the Russian summer offensive was due to commence on June 10. It was also the day when General Montgomery reported to Churchill that he was now safely established ashore to receive a visit.[24]

Happy and eager to be in the thick of fighting again, Churchill accepted General Montgomery's invitation to visit the battlefields. A British and American destroyer awaited him at Portsmouth, and he crossed the Channel without incident, arriving cheerfully with his habitual cigar, accompanied by Generals Smuts, Brooke, Marshall, and Admiral King.

Monty was all smiles when Churchill arrived with his retinue. The general always contrived to make everything look easy, as if it had all happened according to his original plans. It did go according to plan, but not according to timing. He would be held up for longer than he'd scheduled.

The weather was brilliant when Montgomery met them on the beach, still smiling and confident, as they scrambled out of their landing craft. His army had already penetrated seven or eight miles inland. There was very little firing or activity. They drove through fertile agricultural terrain in Normandy, with Monty in high spirits. The battlefront was only three miles away.[25] Montgomery's headquarters was about five miles inland. It had already been bombed, and it received another bombing attack after they met.

Churchill, with his usual aplomb, managed to ignore Montgomery's boasting and shared his triumph with him. Despite his admiration for Monty's audacity and his continual good luck, Churchill found his vulgarity somewhat offensive. And it continued to increase with his successes. But, like Ike Eisenhower with General Patton, Churchill showed considerable forbearance with the posturing of his generals. He knew it went with the territory, and he considered himself fortunate finally to have found one with the attribute he'd sought—the killer instinct. Encouragement kept them on their toes. But neither needed it; they were both so determined and thick-skinned that nothing could deter them from mastering challenges to display their brilliance.

Montgomery moved on two days afterward. His troops were checked by the only panzer division in the area. A second panzer division arrived the next day, then a third. It took a month of fighting before the position was secured. They thrust their way in to Villers-Bocage on the thirteenth but were pushed out again. The German defensive forces were reinforced by a fourth panzer division. It took two more months of heavy fighting to capture Villers-Bocage.

Monty's original plan had been to capture the whole of the peninsula with the port of Cherbourg in two weeks. The breakout would then be made twenty days after the landing. But American advances from their beaches turned out to be slower than expected, although German forces were drawn off to check Montgomery's own assaults. Instead, his breakout came thirty-six days later than he'd originally planned.

As it turned out, the slower-than-planned advance and the "toughness of the resistance" acted in the Allies' favor. German reinforcements arrived a bit at a time and were ground down first, before the next group arrived. Overcoming enemy resistance at that point ensured the Allies a clear run through France afterward. Nevertheless, they would not have had a chance of getting established without supporting naval gunfire, or winning without air supremacy. Another factor in their favor was the conflict of different ideas between Hitler and his generals, and between the German generals themselves.[26]

The German generals argued for hours on D-Day. As General Blumenstein would remark afterward:

> As early as four a.m. I telephoned them [Hitler's headquarters] on behalf of Field-Marshal von Runstedt and asked for the release of this Corps—to strengthen Rommel's punch. But Jodl, speaking for Hitler, refused to do so. He doubted whether the landings in Normandy were more than a feint, and was sure that another landing was coming east of the Seine. The battle of argument went on all day until 4 p.m., when this Corps was at last released for our use.[27]

Clearly, the Allied deceptions had worked. Rommel himself—who was the commander of the Normandy defenses—had casually gone home to Ulm for his wife's birthday at the critical hour.

The enemy had over three thousand miles of coastline to cover. Nevertheless, Hitler dismissed all his generals' warnings in a complacent belief that his new flying bombs would seal the outcome of the war.

The most massive tank attack on the enemy took place on July 18 when three Allied armored divisions took the Germans by surprise. They had assembled stealthily in a small bridgehead over the Orne and poured out in the early morning after a broad area had been bombed by two thousand Allied aircraft for two hours. The Germans were deafened by the continued and massive explosions. They were taken prisoner but were still too stunned to be interrogated for at least a day afterward.

Meanwhile, Hitler's last German reserves had been used in the attempt to stop the British. It allowed the U.S. First Army to launch a fresh offensive on July 25. And General Patton's recently landed Third Army was eager to follow. The American spearhead thrust through the Avranches front on the thirty-first. Patton's tanks poured through the gap and quickly flooded the open countryside. "Remnants of the panzer divisions were scraped together and used in a desperate effort to cut the bottleneck at Avranches." It failed. And many Germans were trapped in the "Falaise Pocket." It was a time of stormy recriminations on the German side. General Kluge, who was in command of the German forces, was sacked, and swallowed a poison capsule on his way home.

Field Marshal Rommel was knocked out of the war when his staff car was strafed by British aircraft. The Allied breakout at Avranches was made on July 31. The bulk of German forces had been kept in the area until they collapsed, as a consequence of Hitler's orders for no withdrawal.

With Patton's tanks pouring through the Avranches breach and the German front in Normandy collapsing, "it was a moment of universal crisis for the Germans." There had also been a deliberate explosion at German headquarters on the twentieth, and tremors spread outward from the attempt to kill Hitler and overthrow the Nazi regime. A number of generals were implicated in an assassination plot that miscarried. There was initial uncertainty as to the outcome, and then fears of retribution, which produced confusion and paralysis in German military headquarters.[28]

Hitler forced Rommel to commit suicide for his alleged part in the plot, with the understanding that they would not murder his family if he complied.

When Churchill heard that Hitler had escaped alive from the attempted assassination, he joked that he was delighted to hear it, since he wouldn't want the Allies to be deprived of Hitler's military genius, which was the biggest factor in ensuring that the Allies would defeat Germany.

26

DRONES OVER LONDON

———————

ONLY A WEEK AFTER D-DAY, PILOTLESS V1 aircraft projectiles began to attack Greater London on June 13, with a continuous spluttering sound from the flames jetting out from their tails. The sound cut out just before they identified and dived down onto their targets. It was the beginning of a long premeditated assault on the civilian population in retaliation for the Allies' breakthrough of the Atlantic Wall at Normandy.

One of the first V1s landed in the suburb of Bethnal Green, killing six people and injuring nine others. The attack was premature, but Hitler was evidently desperate. Londoners began to think of it as just a "flying bomb." Speeding at up to four hundred miles an hour, it carried a ton of explosives and was steered by a magnetic compass and a tiny propeller that measured the distance to its target.

German retaliation for the Normandy defeat built up to more than two hundred missiles, which arrived in twenty-four hours. Over three thousand followed during the next five weeks. It became known familiarly as the "buzz bomb" or "doodlebug." The names reflected Britain's ridicule of Hitler and the Nazis, whom they still tended to picture more as a comic music hall act than real people.

Nevertheless, the new weapons triggered and maintained continual suspense and mental strain on the population. Their impersonal robotic nature created feelings of helplessness, because civilians were sitting targets waiting to be struck down, whereas British troops were constantly occupied in the challenge of outwitting and destroying the enemy.

The missiles hit every part of London. Croydon suffered from the most hits—eight strikes in one day. About 750,000 houses were destroyed. And there was always a danger of some dropping prematurely on the direct route from the Continent to London, in Sussex and Kent, an area known as "Bomb Alley." Barrage balloons caught 232 flying bombs before they could reach more densely populated areas in the center of the defensive ring.

Meanwhile, RAF bombing crews continued to attack launching sites— now known as "ski-sites"—in ninety-six different locations in France; some of them they eliminated.

An assessment made at one point showed that out of 2,754 flying bombs launched with 2,752 casualties, two thousand fell on London. It averaged to a cost of one bomb to kill only one individual. So, despite the advantages to the Germans of not having to use ground troops or pilots, and using disposable slave labor to make the flying bombs, they were far less destructive and less cost-effective than mass bombing raids. Hitler had merely replaced each bullet with an expensive bomb.

The average Londoner didn't need statistics to recognize the absurdity. If Hitler's purpose had been to demoralize Britain into begging for peace, he misjudged the hardiness and resolve of the British people, whose spirit he claimed he was going to break. Among other things he failed to understand about Britain was the sense of humor of the British, which gave them a sense of proportion apparently unknown to the Nazis.

RAF Bomber Command now moved from bombing V1 and V2 launching sites to destroying their factories and storage depots. Early in July their bombers attacked and destroyed the largest one. It was in underground caves around Paris, located at Saint-Leu d'Esserent, in the Oise Valley, and required heavy bombs to break through them. The caverns stored two thousand bombs and supplied 70 percent of all bombs launched in June. Another depot that held a thousand bombs was destroyed by American bombers. But the bombing raids cost the lives of nearly two thousand airmen.

By the end of July, it was decided to move antiaircraft batteries from London to the south coast, and use more fighters with RAF radar detection capabilities. The guns would fire at projectiles over the sea, which would be spotted at night by radar and pinpointed by searchlights. An effective way to reduce the number hitting London with its densely packed population was discovered by RAF pilots on the coast. They would cut them off over the

Channel by flying alongside the pilotless aircraft and gently roll them over with the tip of one wing, so that they fell into the sea. This audacious tactic probably saved thousands of lives.

The results soon became apparent with the improved performance of the gunners and the innovative tactic of the fighter pilots. By the end of August, no more than one bomb in seven penetrated the defensive rings. The best score came on August 18, when ninety-four flying bombs approached from over the sea and ninety were destroyed. It was a triumph of imaginative ideas, organization, and cooperation between fighters and bombers, scientists, Civil Defense, and all the individuals involved. Meanwhile, the rapid advance of the British and Canadian forces on the continent of Europe continued their efforts to reduce the threats on London.

Out of an estimated total of 8,000 flying bombs, only about 2,400 reached their intended targets. But they killed 6,184 Londoners and seriously injured another 17,981.

Long-Range V2 Rockets

The next threat to London came with long-range V2 rockets. They were designed to carry enormous amounts of explosives to distant targets and were still being made at Peenemünde. Professor Lindemann didn't believe it was possible for such a small projectile to carry as much weight in its warhead as some military people supposed. A committee set up to defend Britain against long-range bombs (the "Crossbow" Committee) investigated what the V2 consisted of. They considered the extent of its threat and examined how to counter it. It was code-named "Operation Crossbow."[1] In the meantime, Home Secretary Herbert Morrison considered again whether to evacuate a million people from London.

Then fragments of one of the bombs came into the Committee's hands by accident. They were pieced together by British Intelligence and the Royal Aircraft Establishment, as a consequence of a freak error in their trials at Peenemünde.

The Germans had been using glider bombs against Allied shipping for some time. They were launched from aircraft. German scientists now attempted to discover if they could steer a rocket in the same way by using a remote-control lever. It soon sped out of control range and landed in Sweden. Somehow, the remains were brought to Farnborough in England, where Britain's experts examined the battered fragments with great success.[2] The Crossbow Committee deduced that it weighed twelve tons and had a one-ton warhead. They estimated that, as of August 26, the Germans had about two thousand in stock and were manufacturing about five hundred a month. (Actual German figures would turn out to be only slightly lower.)

As Churchill described it, the rocket was controlled by gyroscopes or radio signals. It rose vertically for six miles or so, then automatic controls turned it over to climb with increasing speed at about forty-five degrees. The missile then flew in a gigantic parabola, reaching a height of about fifty miles and falling about two hundred miles away from the launching point. Its maximum speed was estimated at about four thousand miles an hour. The entire flight took no more than three or four minutes.[3]

The enemy launched their first V2 on London on September 8. It fell on the residential suburb of Chiswick in the evening. Sixteen seconds later, another one fell on Epping. In the seven months before the Allies liberated the launching area in The Hague, where most came from, about 1,300 V2s were fired against England. Their cruising altitude was too low for heavy antiaircraft guns to strike them often, and too high for light guns. Many fell short of their target. Barrage balloons with their trailing metal chains had limited success. In eighty days, two thousand V2s destroyed twenty-five thousand homes and killed five thousand Britons.[4] They caused about double the casualties that the V1s had. If British and U.S. bombing raids and army assaults had not succeeded in destroying some of the factories, their production would have started earlier and killed many more, probably double the number.

Up to twenty thousand slave laborers died in ghastly, inhuman conditions where they were forced to manufacture the rockets while being starved and ill-treated by the Nazis.[5] Both Dr. Albert Speer (Germany's Minister of Munitions) and the British Professor Lindemann maintained that the rockets were a waste of productive capacity and manpower, since they were far less effective as weapons than the aircraft production they had replaced. But Hitler had been obsessed with the program. Fortunately for the Allies, Hitler had been unable to fire them until a week after D-Day, when American, British, and Canadian troops were already ashore on the Continent.[6]

Hitler turned out to be one more example of Lord Acton's observation that "absolute power corrupts absolutely." But after it had lost the First World War, Germany had been cornered by the French and forced to sign the Treaty of Versailles. Its indemnity was too great according to the treaty's terms, and Germany's ability to pay it was prevented by the French confiscation of the country's heavy industries. Support was given to those terms by the ailing U.S. President Woodrow Wilson and the League of Nations in an unsatisfactory conclusion to the First World War. President Wilson arrived at the 1919 Peace Conference like a vengeful figure in black—as everyone dressed, out of respect for the dead—but he was like a puritan out of the pages of a Nathaniel Hawthorne novel, and he dominated the proceedings. He spent six months in Paris before taking a break from the conference and fell ill on the way back for the conclusion. He declined in power as his health deteriorated, and statesmen and the public were impatient to return to their old lives. Economist Keynes, who was present, claimed Wilson was ill-informed on foreign policy. Nevertheless, the President was determined that the Germans be punished for the most inhuman and destructive war in history. So were the French. Hitler had sought to reverse the moment the Treaty was signed. It had been a mental fixation at the core of his delusions all along.

Now Hitler's hopes of destroying the spirit of the British people in the Second World War were thwarted by his present delusions. When a hundred German scientists, technicians, and serving officers met in Berlin on May 4, 1944, they had to decide how to tell Hitler he had failed.[7]

As for the future, Duncan Sandys pointed out the advantages of rocket science, if it could be perfected and used more rationally and tactically. Churchill was quick to recognize it. "The advent of the long-range, radio-controlled, jet-propelled projectile has opened up vast new possibilities in the conduct of military operations," he wrote. He could see how the future possession of superiority in long-distance rockets would count as much as, or more than, naval or air superiority.[8]

27

VICTORY

When General "Ike" Eisenhower took over control of all ground forces from Montgomery on September 1, 1944, he planned a broad advance on Germany. Montgomery was promoted to field marshal on the same day. Monty preferred a narrow thrust "into the heart of the Reich," with his army group. But Patton claimed to be inspired by his own alternative plan with his Third Army leading the way. Bradley insisted his own drive for Frankfurt should be at the center. Evidently the generals were already imagining their legacies according to the history books that would be written about the war. One of the objections to General Bradley was the urgent need to occupy the launching sites of the flying bombs that were increasingly falling on London. That necessitated a broad front.

Ike was well aware that competition between field generals could be an effective spur, when he assigned the U.S. Ninth Army to Field Marshal Montgomery, in addition to the First Canadian and British Armies. He had already experienced Patton's impetuosity, although he knew he was an outstanding tank commander. But some American generals were indignant at Ike's choice of a Limey to command them in battle. And they responded by competing, both personally and professionally—in particular, General Patton with Montgomery. Monty took it in a sportsmanlike way. But Patton secretly thought that he himself was the most brilliant general of the war. Patton was an insecure man, whereas Montgomery was supremely self-confident, and for very good reasons.

Patton's U.S. Army's tanks broke through weak German defenses in the Eifel at the end of the Ardennes on March 7, 1945, and reached the Rhine, near Coblenz. His sixty-mile drive took only three days. General Bradley famously exclaimed, "Hot dog, this will bust him wide open." He meant the enemy, not Montgomery, whom they were eager to overtake. But Eisenhower's operational staff officer shook his head. "It just doesn't fit into the plan."[1]

Patton resented the restraint on his actions. He'd planned to cross the Rhine before Monty. But Montgomery had already said pretty much the same thing to prevent the U.S. Ninth Army from crossing the Rhine four days earlier. Monty's grand attack on the Rhine was carefully planned to go without a hitch on March 24, and not before. He was not prepared to take any risks now the Allies were so close to victory.

Montgomery always took care to ensure that his tactics arose out of the main strategy and matched all the overall predetermined planning, whereas Patton believed in exploiting every new opportunity that came along. And yet, both were audacious soldiers. Although Monty was methodical, he was also flexible in adapting to unforeseen situations. General Patton tended rather to act on his instincts, and could be impulsive. And General Eisenhower was not about to appoint a loose cannon to take command.

But now Patton was eager to get ahead of Monty. So he obtained Bradley's agreement to swing his forces south to "roll up the German forces west of the Rhine." And also to "seek a good spot for an early crossing." Patton cut off the German forces before they could withdraw, and crossed the Rhine on March 22, stealing a march on Montgomery by a couple of days and rolling forward as fast as his tanks would go, to reach their destination before Monty.

Hitler called for countermeasures as soon as he heard that American forces had crossed the Rhine. But he was told there were no resources left.

Meanwhile, Montgomery had prepared his grand assault on the Rhine with twenty-five divisions, compared to the enemy's "five weak and exhausted German divisions," which were all that were available to oppose him.[2] After massive bombardment from more than three thousand Allied guns and waves of Allied bombers, Monty's infantry crossed the river and established bridgeheads. Two Allied airborne divisions were dropped in front to open the way, and bridges were built behind him for reinforcements to cross the river with tanks and transports after him.

Churchill and Brooke watched the Rhine crossing from a nearby hilltop. It was followed by the roaring clouds of Allied aircraft overhead, after which a cluster of mushroomlike parachutes appeared and hovered over the Rhine. Then German shelling began, and Churchill was steered off the battlefield and ushered back home to England.

British and American losses were slight from little opposition. But Montgomery knew the powers of resistance of the stubborn German army, and he needed fighting troops rather than casualties. He was right, since Hitler was ready to destroy everything and everybody without reasonable cause.

Albert Speer was so shocked at Hitler's callous orders that he persuaded the army not to carry them out. He no longer felt any loyalty to Hitler, who cared nothing for people's lives and was morbidly attracted to mass murders, torture, and death. By now, the other generals didn't need much persuading—they had allowed Hitler to live out his delusions, but now it was all over.

Nevertheless, Hitler's fantasies continued to grow—he hoped for a miracle to save him, and he studied horoscopes. They "predicted that disaster in April would be redeemed by a sudden change of fortune." But no one came to his rescue, because there was no one left. General Zhukov's and General Konev's armies were advancing on Berlin, which was already surrounded by a ring of battle-hardened Russian troops, who began searching for the German dictator. Hitler committed suicide two weeks later in Berlin, on April 30, preferring to take his own life rather than be captured and humiliated by the Russians.

The Red Army finally linked up with British and American forces in Berlin. And the United States continued to fight the Japanese in the Pacific.

Frontline war correspondent Alan Moorehead couldn't resist observing that the Americans had now overtaken the British, not only in domination, but in determination. Whereas the British soldier was still risk-averse, the Americans were more confident, uninhibited, and audacious with their cowboy culture. Britain had relied throughout the war on Churchill's own courage, bravado, pugnacity, and his determination to win. He had led them to victory in spite of themselves. For, at heart, they were still the irreverent jokesters they had been in Edwardian times, before the First World War—immature in their attitude to life. Churchill himself, when at his most mischievous or impish, was often described as "grinning like a schoolboy." It was a characteristic that endeared him to many English people. Even so, he was a man among boys.

Mass Murder Camps

As the U.S. Army advanced north on April 5, 1945, they came across a prison camp for the first time, at Ohrdruf. It was piled high with starved and frail corpses. It turned out to be a subsidiary death camp of Buchenwald. Puzzled American troops wondered what the Germans had been up to. Some prisoners were still alive but looked like walking corpses. They had not yet been put to death by the guards, who had been surprised by the swift advance of the American army. General Patton, General Omar Bradley, and Eisenhower visited Ohrdruf a week later and saw thousands of emaciated bodies in shallow graves. One shed was piled up to the ceiling with dead bodies, torture devices, and a butcher's block for smashing gold fillings from the mouths of corpses.

Despite Patton's familiarity with dead bodies in battle, the sickening stench of decomposition and the sinister scene made him throw up. Eisenhower turned pale and remarked to frontline media correspondents, "We are told that the American soldier does not know what he was fighting for. Now, at least he will know what he is fighting against." He ordered American units in the area to visit the camp and informed the media back home. A week later, the American Timberwolf Division discovered three thousand more corpses at Nordhausen. Seven hundred were still barely alive, ill, and starving. They had been used as slave labor in the V2 rocket factories.

The Ninth Armored Infantry Battalion of the American Sixth Armored Division was taken to Buchenwald by some Russians. That death camp contained thirty thousand prisoners who were scheduled for murder because they were communists, Jews, or Gypsies. The inmates were said to be "emaciated beyond all imagination or description. Their legs and arms were sticks with huge bulging joints. . . . Their eyes were sunk so deep that they looked blind. . . . Many just lay in bunks as if dead." Even after the liberation of the death camps, hundreds continued to die daily.[3]

What the Nazis described as concentration camps in 1933 were secret camps where anyone who disagreed with Hitler vanished. Himmler's SS chose guards who were mostly violent criminals or sadists, and gave them a free hand. The Allies discovered twenty thousand such murder camps later on.[4]

Here was the evidence that Hitler intended to massacre about 80 percent of the people in territories he conquered, such as Europe, Russia, and North America, and use the remaining 20 percent as slave labor until they died of malnutrition, exhaustion, and disease. Newly won territories would become part of Greater Germany, colonized by obedient Germans who would do whatever Hitler wanted. He knew from the outset that the Jews would never cooperate with his murderous plans, since the essence of the Jewish faith is the celebration of life, which is unique and precious, so Jews became his first target to isolate and eliminate. He had prepared the way with his anti-Semitic hate-filled speech in 1932 and the construction of concentration camps as holding areas until they found the most economical way to murder all their victims.

The murder camps were the legacy that the Nazis and the German army left behind. It was estimated that they had already murdered at least fifteen to twenty million innocent people, or imprisoned and tortured them in the death camps. They included Germans, Poles, and Russian prisoners of war.[5] Their actions were not only racist; theirs was a class war waged from pathological insecurity and envy against anyone who was successful. They were obsessed with bringing others down in order to raise themselves up, by stealing their jobs, their property, and their lives.

Yalta

By the time of the Yalta summit conference in February 1945, the American military was overbearing, and the British delegation was isolated. President Roosevelt looked in ill-health and was vague and withdrawn. It was likely even then that he was dying. Marshal Stalin was quiet, amiable, and self-assured, as usual. He was also in good humor, having been privy to more secret information from the private conversations of diplomats and generals when in bugged Moscow hotels, the Russian embassy in London, or the Kremlin, than either of the other Big Three. So he knew when his allies lied or told the truth, flattered him or prevaricated. "The scale of Soviet espionage dwarfed that of every other belligerent, and yielded a rich technological harvest from Britain and the United States."[6]

By comparison, despite his exhaustion, Churchill cut the more prominent figure. And only he felt full of compassion for the enemy suffering in the Allied onslaught on the Continent and hampered by fleeing German civilian refugees—although he felt they had brought all the horrors on themselves—because he saw the situation on a far larger scale, as a continued struggle of mice and men to survive onslaughts, rape, murders, and depredation.

After arguing about the plight of Poland, he felt nothing had been accomplished, despite Stalin's silky promises, which had unnerved him, because he remembered Hitler's easy promises in the 1930s, which had been meaningless. But there was nothing he could do, short of another war, this time with Russia. And that was unthinkable. The Americans, on the other hand, accepted that since Russia suffered most to restore peace, Stalin now had a right to protect its borders and ensure its neighbors were pacified. But Churchill's conscience worried him, since he had fought one tyrant only to replace him with another. And news of each oppression of the Poles by Russian troops shadowed his joy when in almost imminent sight of victory.

Roosevelt refused to agree to any form of complaint to Stalin. Nor did Churchill's protests to Eisenhower succeed when the Americans assured Stalin that the Red Army should forge ahead of the Anglo-American allies to free Berlin and deal with Hitler.

In any case, Roosevelt died on April 12, and Churchill had to get to know the quiet but firm and decisive new President, Harry Truman.

The fighting continued for more than nine months after the Allies approached the Rhine, and before the battles on the Western Front and the Eastern Front succeeded in defeating Nazi Germany. On May 7, 1945, the German General Jodl signed the unconditional surrender in France.[7] Churchill broadcast to the nation, "The German war is therefore now at an end." Then, almost overcome with emotion, he called to the public outside, from a Whitehall balcony, "My dear friends, this is your hour."

The British delegation to the Potsdam summit on July 17, included Eden, Attlee, Montgomery, and Alexander. Churchill had his first private meeting with Truman on the previous day. They spoke about Britain's fragile financial situation and its debt to the United States of approximately fifteen billion dollars (at the 1945 exchange rate). The President told him of the testing of the new atomic bomb. Churchill agreed that it should be dropped on Japan in order to save millions of Allied lives. But neither he nor the military fully understood its strategic importance or its aftereffects. Although Churchill was impressed by the new President's toughness, nothing else was achieved.

The Legacy of War

As soon as the end of the war in Europe was announced by the BBC, masses of Londoners poured toward the center of the capital to celebrate victory. Crowds arrived at Piccadilly Circus, where the bronze statue of Eros, the mythical god of love, still stood in his protective wooden overcoat. Extravagantly happy people of many nationalities were drawn to the source of the activity, without knowing where they were going or quite what to expect. And, as they watched the joyous antics of inebriated revelers hugging each other and being embraced or kissed by strangers, they cavorted or were swung excitedly around the famous monument. But it was also clear from a few tearful faces of some who had lost loved ones that they felt even more isolated than before. Those whom they wanted to celebrate with were gone, and their absence was suddenly felt as an anticlimax to the end of war.

Many others had grown up in wartime and almost had taken war for granted as a normal way of life. War provided the simplest of choices—either you strove to win or you gave up and died. They suddenly realized that peace would not be so simple. Hitler had left his shadow behind.

Watching jubilant civilians and servicemen and women in uniform jostling with each other to climb the wooden structure in the most familiar center in London's West End, where Piccadilly, Shaftsbury Avenue, Coventry Street, and the Haymarket meet, those who had experienced some of the worst action were overwhelmed by a similar anticlimax to the one felt at the same time by Winston Churchill—all the striving was finally over.

Despite the triumph and jubilation, the moment of glory was like a flamboyant firework that explodes with passion, to end up sodden, lifeless, and discarded in a puddle of rain. As at the end of the First World War, they were now left to face the havoc wrought by it—the bankruptcy of the nation, the loss of empire, the austerity to come, a starving population in Germany that had to be fed, and the realization in so many households of servicemen and women and civilians who would never return home.

As for the achievement of victory, like all achievements, it possessed a hollow center, since it left in its wake not only the tragedy of lost lives, but also a loss of purpose. After the medals for valor, the promotions in rank, and the knighthoods would come the inevitable autobiographies and memoirs of the victors writing in retirement. And then what?

Just like the German dictator, who put the barrel of a gun into his mouth at half past three in the afternoon and pulled the trigger, Winston Churchill also "lost all power to control events." Nevertheless, Churchill's day opened with his normal office routines in the air-raid shelter beneath the Chancellery at the center of London, almost as if nothing unusual had happened.[8]

But at least there was gallantry left. Five days later, he wrote to Anthony Eden:

> You will by now have heard the news of the tremendous surrender that has been made to Montgomery of all Northwest Germany, Holland and Denmark, both as regards men and ships. The men alone must be more than a million. Thus in three consecutive days two and a half million Germans have surrendered to our British commanders. This is quite a satisfactory incident in our military history. Ike has been splendid throughout. We must vie with him in sportsmanship.

Several days after that, Marshal Stalin wrote to Winston Churchill, "I send my personal greetings to you, stout-hearted British Armed Forces and the whole British people, and I congratulate you with all my heart on the great victory over our common enemy, German Imperialism."

But despite all the accolades, Churchill knew how relief leads—all too soon—to complacency and results in inertia. And yet there was a great deal still to be done. So that when he spoke to the British nation, he opened by saying, "I wish I could tell you tonight that all our toils and troubles are over."

But the electorate cannot stand too much truth, and they wanted to get back to their old lives as quickly as possible. His whole approach was an error of judgment. The British had endured too much reality. Now they suddenly viewed their prime minister as an impediment to resuming their normal lives.

Meanwhile, President Roosevelt was dead, and it was left to President Truman to shoulder the burden of how to save millions of American lives still being lost on the seas and battlefields in the Pacific War. Since the atom bomb had finally become a scientific reality, he had to send one over to Japan to stop the unnecessary wholesale slaughter that still continued. And then, when that had no effect, he sent a second one to emphasize the Japanese military's lack of any other choice but immediate and unconditional surrender.

For Churchill, accustomed to wielding power and working continuously for victory, the end of the war provided a restless interlude before the next General Election. He was well aware that human failings do not disappear overnight, or when a document of surrender is signed. There was still plenty of work to be done, and already there were signs of a chasm opening between the interests of the West and those of Soviet Russia. But he admired Marshal Stalin personally as a leader who had saved the Russian people from slavery and extinction. The feeling appeared to be mutual as Churchill sat at a banquet between President Truman on his right and Stalin on his left, at the Potsdam Conference. He poured a glass of brandy for Stalin and one for himself, and raised his glass as they toasted each other.

But Churchill was still worried about the future tactics and tyranny of the Russians. Having been impressed by the new American President's staunchness, Churchill instructed his chiefs of staff to study the military situation in the West and prepare a strategic plan to push the Red Army back, in order to secure justice for Poland. He also ordered Field Marshal Montgomery to stockpile all captured German weapons for the future. The secret file he opened was coded, "Unthinkable."

Britain's wartime coalition government was dissolved on May 23 and an election scheduled for July 26. Eden felt alienated from his political party and wondered if the system of government was now obsolete. And General Slim, on leave from Burma, warned Churchill not to expect any votes from the army. A new tide was coming in with questions about their future lives, rather than recapturing the past glories of the British Empire. Churchill began to feel he might have lost his touch.

He returned home on July 25, 1945 and went to bed, satisfied in his belief that the British electorate would want him to remain in office as prime minister at the General Election. But when he woke up in the morning, he was suddenly aware that something at the back of his mind had told him differently, and he knew he was facing a fall from power. By noon, a count of votes showed the opposition Socialists would have a majority. Winston Churchill's years of glory were over.

The war in the Pacific ceased abruptly after another five weeks, thanks to the atom bomb, which saved millions of Allied lives. Clement Attlee became Britain's new Socialist prime minister, and Churchill assumed a new role as leader of the Opposition, eager to lead the Conservatives back in power, although he never felt comfortable as a Conservative.

In 1946, Montgomery would become Commander in Chief of the British Army of the Rhine in Germany, then Chief of the Imperial General Staff, be knighted, and then awarded the title of Viscount Lord Montgomery of Alamein. It was created for him to commemorate his crucial victory in the second Battle of El Alamein, which sealed Marshal Rommel's fate.

Pennies from Heaven

Former nations of the British Empire would choose independence. Some would disintegrate, others flourish on their own. The British Isles became what they had always been before the days of empire—a group of scattered offshore islands isolated between the European continent and North America. Once upon a time, England had faced the continent of Europe. Then, with colonies in North America, it had turned its face to the West. Now it was suddenly left to its own despair and devices, confused and alone and with years of socialism and austerity ahead.

What had gotten the British through the war was an ability to laugh at themselves and each other, and consider the ironies of life. Neither the Germans nor the Japanese possessed that gift. The English had it even earlier than the Edwardians and the Elizabethans, since Chaucer—the "father of English literature"—possessed it as early as the fourteenth century.[9]

As for the starving Germans, there was a popular move in the West to "leave them to their fate," as some newspapers advised, because of their cruelty and barbarism. How could Britain feed German civilians with its own austere budget? But others recognized that German civilians had been victims of the Nazis, too. In 1945, left-wing publisher Victor Gollancz campaigned to support the starving Germans and feed their children.

One of the ironies of the war was that the U.S. economy had been in the doldrums since the 1929 Wall Street Crash, with eight million men and women unemployed. Nothing could revive it until Britain's desperate need for arms and armor, tanks, ships and aircraft to keep Nazi Germany at bay in 1938 created a bonanza for President Roosevelt. All the necessities of war, with a budget of a hundred and fifty billion pounds sterling, combined to create full employment in the United States and plenty of overtime, with more women working and earning more than ever before.[10] Wages rose and so did savings. American blue-collar workers were elevated to the middle-classes, and the middle classes enjoyed greater wealth.

Franklin D. Roosevelt is generally remembered today as the jaunty and debonair President with a cigarette in its holder jutting self-confidently from a firm jaw, while his optimistic election campaign song of "Happy Days are Here Again" spread confidence throughout America. And his "New Deal" enabled Americans to share the nation's wealth. An even more appropriate campaign song would have been "Pennies from Heaven." By devising Lease-Lend as an easy-to-pay business deal on credit, the United States came out of the Second World War richer than it went in, whereas Britain's war to defend itself, free Europe, and save the German population from the Nazis, had placed it close to bankruptcy.[11]

In hindsight, it is tempting to consider that just as Churchill led Hitler by the nose to his doom, so did President Roosevelt lead Churchill to his downfall at the hands of the British electorate. Churchill was naive to imagine that he could trust President Roosevelt unreservedly, although he himself was genuinely sincere. History shows Roosevelt to have been a shrewd politician of genius and an astute leader who took office in a global recession with large-scale unemployment—as all the leaders of the 1930s superpowers did—and came out ahead in the race with full employment and prosperity.

And Churchill, the historian, would have known that the American colonists of 1754 habitually tweaked Britain's nose and made fools of the imperial

British from the beginning of their independent thinking and planning. One of the colony's most influential leaders had been Benjamin Franklin, who had openly extolled the virtues of a British Empire containing an American colony. He was apparently proud of being a part of it: "Britain and her colonies should be considered as one Whole, and not different states with separate interests." But that was largely to persuade Britain to chase the French off the North American map, so that the colonies would no longer need the imperial army and navy to protect them against the French and their barbaric Indian mercenaries. Then they could dispose of British rule by claiming independence.[12] It was an intellectual chess game with brilliant players like Washington, Jefferson, and Franklin representing the eighteenth century colonists. Roosevelt enjoyed playing another round in the 1930s.

Roosevelt was not only after Britain's cash reserves and gold bullion to pay for America's industrialization program, he also planned to replace Britain as the global superpower, and he succeeded. By the end of the war, the United States of America was by far the most powerful country in the world. Roosevelt's third great accomplishment was to postpone fighting an unpopular war for as long as possible—as America had managed to do in the First World War—by arming British and Russian troops in the front lines instead of risking compulsory conscription of American boys. Nevertheless, Churchill had no other choice but to befriend the Americans and make them Britain's allies. It is to his credit that he managed to do so for so long as an equal partner with an empire, before imperialism faded into history.

Death of a Hero

On January 30, 1965, more than a million admirers of Sir Winston Churchill poured out into the streets to say their last grief-stricken good-byes to the great man who had saved all our lives and the civilization we cherish, and whose memory has become part of the heritage of the free world.

Churchill had died six days earlier from a stroke at the age of ninety. Crowds lined the streets in silent respect for Britain's greatest wartime leader, as a gun carriage bearing his coffin left Westminster and the procession moved slowly through central London for his funeral service at St. Paul's Cathedral. Then 321,360 mourners, including his widow Lady Clementine, his son Randolph, and his daughters Mary Soames and Lady Sarah Audley filed past his coffin as he lay in state for three days. Her Majesty the Queen attended with members of the royal family and the prime minister. Representatives from 112 nations came to the service. Then Churchill's coffin was piped aboard a launch for a short trip on the Thames to Waterloo, where thousands more met the locomotive named after him. He was finally buried at the parish church of Bladon near Blenheim Palace where he had been born and where his extraordinary career began.

His successful leadership revealed what an extraordinarily talented man he was. And apart from his magnificent shepherding of the free world and the Allied forces in the Second World War, with his inputs into military strategies and tactics and wartime innovations, his skills as an author and an orator, he also possessed several unusual qualities for a politician. He considered the long-term consequences, whereas most politicians know that the electorate wants what it wants right away. That was his one mistake as a politician at the end of the war. And it came about because he was entirely genuine, sincere, and honest. That appealed to the British public, who trusted him and called him "Winnie," with unusual warmth and affection for a politician. But the electorate are fickle. Even so, Winston Churchill is a hero for all time, against whom the memory of others fades.

Obsolescence

There have been all kinds of criticisms aimed at Churchill in the postwar years by people who imagined they could have done many things better than him, but none has amounted to much after considerable scrutiny. And the reality is that leaders are appointed or elected to take risks, not all of which can turn out as intended, because of changing circumstances. And no one can predict the future. What shadows all battles and wars are the unintended consequences of every action—such as the unfortunate sinking of the *Prince of Wales* and the *Repulse* by Japanese fighter pilots. And all of us are much cleverer after the event. In the end, "the Air Ministry now emerged as the real villain in the dispute, while Churchill was treated more as the victim of bad advice than a fundamental cause of the Admiralty's difficulties."[13]

Of course he was "impatient and overbearing." But that was to the advantage of the war. And of course he was inconsistent, since everything was undergoing changes from day-to-day and hour-by-hour, and he was provided with the consequences of actions that turned out to be less effective than intended or hoped. Just like General Montgomery at the battlefront, Churchill had to change his plans constantly as he confronted the challenges of new conditions. As historian Professor Bell remarked, sending the *Prince of Wales* to Singapore "against naval protests" was an exception rather than the rule. According to Bell's study of the situation, Churchill acted on political considerations with strong support from Eden and other civilian members of the Defense Committee.[14] Professor Bell ends his book *Churchill and Sea Power* by stating that "the nation was fortunate that he was so frequently and prominently involved in managing its naval affairs."[15]

Prior to the commencement of the Second World War and for several subsequent years, Britain had been at the center of the world as the only superpower. It owed much of that power and prestige to the formidable battleships and crews of the unbeatable Royal Navy—even as early as the Elizabethan Renaissance, but certainly after the Battle of Trafalgar when Admiral Nelson demonstrated that "Britannia Ruled the Waves." But in only a few hours at the very end of 1941 the power and prestige of the Royal Navy sank with HMS *Prince of Wales* and HMS *Repulse*. Churchill must have reflected ruefully on that moment for long afterward, since his reputation before becoming the wartime prime minister had rested very largely on being First Lord of the Admiralty. It was at that point in the Second World War when the torch of world leadership was passed to the United States of America with its aircraft carriers in the Coral Sea that had to fight hundreds, or even thousands, of striking Japanese Zero kamikaze suicide pilots in the Battle of Midway in May and June 1942.

Churchill was ahead of the Admiralty in recognizing that fleets of battleships were now obsolescent. Nevertheless, the very idea of an obsolete Royal Navy caused them to hang on to an optimistic belief that the future of the Senior Service lay in aircraft carriers that would be wanted "to provide cover to naval forces operating at sea."[16] And they could take British air superiority further out to sea as bases or fortresses in other territories. But Churchill felt differently from the Admiralty after the shock of defeat at Singapore. All services would be combined in future to bring about a coordinated blitzkrieg, with the threat of an atom bomb hovering implicitly overhead. Hopefully, it would deter Britain's enemies better than the old-time gunboat diplomacy.

All that was left of the memory of the indomitable Royal Navy was a charming little ditty called "Rule Britannia, Britannia Rule the Waves" that Britons with their wry sense of humor, still love to sing. It was their irreverent sense of fun as they targeted personal pomposities that had brought them through the ugliness and the horrors of the Second World War. Now it was part of the mythology of the tarnished and faded British Empire and its obsolete Royal Navy.

How can we account for the time and circumstances and mix of temperaments and skills that produced those great generations who won two world wars? As we know, many were descended from a varied mixture of Picts and Scots, Angles, Frisians, and Jutes—all the way back to two Germanic brothers named Hengist and Horsa, who arrived in the British Isles in the fifth century (according to Bede, and as Churchill would have been taught as a schoolboy).[17] Most absorbed the essence of Judeo-Christian values and attitudes toward life, which could be summed up in the message of the Sermon on the Mount, the Ten Commandments, or their essence in the Golden Rule—as Winston Churchill did. But that was not all; they and he owed their character also to the Elizabethan Renaissance, the Victorian Era, and Edwardian England. Molded by all those forces and influences, it would be impossible to produce the same Happy Breed ever again. Closest to them are their cousins, who were formerly called the British Commonwealth, and are very largely composed of Canadians, Australians, and New Zealanders.

There are now fifty-three independent nations that voluntarily became members of the Commonwealth of Nations, headed by the Queen of England. Their sentiment at having been a part of the former British Empire and, hopefully, shared its values, has made them reluctant to part from its magic.

And each year on the last night of the BBC Proms (summer concerts) in the Albert Hall, in London's Royal Borough of Kensington, 5,272 cheerful English-speaking voices rise up with pride to sing the eighteenth century ditty "Rule Britannia" as if their lives depended on securing an image in their minds and hearts of a long-lost paradise. It is a fixture of the proms— as much a part of it as Elgar's "Land of Hope and Glory, Mother of the free." And there are accessibility links beyond the Albert Hall to millions of TV, radio, and cross-platform online audiences all over the world, as well as excited crowds standing outside to watch the televised performances in Hyde Park and elsewhere.

No doubt Winston Churchill, who loved Britain, imperialism, and the monarchy, as well as America, would have loved heartily to join in the chorus.

When Britain first, at Heaven's command
Arose from out the azure main;
This was the charter of the land,
And guardian angels sang this strain:
"Rule, Britannia! Britannia rule the waves:
"Britons never, never, never will be slaves."

28

COLLECTIVE GUILT

AFTER EVERY GREAT ENDEAVOR WHEN OPPOSING forces have to be challenged and defeated, there is a period when scapegoats are sought, to explain why the problems occurred and who is to blame. The question of who and what was responsible for the Second World War and its atrocities—the Nazis or the Germans as a whole—continues to be raised. Collective guilt became the subject of debate during the war and as soon as it ended, when it formed the basis for newspaper headlines that claimed the German population should be left to starve as a punishment for the war, or whether Britain and the United States were morally bound to supply German civilians with food. Discussions and conclusions were influenced also by a rigid Russia, and Soviet-controlled Poland and Czechoslovakia.

According to publisher Victor Gollancz, the West was also guilty in that it "annexed, expelled, and stole: we exhibited an extreme of national intolerance; we bore ourselves with offensive superiority."[1] The continuous debate was also steered by a belief in the creation of a victim culture in Germany.[2] It developed at the end of the war and received considerable publicity due to Victor Gollancz's "Save Europe Now" campaign, which was aimed at creating stability in postwar Europe. Although there is some doubt that he influenced public opinion, it is likely he influenced British foreign policy during the postwar occupation of Germany.

The discourse has since veered from *The Times* of London, which claimed in 1945 that "it is surely not enough to say that the Germans brought these miseries upon themselves,"[3] to historian Wasserstein's assertion that the Germans "were, for the most part, victims of a calamity of which they were themselves part authors."[4] No doubt it will continue for some time to come, casting way back to the shock of defeat by Roman legions from Germanic tribes in the Teutoburg Forest in the seventh century of the Common Era. It was Rome's greatest defeat, and it would affect subsequent European history. It would cause France—when it became the most powerful nation in Europe—to ensure that German tribes were kept separated from each other to prevent an aggressive German race from dominating the Continent. Hitler's intention was to unite them in a Greater Germany even before 1933. But that is far too large a subject for the remainder of this book.

One thesis draws our attention to the fact that "Churchill was the first to officially support the policy of expulsion in Europe as a means of dealing with the [German] minority problem."[5] Certainly Churchill stated in the House of Commons on December 15, 1944, "I am not alarmed by the prospect of the disentanglement of populations, nor even by these large transferences, which are more possible in modern conditions than they ever were before." And yet, only a year later, he complained that the Russian-dominated Polish government expelled millions of Germans.[6] But the former situation obtained before the end of the war, whereas the second was during its aftermath in the Cold War with Soviet Russia, when the Allies were obliged to settle postwar Central Europe. One of Churchill's problems was what to do with Germans that the Nazis had settled in countries they invaded, like Czechoslovakia and Poland, where they were not welcome.[7]

Then and Now

Winston Churchill's span of public service was so long that critics of all types have had plenty of opportunities to examine his past for at least a hundred years in order to criticize him for any alleged failings. And yet, to judge from the following list, it is remarkable how little they have come up with after all this time. What is also extraordinary is that, although his supporters generally provide reasonable answers, there is already a general lack of perception of the time he lived in and its typically accepted values. There is a tendency for a younger generation to imagine that most people and their attitudes then were much the same as they are now. The following observations about the past should demonstrate how different they really were.

If we list as a shorthand, for example, the four unmentionables in Victorian society when Churchill was born—or Edwardian England in which he grew up, and even the post-Edwardian period when he became a political leader— our attitudes toward sex, money, politics, and religion have changed vastly. They were dirty little secrets then, each one a Pandora's box that no one wanted to open for fear of what they might find inside.

Sex, and the prevalence of venereal disease, was never mentioned in polite society, nor properly understood—whereas over half the searches made on the Internet today are for sessions with online pornography sites. We can hardly avoid encountering sex shops today, and sexual innuendos in advertising, social media, and conversation are frequent.

The taboo on mentioning money in polite society then was largely to avoid any possibility of embarrassing a guest whose ancestors might have made or inherited their fortunes from, for example, the opium trade in China, or war munitions, gambling, fraud, embezzlement, prostitution, even the slave trade—who knew! It was easier to treat money disdainfully by not mentioning it. Newly rich stockbrokers, with their faux-Tudor houses, were viewed with intense suspicion—you wouldn't want to invite one to your home. That didn't apply to the industrial north of England, however, where the familiar phrase, "where there's muck there's money," encouraged nouveau riche entrepreneurs in Bradford or Manchester to boast of their success, more like Americans who were proud of being self-made. But in England then, there was a sharp social distinction between old money and new money. Today electronic media and major newspapers now feature regular programs or pages on finance, and masses of people envy wealthy celebrities who own the top 1 percent of the nation's capital for their ability to accumulate money. Businessmen in Victorian or post-Edwardian England would have shunned any idea that they were motivated by greed, whereas greed was proudly proclaimed in the United States beginning in the 1980s as being the best motivator for success.[8]

Most people, including many politicians, did not understand politics, certainly not foreign affairs from which they kept a skeptical distance, so it was safer then to avoid looking foolish by not mentioning it—whereas today, politics are a regular feature on television, the online news, or with discussions by bloggers in newspapers. And news from the White House never ceases to amaze us.

Then there was a web of disconnected myths, poetry, and metaphors, which were blindly accepted as religion, but seldom discussed, since few understood it, including the clergy. So raising the subject could cause embarrassment. Now science refutes their lifelong beliefs almost daily. So it should come as no surprise that most of the criticisms aimed at Winston Churchill are similarly out of date in terms of relentless historical changes that trigger new attitudes, new scientific discoveries, and passing fashions.

Public Service

As recently as the fiftieth anniversary of Sir Winston Churchill's death, on January 26, 2015, Tom Heyden listed "The Ten Greatest Controversies of Winston Churchill's Career," in *BBC News Magazine* online. And despite the high regard still felt for him by many (he was rated the greatest Briton in 2002), they reveal that he is still a controversial historical figure. So such lists are all part of a blame game in which uninformed and misinformed people who previously felt powerless can denigrate anyone they want from the safe online pages of social media. Bickering opinions of Churchill have become almost a national sport in Britain. And bickering from the United States is almost like 1776 again. Even so, it needs to be addressed.

1. Racism

Churchill told the Palestine Royal Commission in 1937 that he did not consider "a great wrong had been done" to indigenous peoples when a stronger race, or a more worldly one, took over their territory. To use the words of historian John Charmley, the newcomers were, in effect, "winners in a social Darwinian hierarchy." That would have been how Churchill, as a historian, would have viewed a process that has been going on all over the world, wherever there was human or animal or insect life, for hundreds of thousands of years. He would have grown up with anthropologist Herbert Spencer's famous phrase "the survival of the fittest" still ringing in his ears.[9]

To accuse him of being a racist for making a scientific, or anthropological, or historic observation, is patently absurd. Nevertheless, today's whimsical fashion of so-called political correctness would, no doubt, label him as such. But attitudes and language were very different in the 1930s when eugenics was being earnestly explored as a possible scientific solution to the problem of overpopulation, from which it was thought the world would run out of sufficient resources to feed them all. But Churchill did not invent eugenics; it was simply part of the conversation of educated people at the time. And there is no evidence that he held destructive racist theories, such as the Nazis and Fascists did, during his political career: on the contrary.

2. Use of Poison Gas

What Churchill was discussing in 1919 was a relatively harmless new weapon with which to defeat the enemy without the fatalities caused by machine guns or close combat with fixed bayonets. According to Warren Dockter, the gas he referred to was only temporarily disarming, since it was tear gas, as used today in the West by police riot squads protecting property and innocent citizens from violently destructive crowds. "Loss of life should be reduced to a minimum," were the words Churchill wrote in his memo, when governments, the public, and generals were horrified at the ghastly effects of mustard gas that German armies used. To clarify what he had in mind, he made the notation: "would leave no serious permanent effect."[10]

3. The Bengal Famine

More than three million people are believed to have died in the famine in India that resulted from the Japanese occupation of Burma in the Second World War. Author Madhusree Mukerjee claimed that Churchill refused to export wheat to India. She failed to understand that he had to deal with conflicting priorities during his wartime leadership. There were two major ones— directing all possible resources to winning the war, and also stockpiling wheat in order to be able to feed starving European civilians after liberating them from Nazi dictatorship—as his war cabinet was doing. His continual focus on the war effort to defeat Hitler's armies was a recurring theme throughout. He considered that anything else would distract and prevent the Allies from winning it. And author Arthur Herman claimed that the Bengal famine would have been worse without Churchill's help: "Churchill and his cabinet sought every way to alleviate the suffering without undermining the war effort."[11] And when Field Marshal Wavell became governor general and viceroy of India on October 1, 1943, his first act on taking office was to have relief supplies distributed to starving rural Bengalis.

4. Churchill's Attitude toward Gandhi

Churchill in the 1930s did not view Gandhi in the same light as some people who venerate him today. Instead, he thought of Gandhi as a respectable lawyer who had suddenly lost his mind and taken off all his clothes to appear in a loincloth at official functions where he advocated Indian self-determination. He was not the only one to wonder at the time if Gandhi was a fake. And, to the imperialistic Churchill, India was the "jewel in the crown" of the British Empire, and surely required a more dignified and modern leader who would not stir up trouble between the Hindu majority and the Muslim minority. Churchill was behind the times regarding colonies and dependencies in 1931. And, unfortunately for him, Gandhi was ahead of him in manipulating world opinion.

It is tempting to reflect on what might have happened in 1938 if Britain had not been distracted by having to prepare for war with Germany, since the two files at the top of Britain's foreign policy agenda at that time were the problem of the self-determination of India (which was made impossible by the hatred between Muslims and Hindus), and Home Rule for Ireland (which was complicated by the hatred between Protestants and Catholics). Neither could just be abandoned to kill each other off.

Gandhi and Churchill shared a common failing in that they were both romantics. Gandhi's dream was unrealistic without amicable coexistence between Muslim and Hindu populations. It ended in civil war and mass murders, and the fragmentation of India. But for some unknown reason, according to Charmley, "Churchill's views on India between 1929 and 1939 were quite abhorrent." There are two possible reasons for this: One was his esteem for Indian Muslims, and Gandhi was a Hindu. The other could well have been the general revulsion at atrocities committed by army rebels who were Hindus. The British in India lost trust in, and became afraid of, the majority population when thousands of English women and children were abused and massacred in the Indian mutiny of 1857–58, when Churchill was seventeen. He was old enough and young enough for it to make a lifelong impression. It certainly had a devastating effect on many others who served in India at the time. Nevertheless, there can be little doubt that the affair was insensitively handled by unimaginative civil servants and British army officers.

5. Jewish Rights

According to Churchill's official biographer, the historian Sir Martin Gilbert, he "supported the idea of a Jewish state." Churchill was a fervent Zionist, writing in a 1920 article that "they [the Jews] are beyond question the most formidable race which has ever appeared in the world." Despite that, "casual anti-Semitism was rampant" in English society at the time. But that foolish aberration had nothing to do with Winston Churchill, who dismissed it—like his father did—as ignorance.

Regardless of Churchill's admiration and respect for the Jews, Allied governments have frequently been accused of not reacting quickly enough to victimization of Jews by the Nazis. Gilbert addressed that by stating that Churchill supported boycotts of German goods, "to bring pressure, economic and financial, to bear upon the governments which persecute them." When Winston Churchill became prime minister in 1940, he opposed those who were preventing Jewish refugees from reaching Palestine and attempted to guide Britain's Colonial Office accordingly. When he broadcast to the nation in November 1941, he raised the matter of thousands of Jews being murdered by German forces invading the Soviet Union.

Gilbert's comments ranged from such incidents in 1942 and 1943 that Churchill reacted to immediately when the pro-Nazi French Vichy government began deporting Jews to be murdered at the Auschwitz death camp, including four thousand children. Churchill insisted that the Vichy-French laws against Algerian Jews should be repealed. He opposed Spain closing its frontiers with France to fleeing Jews, warning the Spanish government that it would never be forgotten if they handed refugees back to the German authorities.

When Allied troops crossed the Rhine and discovered secret Nazi murder camps, General Eisenhower phoned to tell Prime Minister Churchill what they had found, and Churchill telegraphed him right back that evening. "From the first to the last days of the war," wrote Gilbert, "the fate of the Jews was something on which Churchill took immediate and positive action whenever he was asked to do so.[12] Meanwhile, he refused to be deterred from attempting to defeat Hitler, or even think of discussing peace terms with him.

6. Islam

To introduce as criticism of Islam what Churchill wrote in his 1899 book *The River War* is as absurd, dishonest, and misleading as citing today's general criticisms of fundamentalist terrorists like ISIS or al Qaeda or the Taliban as views on Islam. Churchill considered his enemies in that nineteenth-century war as backward and lazy, as most other people did. It was a view of the times. But he was fascinated by Islam. Years later, he would recognize the services of Muslims who fought for Britain by having his 1940 war cabinet budget a hundred thousand pounds toward building a mosque in London's Regent's Park. It has since become a landmark.

7. Churchill's Anti-union Views

The way he handled the Tonypandy miners' strikes in 1910, when he was home secretary, brought him ill-feeling from the south of Wales for the rest of his life. And yet, he was one of the few who would have known the political and historic background to his hurried decision to reinforce the outnumbered local police force. The disputes with mine owners lasted nearly a year. And when the strikers clashed with local police, he sent in the army. But no shots were fired.

Churchill had no time for trade unions then or later. *The Communist Manifesto* by Karl Marx and Friedrich Engels had already been published in 1848. It encouraged the British working classes to revolt, and it triggered the revolution of 1848 right across Europe. The revolution is known today as the Spring of Nations. And it was the most widespread wave of revolutions in the history of Europe. It was savagely resisted by some nations and took a year to collapse. Meanwhile, it spread across the Continent and caused hundreds of thousands of refugees to flee for safety to the United States and Britain. Churchill's responsibility as home secretary was to maintain law and order in Britain. Fortunately, he acted speedily to prevent further unemployment in Britain, social unrest, and even a possible class revolution. Meanwhile, his critics took a typically parochial view of British working-class rights without having any idea of what was going on in the larger world outside.

8. The Siege of Sidney Street

The same broad circumstances and attitude applied to Churchill's reaction to a shooting in the East End of London only a year later, in January 1911, when two hundred police surrounded an anarchist hideout after "Peter the Painter" had killed three policemen. Violent crimes of that sort were rare, and British police were not issued with firearms. But in this case, where the anarchists had organized a bank raid to obtain funds for their activities, a few police had been armed with rifles, and a gun battle ended after the anarchists set fire to the building, probably intending to flee in the commotion. Resistance ended in their deaths in the flames. Churchill crushed terrorism before it could gain the upper hand.

For critics of Churchill (who appeared at the scene), it may have looked just like an ambitious photo opportunity. But it was only three years before the German war broke out. Until then, London was a safe haven for anarchists and communists from Europe, so the capital city was like a tinder box awaiting a spark to ignite it—as would happen in Tsarist Russia with a Bolshevik revolution only seven years later. And Churchill would have possessed presentiments about insurrections and war after recently reviewing German troops with the Kaiser in Germany. In short, he understood the possible dangers more than anyone else in Britain. And when it came to protecting Britain, he missed little.

9. The Irish Troubles

The First World War had already begun when Churchill was secretary of state for war and air. The Irish War of Independence broke out in January 1919. Churchill had supported Home Rule for Ireland as early as 1912. But it was far too dangerous while a state of war existed with Germany, so he advocated partition in the meantime. He also played a leading role in the Anglo-Irish Treaty of 1921 that ended the war there. Meanwhile, it was feared that Britain would be stabbed in the back by pro-German forces in Ireland, like the Irish Republican Army (IRA). His character was to fight hard when necessary and pursue peace by dialogue at the earliest opportunity.

10. Inappropriate Influence

Rules against politicians lobbying for a fee were not in place in 1923 when Churchill was paid five thousand pounds by Shell and Anglo-Persian Oil to represent them to the government in a merger. But he was accustomed to being paid for his freelance services as a journalist and an author. Today it would be recognized as an unacceptable conflict of interest. But there was a different political and ethical environment nearly a century ago.

Despite today's custom of the media searching out human frailties or transgressions of celebrities or politicians, scandalmongering was barely known in the Edwardian era, because there was no money in it for the news media. Even if the press had wanted to discover Churchill in embarrassing situations, he was a faithful husband and appeared to have had little interest in involving himself in sexual scandals. He enjoyed cigar smoking and alcohol, but could hold an enormous amount without immediate or later ill effects. Moreover, he was so well-known that his life was transparent. He enjoyed his home, where he wrote history or pursued his hobby as an amateur bricklayer, which gave him a sense of creative accomplishment. And he painted artistic watercolors of landscapes when on vacation. About the only weakness in his constitution was the deep depression that assailed him from time to time, which he called his "black dog," that habitually followed him around. It overwhelmed him, by and large, during anticlimaxes in his life, when he felt despondent at having nothing creative or constructive to occupy himself with, since he was an overachiever with a highly developed sense of responsibility.

The Matter of Empire

The specter of empire still hovers over European history—just as it does with ancient Rome's—because it touches on many issues, from the ideal of human rights to simple economics, and from romantic and uplifting ideals to the brutal realities of the flawed human condition. White imperialism finally went out of fashion when the United Nations (UN) passed sanctions on the nationalistic Afrikaans-speaking government of South Africa for its apartheid regime that restricted the lives of the much larger black population, while abusing and humiliating them. Although that was as recent as the 1970s, it was actually promoted by the British white supremacist Cecil Rhodes, who founded De Beers diamond mines in 1888. It was continued by descendants of Dutch colonists. It took a number of years before Nelson Mandela was freed from prison (as an alleged Communist terrorist in 1990), and acclaimed a more ideal "rainbow society," where all colors of skin and shades of culture were welcome.

But Winston Churchill was born even before that, in 1874, when the imperial Austro-Hungarian Habsburg dynasty, the Russian Romanovs, and the Prussian Hohenzollerns still ruled, and the British Empire was the biggest and most powerful empire in history. So Churchill's beliefs, values, and attitudes were influenced by those of the times, and he had known nothing else. Idealistic Britons sought to improve British colonies and the lives of their inhabitants. That not many of the colonial leaders or administrators were competent enough to fulfill their responsibilities or handle power resulted in a backlash that ended the three other dynasties at the end of the First World War. Only the British Empire remained after 1919.

Western society has changed vastly since then. In the so-called "permissive society" of the 1960s, for example, there were suddenly twice the number of violent crimes in Britain, and its prison population tripled. All kinds of sexual corruption and criminal gangsterism ensued, forcing the police to be issued with regular firearms for the first time in British history in order to protect the public and themselves. However, the outcome of the social revolution was a more classless society in Britain. It brought with it a more popular form of free rein– or laissez-faire-attitude rather than the old Victorian sense of responsibility or the pessimistic existentialism of Jean Paul Sartre in France.

With it came a recognition of the randomness and absurdity of life. So that, in 1965, no less than three major theaters in London presented plays that represented the "theater of the absurd"—all in the Aldwych and Covent Garden area. Samuel Becket's famous *Waiting for Godot* vied for audiences with Harold Pinter's *The Caretaker*. The third play, featuring Sir Laurence Olivier, was Ionesco's *Rhinoceros*—a grim satire on racism. Evidently there were enough audiences in London to make those three productions viable.

At the same time—and from even earlier—recognition of a previously ignored underclass came about with Joan Littlewood's Theatre Royal ensemble productions at the Stratford-atte-Bow district in London's East End. It owed much to the Berlin ensemble theater of Bertolt Brecht. One of her most successful plays would be filmed in 1969. It was a down-to-earth satire put to music and entitled *Oh, What a Lovely War!* It sought, and succeeded, in featuring the boneheadedness of the English generals of the First World War, like Haigh, French, and Kitchener, who apparently had no idea of the effects of modern weaponry or trench warfare, and blithely sent hundreds of thousands of young soldiers to their deaths on the Western Front.

They were the type of authority figures depicted as not possessing the faculties to fulfill their responsibilities. With the success of an emerging so-called "working class" theater and film industry, it was not long before other imperial authority figures were displayed with all their character flaws and dysfunctions, to be scorned by the public. Inevitably, they included the allegedly half-mad Brigadier Reginald Dyer who supposedly ordered his Indian and Gurkha rifleman to shoot volley after volley into a peaceful crowd of civilians in Amritsar, in the Punjab, on April 13, 1919, when Britain was at war with Germany. What also appeared to be shocking was the praise and support offered to Dyer after the army stripped him of his rank and retired him to return home as a sick man.

Winston Churchill called the Amritsar affair "monstrous."

It is the main story used to criticize an allegedly "vicious" British Empire. And it would certainly be monstrous, if true. But, as with most rumors, gossip, and national or political mythologies used for propaganda, it was not what it seemed to be at all. Nor was it so-called "imperial terrorism."[13] According to the most recent account, Dyer arrived with too small a force to quell a riot by a far greater mob than he'd expected. He had only ninety men (including forty without rifles) to face off an unruly mob of twenty-five thousand young men who were angry and violent enough to attack them. The odds against Dyer's men coming out alive were 275 to 1. And he knew that if he hesitated to react for a moment, he and his small force would be torn apart in minutes.

As a career officer, he was required to act to protect his men by quelling the riot. And no British officer had ever forgotten the atrocities and massacres of thousands of British women and children in the rebellion of Indian mercenaries in 1857. He probably knew he would be criticized if he acted, but dead if he didn't. In the previous three days, such mobs of "bored, sullen, and hostile" groups of youths had killed five Europeans, lynched three bank employees, and burned their bodies. Two others were murdered. And an elderly missionary named Miss Sherwood had been torn from her bicycle and beaten to the ground by a mob.

It was not a peaceful crowd that faced him. It was mostly composed of young men, many of whom were armed with metal-tipped sticks known as *lathis*. Some wielded billhooks, swords, or other cruder weapons. They also possessed kerosene to set the buildings on fire. They were clearly intent on more violence. As a result of other violent riots and unrest, Dyer had previously sent out warnings in nineteen different places that no demonstrations were allowed to take place in the streets. And yet, they had already been surrounded and spat upon by such hostile young men. If he allowed them to, they would kill thousands of innocent Sikh shopkeepers in the conflagration. And there were 150,000 inhabitants in the city who might also burn to death. Dyer knew he had to stop them from getting out of control before that happened. He and his small detachment would have to shoot their way out of a tight corner. And that is what they did.

What he did not know about the walls of the city was that, when he fired to clear the mob, there was no way out for them to scatter and disperse.

He was distraught for months afterward—even though the Indian shopkeepers thanked him formally for preventing a riot and subsequent looting. They even invested him as an honorary Sikh in the Golden Temple. Nevertheless, the incident was made out to be a vicious onslaught by a callous imperialist army. And in more contemporary times, Richard Attenborough's anti-British-establishment film romanticizing Gandhi distorted the story further.

Closer to our own time, in 2015, a dramatic TV serial about socialites in the decline of the British Raj, entitled *Indian Summers*, was screened with all the exoticism of a romantic and sensual movie with beautiful and sexy young women. It also portrays some of the typical protagonists of the times, with a viceroy of India and his young and ambitious protégé who love India, which they find a paradise, as long as they are in charge, but are too thick-skinned to recognize that they are not loved in return. Neither has any wish to go home to damp and rainy England. The viceroy even admits to his protégé that, as a member of the ruling class, he is not loved in England either.

Churchill, on the other hand, was loved by most of the British people, but they recognized by war's end—as he did not—that his attitudes toward restoring the British Empire were now obsolete.

One of the accusations against British rule in India was that it polarized the continent; in fact, it had already been forcibly split by the previous Moghul Empire, which had destroyed itself.

The TV movie is well supplied with a variety of cultural, racial, religious, and class clashes among both the Indian population and the British, which arose from the human paradoxes we have to contend with every day as facts of life that we inherited. The prototype of the anti-imperialist genre appears to be the 1924 novel *A Passage to India*, by E. M. Forster, which showed up the injustices of the British Raj by its dull-witted civil servants, including its viceroys. The highly successful *The Jewel in the Crown* established it in the minds of television audiences in 1984. It prompted filmmaker Sir David Lean (who had already filmed *Lawrence of Arabia* in December 1962) to sigh and remark offhandedly at the release of his film of Forster's novel in 1984, "I'm afraid the British have a bad time of it again." But no one can spoof British pomposity as well as the British themselves.[14] Even so, the anti-imperialist cinema and television stories are fictions.

Winston Churchill's own duality was that, although he took a romantic and idealistic view of the British Empire that we might consider inappropriate today, it was precisely that which made him an effective leader to defend the British Isles in wartime. And no one else was available who could do it. The six appeasers in the 1930s Conservative government thought of themselves as realists, but could not handle reality when they met it close up and were found to be romantics of another type, whereas Churchill was the realist when it came to total war. So, while we may regard Winston Churchill's joyful imperialism as a character flaw, it did not make him dysfunctional as a wartime leader—on the contrary, his defense of Britain and human rights depended on that very attribute.

The War Crimes Trials

Soon after the end of the Second World War, the enemies of human rights—at least, a number of leading Nazis who were still alive—were arraigned for their war crimes at an international court in the city of Nuremberg. According to German law for punishing murderers, their criminal acts would have merited their execution by means of an axe. The Russians had already requested nothing less than the death penalty for the murders of some twenty million

Russians massacred in the war by Germans. The Nazis themselves expected nothing less, because they had lost the costly war they had started. And who knew better than they the extent of their crimes! Seeing them in court, it was hard to think of them as human beings at all; they looked so grotesque.

The grossly fat Göring had already lost considerable weight from prison rations, so that his belly sagged, "giving him an air of pregnancy," according to official correspondent Rebecca West. She described his face as *unreal,* "like the head of a ventriloquist's dummy." It was an apt description, since the Nazis had always been senseless dummies, ready to obey Hitler's manic instructions.

Without the sartorial splendor of their custom-designed uniforms, which had been deliberately cut and decorated to transform them from criminals into heroic figures, they all looked drab and devoid of human personality. They were more like waxwork effigies of themselves, ready to be displayed as serial murderers in the Chamber of Horrors at Madame Tussaud's exhibition in London. Hess's skin was ashen, and he habitually fell into fixed lunatic postures that made him look like an inmate in an asylum. Schacht made a deliberate point of sitting at an angle leaning away from his fellow criminals— in an attempt to disassociate himself from them—by looking past them or over their heads, because he judged himself to be superior to Hitler's thugs who would stop at nothing for power and gain. He was enraged at the court for placing him among a bunch of violent criminals. Speer was a pale shadow of his former self. Streicher, the former Nazi propagandist and self-styled "Jew-baiter," was described by Rebecca West as the type of dirty old man who causes trouble in public parks. The former youth leader, Baldur von Shirach, sat like "a neat and mousey governess."

Hitler had killed himself, not so much to avoid a public trial as to prevent capture by the Russians whose armies had entered Berlin ahead of the other allies. No doubt he expected they would torture him in revenge for German atrocities on the Russian front. Reinhard Heydrich, who was responsible for the Holocaust, was assassinated in 1942 by exiled Czech intelligence agents. Heinrich Himmler, who had led the infamous SS and managed the death camps, committed suicide with his cyanide capsule after arrest in 1945.

Uniformed guards stood stock-still, gripping their white truncheons behind their backs, while eight judges sat on the bench in the Palace of Justice.

French, English, and Russian versions of the trial described the proceedings through spectators' earphones, while the words of Sir Hartley Shawcross's closing speech described in succinct and unemotional terms the evils perpetrated by each criminal in the dock.

Youth leader Schirach removed his headphones at the mention of his responsibility for deporting forty thousand Russian children. When Shawcross quoted one of the witnesses who had described a Jewish father standing before a firing squad with his small son and trying to divert him from the scene by engaging him in normal conversation and pointing up at the sky while gently stroking his hair, the faces of the accused in the dock seemed to age, while they wriggled uncomfortably in their seats in the face of unaccustomed reality.

Media correspondent Rebecca West expressed amazement afterward at the extent of the sadism amongst the Germans. There was the French doctor they tortured month after month at Mathausen, the number of lamp shades they made out of tattooed human skins, and there had been unnecessary operations carried out on children without anesthetics. Human beings had been frozen to determine how low a temperature they could withstand before they died. Some doctors and medical orderlies had even shown annoyance with their victims for continually screaming as they were frozen to death. They had acted like mindless imbeciles pulling the legs off of people as if they were insects.

Anticlimax

Peace had come as an anticlimax to many who had fought in the war, and to civilians who had suffered from continual bombing raids or occupation by enemy troops, hostage-taking, arrests, firing squads, starvation, and mass burials. The final day of the Nuremberg trial was reduced to a similar anticlimax. Fritzsche, former chief of radio at the Propaganda Ministry, was found not guilty of atrocities. So were Papen and Schacht. Deputy Führer Hess was allowed to live in prison for the rest of his life as a mentally defective imbecile.

All the accused were under close supervision by psychiatrists, because it was still unclear to the public how sane people could have perpetrated such gross and perverted acts on such a monumental scale. What could possibly have been going on in their minds? Were they biological monsters or psychopaths? All the psychiatrists could say to the media was that, with the exception of the ignorant opportunist Streicher, they were not stupid. In fact they were found to possess above-average intelligence quotients when tested.

Dr. Gustave Gilbert, an American psychologist who interviewed the Nazi leaders over a period of a year, until they were hanged, told of his experience with Göring. Although Göring knew he would be condemned to death as the Nazi second-in-command anyway, and that Dr. Gilbert had no influence with the judges, he would ask to see the psychologist every day. He continually repeated the same message: "Look, I'm not as bad as all that. I'm not as bad as Hitler. He killed women and children. I didn't. Please believe me."

It was not a matter of remorse. Reports from the British and US Army of Occupation reported most Germans as being "sullen and dangerous." And Nazi leaders had shown no signs of remorse for what they had done. Psychological profiling of the killers, including Hitler, were sought during the war crimes trial, during which American psychologist Dr. Gustave Gilbert became Göring's and Ribbentrop's confidant. He attested that Hess was sane and described Göring as an "amiable psychopath."[15] During a discussion with Göring, Göring remarked:

> Naturally, the common people don't want war... But, after all, it is the *leaders* of the country who determine the policy and it is always a simple matter to drag the people along, whether it is democracy, or a fascist dictatorship... the people can always be brought to the bidding of the leaders... All you have to do is tell them they are being attacked, and denounce the pacifists for lack of patriotism and exposing the country to dangers.[16]

Göring escaped hanging in the end by swallowing a cyanide capsule he'd managed to conceal in a hollow tooth until the last moment. The other ten men were hanged. They struggled for air as they slowly choked to death. Ribbentrop took twenty minutes to die.

Despite the Allied victory and the trials to seek justice, the Allies were left with an uneasy feeling that the punishments failed to fit the horrendous crimes, since they could not bring back to life the many millions of Nazi victims. The

Allies were left with a sense of helpless anger and frustration that lingered on for decades afterward, while new information of Nazi atrocities continued to emerge.

THE COST IN LIVES

	Total Deaths*	Including
Soviet Russia:	26.6 million	13.2 million civilians
Poland:	5.6–5.8 million	2.4 million civilians
Czechoslovakia:	340,000–355,000	
China:	15–20 million	7.8 million civilians
Germany:	6.9–7.4 million	Over 2 million civilians
France:	600,000	67,000 civilians
French Indochina:	1.6 million	
India:	1.6–2.6 million	2 million civilians
Italy:	444,500	
Japan:	2.5–3.2 million	580,000 civilians
Yugoslavia:	1–1.7 million	514,000 civilians
TOTAL DEATHS (All Countries) (About 3 percent of global population):	72.5–85 million	34 million civilians
Britain:	591,634 + 92,700 civilians (UK War Graves Commission).	
United States:	419,400 + 6,000 civilians	

* Published statistics vary and are estimated according to the ways they are calculated, and are therefore controversial. These are estimations and include military deaths in combat and civilian deaths either on battlefields or deliberately murdered, as well as deaths from malnutrition, diseases, and famine directly resulting from the war. From a multitude of authoritative sources, including the *League of Nations Yearbook*, UK Ministry of Defence, *The Oxford Companion to World War II*, the World War II Foundation, UK National Archives, U.S. National Archives, U.S. Library of Congress, and others.

Note: Most statistics are calculated as the difference between 1939 populations and postwar ones. They include Prisoners of War murdered by the Germans (3.1 million), POWs murdered in the Soviet Union (3.5 million), Jews (5.7 million), Non-Jewish Holocaust victims (5 million), Roma genocide victims (500,000–1.5 million), nearly 250,000 handicapped persons murdered, and 10,000 to 15,000 homosexual men. Those statistics include a multiplicity of overlaps.

Civilian Deaths (compared to military dead in both world wars). WWI: 95 percent military deaths to 5 percent civilian. WWII: 33 percent military deaths to 67 percent civilian. **Air Raid Deaths:** Britain (60,400). Germany (543,000).

ACKNOWLEDGMENTS

RATHER THAN LIST SCORES OF TITLES on war in a long bibliography that may not be appropriate for readers who want more comprehensive details about what happened in the Second World War, the author acknowledges the following eight books in particular. Those are the ones that formed the foundation for this book, by activating memories that had never entirely left him—so that this narrative unrolled seamlessly, as if on its own.

- *A History of the Second World War* by Captain Sir Basil Liddell Hart (Cassell, London 1992). Military historian. (829 pages)
- *The Second World War* by Winston S. Churchill (Houghton Mifflin, Boston 1948). Britain's Prime Minister during World War Two. (In 6 Volumes of close to 5,000 pages).
- *Churchill: An End to Glory* (A Political Biography) by John Charmley (Hodder, London 1993). Historian. (742 pages)
- *Stalin's General: The Life of Georgy Zhukov* by Geoffrey Roberts. (Random House, 2012). Historian. (400 pages)
- *The Storm of War* by Andrew Roberts. (Penguin UK, 2009). Historian (712 pages)
- *Churchill & Sea Power* by Christopher M. Bell. (Oxford University, 2013). Professor of History (429 pages)
- *The Second World War* by Antony Beevor. (Weidenfeld & Nicolson, London 2012). Military historian. (863 pages)
- *Finest Years: Churchill as Warlord 1940-45* by Sir Max Hastings. (Harper UK, 2009). War Correspondent and Military Historian. (664 pages)

The author also studied most books by and about Field Marshal Bernard Montgomery's soldiering years, among many others like *The Art of War* by Clausewitz. He also used strategies and tactics of great generals in the field as metaphors in his two previous books on leadership and management.

Readers interested in the American war in the Pacific, which is not featured here, will also want to read about Admirals Nimitz, King, and Halsey, General Macarthur, and President Dwight D. Eisenhower.

ABOUT THE AUTHOR

JOHN HARTE WAS BORN IN LONDON, England, between the two World Wars. He absorbed the experiences and lessons of the 1914-1918 World War while growing up in its aftermath and studying it at a time when magazines, books, and encyclopaedias were still absorbed by it. He then observed the phenomenon of the growing dictatorships emerging on the Continent of Europe, which resulted in the outbreak of World War II.

He witnessed the bombing of London and the Battle of Britain from a rooftop in the West End of London, and volunteered for the RAF while still underage. Stationed at the same aerodrome where Winston Churchill learned to fly, he was invalided out after hospitalization. Working in Hastings, he was able to observe the arrival of American troops for training inland on the southeast coast for the D-Day landings. Returning from time to time to London during the subsequent invasions by Hitler's so-called secret weapons, he experienced the effects of the enemy's V1 and V2 rockets launched from across the English Channel to destroy London and its population.

Harte began his writing career as a freelance investigative journalist for three leading publications in the UK, while as a playwright he had four of his plays produced in London and elsewhere. After moving to South Africa to work in the advertising industry with J. Walter Thompson, he also wrote freelance feature articles under his own byline for the two leading newspapers there, which were syndicated worldwide by *Reuters*. He also broadcasted his own stories on the SABC. He now lives in Ottawa, Canada.

This is the author's third published nonfiction book. His fourth was bought by Skyhorse Publishing in New York and is scheduled for release, entitled *Churchill The Young Warrior*.

SOURCES AND ENDNOTES

Author's Preface

1 On Wednesday August 2, 1940.

2 *The Map and the Territory.* (Penguin NY, 2013).

3 *MI6: The Real James Bonds 1909–39.* Michael Smith. (Biteback Publishing, London 2011).

1. England at the Center of the World

1 *Wodehouse: A Life.* Robert McCrum. (Norton, NY 2004).

2 Diagnosed by Sigmund Freud when invited to study victims by the Austrian army in 1917. Now known as PTSD or post-traumatic stress disorder.

3 It could be said that the Edwardian era in England lingered on as long as prime minister and respected statesman Lloyd George headed the Liberal government, but it faded away with his fall from power by 1922.

4 *Lords of Finance.* Liequat Ahamed. (Penguin, 2009). P. 5.

5 *Lords of Finance.* Ibid.

6 W. H. Auden.

7 British complacency began much sooner, around 1850, before the middle of Queen Victoria's reign. There was lack of follow-up in trade and commerce after the English Industrial Revolution was copied by Germany, America, and Japan. It was partly a generational issue, and economist Adam Smith warned in 1776 in *The Wealth of Nations* that professional managers would be unlikely to be as vigilant in looking after other people's money as the owner of an enterprise would. Britain steadily lost market share to Germany who seemed to be better at science (which Britain's universities failed to encourage) and Americans who were better at commercialization, which the British found distasteful. British speculators, who had already made money, lost interest in business

after building themselves splendid country homes and town houses. The complacency of imperial power resulted in the Great Depression of 1870 with large-scale unemployment.

8   Winston S. Churchill. *The Second World War:* "The Gathering Storm." (Houghton Mifflin, Boston 1948).

9   *Flight of the Eagle.* Conrad Black. (Random House, 2013). Pp. 358–363.

10   *The Storm of War.* Andrew Roberts. (Penguin UK, 2009). P. 1.

11   W. S. Churchill. Ibid.

12   John Charmley. *Churchill: The End of Glory.* (Hodder, London 1993).

13   "The Gathering Storm." Ibid.

14   "The Gathering Storm." Ibid.

2. The Master of Germany

1   "Crazy violence," or "Rage Disorder" (like running amok in Malaya). Hitler would resort to an uncontrollable rage to terrify subordinates and get his own way.

2   "The Gathering Storm." Ibid.

3   John Charmley. Ibid.

4   John Charmley. Ibid.

5   Former British military intelligence officer Lord (Noel) Annan. Quoted by Sir Max Hastings in *The Secret War.* Ibid. P. 350.

6   The British Admiralty was headed by Lord of the Admiralty, Sir Bolton Eyre-Monsell on June 21, 1935.

7   W. S. Churchill. Ibid.

8   "The Gathering Storm." Ibid.

9   *The Storm of War.* Ibid. P. 6.

10   W. S. Churchill. Ibid.

11   *Mein Kampf.* Adolf Hitler (with the help of Rudolf Hess). 1925. P. 603.

12   Greenwood Press.

3. A Force of Nature

1   *The Churchill Factor.* Boris Johnson, London's Mayor from 2008. (H&S, London 2014).

2   *My Early Life.* Winston S. Churchill. (Scribner NY, 1996).

3   W. S. Churchill. Ibid.

4   Immortalized in George Formby's popular song: *I'm leaning on a lamp post on the corner of the street, in case a certain little lady comes by.*

5   (Dover Publications, NY 1908). Henry Mayhew later founded *Punch* Magazine.

6   December 18, 1936, with the Public Order Act of 1936.

4. The Art of Deception

1   "The Gathering Storm." Ibid.

2   John Charmley. Ibid.

3   John Charmley. Ibid.

5. A Thin Slice at a Time

1   W. S. Churchill. Ibid.

2   Largely written by his close friend Rudolf Hess.

3   W. S. Churchill. Ibid.

4   Max Hastings. *Finest Years.* (Harper UK, 2009). P. 109.

5   *Ein Requiem in Rot-Weiss-Rot.* P. 37ff. Schuschnigg.

6. The Munich Crisis

1   W. S. Churchill. Ibid.

2   *The Storm of War.* Ibid. P. 8.

3   W. S. Churchill. Ibid.

4   "The Gathering Storm." Ibid.

5   "The Gathering Storm." Ibid.

7. The Phony War

1   That was the culture that inspired all the early novels of P. G. Wodehouse with their upper-class heroes of negligible intellect, based largely on people of his generation whom he knew (Wodehouse was educated at Dulwich) and the satirical novels by Evelyn Waugh that often featured helpless young schoolmasters who couldn't teach. Waugh himself had attempted and failed as a young schoolteacher. It might also be claimed that many of those teachers hated boys who were disinterested in sports and wanted to learn instead.

2   Journalist and author of *Animal Farm* and *1984.*

3   John Charmley. Ibid.

4   Money left by one of its members funded the left-wing London School of Economics.

5   *The Secret Agent,* 1907.

6   Reaction in England toward the Communist Revolution in Russia was calm and reflective in consideration of the fact that the new regime had replaced the Tzar's police state, which was the most oppressive in Europe. And Europe had already experienced different types of brutal religious and political phases that had passed in time. The attitude in America was very different; it was one of befuddled panic at a time when American governments purposely isolated themselves from Europe with its old hatreds. It led to fear, spy hunts, and arrests for years, and a terror of finding "a Red under every bed." America did not understand Europe and didn't want to, whereas Britain, on the other side of the Channel, had to watch it carefully.

7   The fact that they passed information to the Soviet Union during the Second World War may have helped the Allies to win. But they continued during the Cold War afterward between Soviet Russia and the West. When suspicion turned on Philby, he was obliged to resign from MI6 to become a journalist in the 1950s, then defected to Russia. Burgess and Maclean defected in 1951. Blunt was interrogated by MI5 in 1964. Later on, it was discovered there was not only one more traitor in the spy ring, but several.

8   *Eminent Victorians* (1918) featured revealing biographies of General Gordon, Florence Nightingale, Cardinal Manning, and Thomas Arnold. Lytton Strachey was an older member of the notorious Bloomsbury Group of intellectuals and artists.

9   *The Psychology of Revolution.* (1894). *The Psychology of the Crowd.* (1896).

10   John Charmley. Ibid.

11   At the end of August 1939, Hitler concocted a lie that the Poles had attacked Germany, so that he could claim he invaded Poland in self-defense. To do so, an inmate of a German concentration camp was dressed up in Polish uniform and shot, to provide so-called evidence. He was thought to be the first victim of World War II. But according to historian Beevor, "the first clash of the Second World War . . . began in the Far east," with the Japanese invasion of China. (Antony Beevor. Ibid. P. 10).

12   *The Storm of War. Ibid.* P. 17.

13   *Panzer Battles.* P. 4.

14   *The Storm of War.* Ibid. P. 19.

15   *The Storm of War.* Ibid.

16   *The Storm of War.* Ibid.

17   W. S. Churchill. Ibid.

18   The Nuremberg documents, Part 1. Pp. 167–8. *Scraps of Paper.* Harlow A. Hyde. (Harlow, 1988).

19   *The Storm of War.* Ibid.

20 *The Storm of War.* Ibid. P. 22.

21 Source: Keitel's Nuremberg Papers.

22 Although French troops invaded Germany on September 6, they only captured a dozen abandoned villages. *The Storm of War.* Ibid.

23 *The Storm of War.* Ibid. P. 24.

24 Source: Count Mirabeau.

25 B. H. Liddell Hart. *History of the Second World War.* (Cassell, London 1979 & 1992).

26 *The Storm of War.* Ibid. P. 25.

27 Liddell Hart. Ibid.

28 *The Storm of War.* Ibid. P. 25.

29 *The Storm of War.* Ibid.

30 Major-General Mellenthin.

31 *Second World War.* Gilbert. P. 30.

32 *The Storm of War.* Ibid. P. 27.

33 *The Storm of War.* Ibid. P. 28.

34 W. S. Churchill. Ibid.

35 W. S. Churchill. Ibid.

36 *Second World War.* Michel. P. 75.

37 *The Storm of War.* Ibid. P. 43.

38 *The Storm of War.* Ibid. P. 43.

39 *The Storm of War.* Ibid. P. 43.

40 *The Storm of War.* Ibid. P. 29.

41 *Total War.* Calvocoressi & Wint. P. 103.

42 *The Storm of War.* Ibid. P. 31.

43 *The Storm of War.* Ibid. P. 32.

44 *The Storm of War.* Ibid.

45 Liddell Hart. Ibid.

46 Liddell Hart. Ibid.

47 John Charmley. Ibid.

8. Blitzkrieg

1 *The Storm of War.* Ibid. P. 46.

2 Or, as Churchill often said, "It's better to have him inside the tent, pissing out, than outside pissing in."

3   W. S. Churchill. Ibid.

4   *The Storm of War.* Ibid. P. 1.

5   W. S. Churchill. Ibid. Vol. 3. Pp. 3–4.

6   W. S. Churchill. Ibid.

7   *The Storm of War.* Ibid.

8   *The Storm of War.* Ibid. P. 52.

9   *The Storm of War.* Ibid.

10 *Panzer Battles.* Field Marshal Melenthin. P. 24.

11 Source: Lieutenant-General Henry Pownall, General Gort's chief of staff.

12 *The Storm of War.* Ibid. P. 55.

13 Alan Brooke commanding British troops, and General Georges the French; also General
    Billote. Source: *The Storm of War.* Ibid. Pp. 55–6.

14 Liddell Hart. Ibid.

15 Liddell Hart. Ibid.

16 *The Storm of War.* Ibid. Pp. 56-7.

17 Antony Beevor. Ibid. P. 94.

18 Liddell Hart. Ibid.

19 *Nuremberg Interviews.* Goldensohn. P. 342.

20 *Other Side.* Liddell Hart. P. 140.

21 *World at War.* Holmes. Pp. 107–8.

22 *Other Side.* Liddell Hart. P. 140.

23 *The Storm of War.* Ibid. P. 60.

24 *The Secret War.* Ibid. P. 356–7 caption beneath a photo of Hitler studying a map with his
    courtiers.

25 Liddell Hart. Ibid.

26 Liddell Hart. Ibid.

27 Liddell Hart. Ibid.

28 W. S. Churchill. Ibid.

29 *Churchill & Sea Power.* Christopher M. Bell. (Oxford University Press, 2013). P. 195.

30 Mollie Panter-Downes.

31 W. S. Churchill. Ibid.

9. The Battle of Britain

1   *Holy Fox.* Roberts. Pp. 221–4.

2   Peter Fleming. Ibid. P. 199.

3   W. S. Churchill. Ibid.

4   W. S. Churchill. Ibid.

5   W. S. Churchill. Ibid.

6   *Churchill & Sea Power.* Ibid. P. 144.

7   Max Hastings. Ibid. Sir Stewart Menzies was Chief of British Intelligence ("C") at that time.

8   Although equally contemptuous of Latin races, like the French and Italians, he was prepared to tolerate them as long as they did what they were told.

9   *The Second World War.* Antony Beevor. (Weidenfeld & Nicolson, London 2012). P. 5.

10   Liddell Hart. Ibid.

11   Liddell Hart. Ibid.

12   Liddell Hart. Ibid.

13   Liddell Hart. Ibid.

10. France Falls

1   W. S. Churchill. Ibid.

2   *Sunday Times.* Alan Judd. Book Section. P. 5. 12/10/1997.

3   *World at War.* Holmes. P. 102.

4   W. S. Churchill. Ibid.

5   W. S. Churchill. Ibid.

6   John Charmley. Ibid.

7   General Beaufre. Source: *World at War.* Holmes. P. 97.

8   *The Storm of War.* Ibid. P. 77.

9   W. S. Churchill. Ibid.

10   Source: David Pryce-Jones, *Literary Review,* April 2001. P. 22.

11   *The Storm of War.* Ibid.

12   *The Storm of War.* Ibid. P. 84.

13   *Pétain.* Williams. Pp. 441–2.

14   *Fighters in the Shadows.* Robert Gildea. (Harvard University Press, 2015).

15   *Collaboration in France.* Ed. Hirschfeld & March. P. 14.

16   *The Storm of War.* Ibid. P. 84.

17   *Sunday Times,* 18/1/1999.

18   General André Beaufre, 1940. P. 214. Source: *The Storm of War,* P. 84.

19   *The Storm of War.* Ibid.

11. Anglo-Saxon Attitudes

1   *The Storm of War.* Ibid. P. 87.

2   Directed by William Wyler. Novel by Jan Struther.

3   Directed by Zoltan Korda.

4   Written by Robert Ardry. Directed by Elia Kazan.

5   Most probably the Chanticleer Theatre with only one hundred seats.

6   King George V changed his family's name in 1917 from Saxe-Coburg and Gotha.

7   Thomas Gray. *Elegy Written in a Country Churchyard.*

8   *Leviathon.* Thomas Hobbes. (1651).

9   Traudi Junge was twenty-one when she was one of three secretaries for Hitler. In an interview about the collective responsibility for the Holocaust, she claimed she was kept in ignorance, and when she asked about the concentration camps she was told they were for criminals. Struggling for her opinion, she said, "he tried to manipulate the conscience of the entire German people."

10   The first was directed by Noel Coward and David Lean, the second by David Lean.

11   *Operation Sea Lion.* Peter Fleming. (Simon & Schuster, NY 1957). Opposite pages 32 & 80.

12. War in the Air

1   *Finest Years.* Max Hastings. Ibid.

2   *The Storm of War.* Ibid.

3   Source: General Blumentritt, after the war.

4   *Operation Sea Lion.* Peter Fleming. Ibid. *The Storm of War.* Ibid. Pp. 90–1.

5   *The Storm of War.* Ibid. P. 91.

6   *The Storm of War.* Ibid. P. 92.

7   W. S. Churchill. Ibid.

8   Peter Fleming. Ibid.

9   *Battle of Britain.* Ray. P. 43.

10   *The Storm of War.* Ibid.

11   Peter Fleming. Ibid. P. 220.

12   The German patriot was arrested and murdered in April 1945 by the Nazis as a traitor after the attempted assassination of Hitler. *The Canaris Conspiracy.* Roger Manvell & Heinrich Fraaenkel. (Heinemann London, 1969).

13 Peter Fleming. Ibid. P. 239.

14 Source: Dupuy and Dupuy, *Encyclopedia,* P. 1166. (Simon & Schuster). P. 81.

15 *The Storm of War.* Ibid. P. 94.

16 *World at War.* Ibid. P. 134.

17 *The Few.* Kershaw. P. 65.

18 *Memoirs.* Bridgeman. P. 184.

19 Spitfire designer; R. J. Mitchell. Hurricane designer; Sydney Cammus. Source: *The Storm of War.* Ibid.

20 ED. Parrish. (Simon & Schuster). P. 290.

21 *Duel of Eagles.* Group Captain Peter Townsend. Pp. 361–2.

22 *The Storm of War.* Ibid. P. 99.

23 *Battle of Britain.* Ibid. P. 82.

24 *The Storm of War.* Ibid. P. 99.

25 Liddell Hart. Ibid.

26 Liddell Hart. Ibid.

27 *Battle of Britain.* Ibid. P. 93.

28 *The Storm of War.* Ibid. P. 101.

29 *Living through the Blitz.* Harrison.

30 *World at War.* Ibid. P. 111.

31 *Why the Allies Won.* Overy. P. 109.

32 *World at War.* Ibid. P. 132.

33 *Halder War Diary.* Ed. Burdick & Jacobsen. P. 256.

34 W.S. Churchill. Ibid.

35 W. S. Churchill. Ibid.

36 W. S. Churchill. Ibid.

37 W. S. Churchill. Ibid.

38 W. S. Churchill. Ibid.

39 According to Colonel Galland. Source: *Decisive Battles.* Young. P. 61.

40 *The Second World War.* W. S. Churchill. Vol. 2. "The Grand Alliance." (Houghton Mifflin, Boston 1950). P. 41.

41 *The Storm of War.* Ibid. P. 106.

42 W. S. Churchill. Ibid.

43 *Finest Years.* Ibid.

44 *Finest Years.* Ibid. Pp. 268–270.

45 In fact, Byng had been persecuted and used as a scapegoat by the prime minister, the Duke of Newcastle. But Byng's execution by a firing squad has since been mythologized to warn timid admirals in the Royal Navy what to expect if too cautious in battle. *Flight of the Eagle.* Conrad Black. Ibid. Pp. 13 & 18.

46 *Finest Years.* Ibid. P. 267.

47 *Finest Years.* Ibid. P. 277.

13. Secret Service

1 Peter Fleming. Ibid.

2 *The Secret War.* Ibid.

3 *What Britain Has Done.* Ministry of Information. P. 110.

4 W. S. Churchill. Ibid.

5 *The Storm of War.* Ibid

6 *The Storm of War.* Ibid. P. 113.

7 *Eye of the Hurricane.* Schwarz. P. 125.

8 *Moscow 1941.* Braithwaite. P. 48.

9 *Wept Without Tears.* Greif. P. 97.

10 *Wept Without Tears.* Ibid. Pp 11–16. P. 97.

11 *The Storm of War.* Ibid. P. 114.

12 *A Spy Among Friends: Kim Philby and the Great Betrayal.* Ben Macintyre. (Penguin, 2014). P. 63.

13 *Inside SOE.* Foot. Pp. 219–220.

14 Major-General Colin Gubbins was in charge.

15 Michael Smith. Ibid.

16 Michael Smith. Ibid.

17 On August 21, 1940. Trotsky had been commander in chief of the Red Army and an advocate of international communism.

18 *The Secret War.* Ibid. P. 352.

19 *The Secret War.* Ibid. P. 350.

14. The Desert War

1 *Finest Years.* Ibid. P. 124.

2 *Finest Years.* Ibid. P. 137.

3 *The Storm of War.* Ibid. P. 120.

4   *The Storm of War.* Ibid. P. 120.

5   *The Storm of War.* Ibid.

6   *The Storm of War.* Ibid.

7   W. S. Churchill. Ibid.

8   W. S. Churchill. Ibid.

9   W. S. Churchill. Ibid.

10 John Charmley. Ibid.

11 *The Storm of War.* Ibid.

12 Liddell Hart. Ibid.

13 Liddell Hart. Ibid.

14 *Hitler's Mediterranean Gamble.* Porch. P. 662.

15 *First Victory.* Lyman. P. 2.

16 *The Storm of War.* Ibid. P. 131.

17 W. S. Churchill. Ibid.

18 W. S. Churchill. Ibid.

19 *Rommel as Military Commander.* (Ballantine, 1970).

15. The Killer Instinct

1   Liddell Hart. Ibid.

2   Liddell Hart. Ibid.

3   Christopher M. Bell. Ibid. P. 231.

4   Christopher M. Bell. Ibid.

5   He was not only stunned by guilt, but by the sudden realization that the historic usefulness of the Royal Navy was now jeopardized by being a sitting target for dive-bombers.

6   Christopher M. Bell. Ibid. Pp. 248–253.

7   *Finest Years.* Ibid. P. 240.

8   Antony Beevor. Ibid. P. 282.

9   Antony Beevor. Ibid. P. 288.

10 Christopher M. Bell. Ibid. P. 283.

11 Antony Beevor. Ibid. P. 313.

12 *The Storm of War.* Ibid.

13 *The Storm of War.* Ibid. P. 135.

14 Antony Beevor. Ibid. P. 322.

15 *The Storm of War.* Ibid. P. 281.

16 *Finest Years.* Ibid. P. 316.

17 Antony Beevor. Ibid. P. 318.

18 *The Storm of War.* Ibid. P. 283.

16. The Desert Fox

1   *The Storm of War.* Ibid. Pp. 283–4.

2   Liddell Hart. Ibid.

3   Liddell Hart. Ibid.

4   *Brute Force.* Ellis. P. 264.

5   *With Rommel.* Schmidt. P. 175.

6   B. H. Liddell Hart. *The Rommel Papers.* (Collins, London 1953). P. 312.

7   Liddell Hart. Ibid.

8   *The Storm of War.* Ibid. P. 297.

9   *The Storm of War.* Ibid.

10 *Decisive Battles.* Ed. Young. P. 182.

11 W. S. Churchill. Ibid.

12 *The Rommel Papers.* Ibid. P. 366.

17. The Anglo-American Alliance

1   *Finest Years.* Ibid. P. 214.

2   W. S. Churchill. Ibid. Vol. 3. P. 584

3   W. S. Churchill. Ibid.

4   *Winston's War.* Max Hastings. (Penguin, UK 2011). P. 179.

5   *War Diaries.* Eds. Danchev & Todman. P. 407.

6   *Army at Dawn.* Ibid. P. 36.

7   W. S. Churchill. Ibid.

8   Antony Beevor. Ibid. P. 344.

9   Antony Beevor. Ibid.

10 *The Storm of War.* Ibid. P. 488.

11 Liddell Hart. Ibid.

12 Liddell Hart. Ibid.

13 Liddell Hart. Ibid.

14 Laurence Burgis Papers (at Churchill Archives Centre, Churchill College, Cambridge).

18. Race for Tunis

1   Liddell Hart. Ibid.

2   W. S. Churchill. Ibid.

3   He was hurriedly shot, leaving a mystery behind him as to who had put him up to it.

4   *The Storm of War.* Ibid. P. 310.

5   *The Storm of War.* Ibid. P. 310.

6   Liddell Hart. Ibid. P. 432.

7   *U.S. Army in World War II.* Howe. *Northwest Africa: Seizing the Initiative in the West.* P. 456.

8   *The Storm of War.* Ibid. P. 312.

9   *The Storm of War.* Ibid. P. 312.

10 *Spectator.* Foot. 5/4/2003. P. 40.

11 *The Storm of War.* Ibid. P. 314.

12 Dwight D. Eisenhower. *Crusade in Europe* (Doubleday NY, 1948).

13 Liddell Hart. Ibid.

14 Liddell Hart. Ibid.

19. The Russian Campaign

1   *Stalin's General: The Life of Georgy Zhukov.* Geoffrey Roberts. (Random House, 2012).

2   *The Storm of War.* Ibid. P. 157.

3   *Barbarossa.* Glantz. P. 40.

4   *Stalin.* Service. P. 417.

5   *Army at Dawn.* Atkinson. P. 8.

6   W. S. Churchill. Ibid.

7   W. S. Churchill. Ibid.

8   John Charmley. Ibid.

9   Liddell Hart. Ibid.

10 W.S. Churchill. Ibid.

11 *The Storm of War.* Ibid. Pp. 145–6.

12 John Charmley. Ibid.

13 *The Battle of the Atlantic 1939-1945.* Eds. Howarth & Law. (Greenhill, London 1994). Pp. 516–37.

14 April 11, 1941 correspondence from FDR to WSC.

15 July 23, 1941 correspondence from Portal to WSC.

20. Battle for Stalingrad

1   *The Storm of War*. Ibid.

2   Antony Beevor. Ibid. P. 283.

3   Antony Beevor. Ibid. P. 286.

4   Antony Beevor. Ibid. P. 362.

5   *The Storm of War*. Ibid. P. 161.

6   Geoffrey Roberts. Ibid.

7   Geoffrey Roberts. Ibid.

8   Antony Beevor. Ibid. P. 11.

9   B. H. Liddell Hart. *The Other Side of the Hill*. (Macmillan, London 1948).

10 Liddell Hart. Ibid.

11 *The Storm of War*. Ibid. P. 340.

12 Liddell Hart. Ibid.

13 Liddell Hart. Ibid.

14 *The Storm of War*. Ibid. Pp. 136–7.

15 *The Storm of War*. Ibid.

16 Source: *Barbarossa*. Clark. P. 48.

17 Source:Ian Sayer Archive.

18 *Halder War Diaries*. Burdick & Jacobsen. 13/7/1940.

19 On June 14, 1941. Source: *Hitler: Nemesis*. Kershaw. P. 385.

20 *Halder War Diary*. Ibid. P. 645.

21 W. S. Churchill. *The Second World War*. Ibid. Vol 4. P. 712.

22 W.S. Churchill. Ibid. Vol. 4. P. 714.

21. The Way Ahead

1   W. S. Churchill. Ibid.

2   John Charmley. Ibid.

3   John Charmley. Ibid.

4   It didn't come off.

5   *Finest Years*. Ibid. P. 359.

6   *On War*.

7   Christopher M. Bell. Ibid. Pp. 285–6.

8 *Flight of the Eagle.* Ibid. P. 61.

9 Antony Beevor. Ibid. P. 281.

10 Christopher M. Bell. Ibid. Pp. 297–301.

11 Only air power and the atom bomb, he declared, would provide strategic superiority. What to do in the event of a preemptive strike by an enemy? Nations would require a second-strike capability to overwhelm the enemy immediately. (Christopher M. Bell. Ibid. P. 310).

12 John Charmley. Ibid.

13 John Charmley. Ibid.

14 *The Secret War.* Ibid. P. xvi.

15 John Charmley. Ibid.

22. Gateway to Europe

1 Liddell Hart. Ibid.

2 Liddell Hart. Ibid.

3 W. S. Churchill. Ibid.

4 W. S. Churchill. Ibid.

23. The Soft Underbelly

1 W. S. Churchill. Ibid.

2 John Charmley. Ibid.

3 *Finest Years.* Ibid. P. 522.

4 Liddell Hart. Ibid. P. 470.

5 *The Storm of War.* Ibid. P. 378.

6 *The Storm of War.* Ibid. P. 378.

7 *Anzio.* Ibid. P. 24. *The Storm of War.* Ibid. P. 380.

8 Liddell Hart. Ibid. P. 478.

9 W. S. Churchill. Ibid.

10 W. S. Churchill. Ibid.

11 Liddell Hart. Ibid.

12 *The Storm of War.* Ibid. P. 380.

13 *Anzio.* Ibid. P. 41.

14 *Swordpoint.* Harris. P. 12.

15 W. S. Churchill. *The Second World War.* Ibid. Vol. V. P. 380.

16 W. S. Churchill. Ibid.

17 W. S. Churchill. Ibid. Vol. 5. "Closing the Ring." P. 480

18 *The Storm of War.* Ibid. P. 384.

19 *Encyclopedia.* Dupuy & Dupuy. P. 1207. *Anzio.* Ibid. Pp. xxiii, 188. *Memoirs.* Ross. P. 209.

20 Liddell Hart. Ibid.

21 Liddell Hart. Ibid. P. 559.

22 *Decisive Battles.* Young. P. 250.

23 Liddell Hart. Ibid.

24 *Anzio.* Ibid. P. 23.

25 *The Storm of War.* Ibid. P. 509.

26 *The Storm of War.* Ibid. P. 509.

24. Hitler's Secret Weapons

1 W. S. Churchill. Ibid.

2 W. S. Churchill. Ibid.

3 W. S. Churchill. Ibid.

4 W. S. Churchill. Ibid.

5 W. S. Churchill. Ibid.

6 W. S. Churchill. Ibid.

7 Dwight D. Eisenhower. *Crusade in Europe.* Ibid.

8 *The Storm of War.* Ibid. P. 429.

9 *Why the Allies Won.* Overy. P. 107.

10 Liddell Hart papers, King's College, London. 15/15/26.

11 Portal Box A File 11.

12 *Storm of War.* Ibid. P. 435.

13 *Wages of Destruction.* Tooze. P. 600.

14 *The Storm of War.* Ibid.

15 Antony Beevor. Ibid. P. 450.

16 Antony Beevor. Ibid.

17 Joseph Heller. (Simon & Schuster NY, 1961).

18 Antony Beevor. Ibid. P. 445.

19 Antony Beevor. Ibid. P. 445.

25. D-Day

1 W. S. Churchill. Ibid.

2 *The Storm of War.* Ibid. P. 461.

3 *Finest Years.* Ibid. P. 480.

4 *How the Allies Won.* Ibid. P. 151.

5 W. S. Churchill. Ibid.

6 W. S. Churchill. Ibid.

7 Liddell Hart. Ibid.

8 *Masters and Commanders. Passim.* Roberts.

9 He removed it from later editions.

10 *Times Literary Supplement.* Nicolas Rowan. 23/11/2004. P. 12. *Fortitude.* Hesketh. Pp. 186–8.

11 *The Storm of War.* Ibid. P. 470.

12 *Rommel Papers.* Liddell Hart. Pp. 476–7.

13 U.S. Army Military History Institute, PA. Foreign Military Studies, MSS B-720.

14 *The Other Side.* Liddell Hart. P. 248.

15 W. S. Churchill. Ibid.

16 *Overlord.* Hastings. P. 88.

17 *Overlord.* Ibid. P. 89.

18 *Overlord.* Ibid. P. 88.

19 *The Storm of War.* Ibid. P. 475.

20 *Overlord.* Ibid. P 95.

21 *The Storm of War.* Ibid. P. 476.

22 Ed. Parrish. Simon & Schuster. P. 304.

23 Liddell Hart. Ibid.

24 W. S. Churchill. Ibid.

25 W. S. Churchill.

26 Liddell Hart. Ibid.

27 Liddell Hart .*The Other Side of the Hill.* Ibid.

28 Liddell Hart. Ibid.

26. Drones Over London

1 Frederick Lindemann (Lord Cherwell). *Closing the Ring.* PP. 231–232.

2   W. S. Churchill. Ibid.

3   W. S. Churchill. Ibid.

4   *The Storm of War.* Ibid. P. 518.

5   *The Storm of War.* Ibid. Pp. 518–9.

6   *The Storm of War.* Ibid. P. 519.

7   W. S. Churchill. Ibid.

8   W. S. Churchill. Ibid.

27. Victory

1   Lidell Hart. Ibid. Pp. 707–708

2   Liddell Hart. Ibid.

3   *Encyclopaedia Judaica.* (The Gale Group, 2008).

4   United States Holocaust Memorial Museum.

5   W. S. Churchill. Ibid.

6   *The Secret War.* Ibid. P. xvi.

7   Liddell Hart. Ibid.

8   W. S. Churchill. Ibid.

9   *The Canterbury Tales.*

10 Antony Beevor. Ibid. P. 281.

11 By comparison, from September 1931 to June 1932 US production had fallen 25 percent and unemployment had reached ten million.

12 *Flight of the Eagle.* Ibid. Pp. 38–9.

13 Christopher M. Bell. Ibid. P. 336. On the "Stephen Roskill Controversy."

14 Christopher M. Bell. Ibid P. 336.

15 Christopher M. Bell. Ibid. P. 341.

16 Christopher M. Bell. Ibid. P. 315.

17 *Historia Ecclesiastica Gentis Anglorum.* According to which the two brothers became chiefs fighting on the side of the British King Vortigern against the indigenous Picts.

28. Collective Guilt

1   *Our Threatened Values.* Gollancz London, 1946. P. 92.

2   Melanie Phillips. (*Jewish Chronicle Online*). *Germans and Victims: Remembering the Past in Contemporary Germany.* Ed. Bill Niven (Palgrave Macmillan, 2006). Pp. 195–197.

3   September 11, 1945.

4 *Barbarism and Civilization: A History of Europe in Our Time.* Bernard Wasserstein. (Oxford University Press, 2007). P. 416.

5 From a German Expulsion Thesis for an MA from files.figshare.com Also *Expelling the Germans.* Matthew Frank. P. 82.

6 *Germany and Eastern Europe Since 1945.* Keesing's Research Report (Scribner's NY, 1973). P. ix.

7 *Dark Continent: Europe's Twentieth Century.* Mark Mazower. P. 233.

8 For example, the 1987 Hollywood film *Wall Street* and *The Wolf of Wall Street* in December 2013.

9 *Principles of Biology* (1864).

10 Dockter is a research fellow at the University of Cambridge and the author of *Winston Churchill and the Islamic World.*

11 *Gandhi & Churchill.*

12 *BBC History Online. Feb. 17, 2011*

13 *Story of One Fateful Day.* Nick Lloyd (2012).

14 Sometimes attributed to the historic clash between the invading Normans in 1066 and the downtrodden Anglo-Saxons who continued to have fun at their expense by exposing their romantic pomposities with their own down-to-earth wit. For example, in 1969, by the popular BBCTV show called *Monty Python's Flying Circus,* which poked fun at as many pomposities of authoritarian figures as they could think of, including mocking depictions of crucifixions to assure self-righteous church followers that they romanticized themselves far too seriously for more earthy Anglo-Saxon sensibilities. Nothing was too sacred for them to parody in order to get a belly laugh in response.

15 *Psychology of Dictatorship.* Gustave Gilbert. (The Ronald Press Company, NY 1950)

16 *The Nuremberg Diary.* Gustave Gilbert. (Farrar, Strauss, NY 1947).

INDEX